ahead of the curve

The Power of Assessment to Transform Teaching and Learning

Solution Tree | Press

a division of
Solution Tree

555 North Morton Street
Bloomington, IN 47404
800.733.6786 (toll free) / 812.336.7700
FAX: 812.336.7790

email: info@solution-tree.com
solution-tree.com

Printed in the United States of America

ISBN 978-1-934009-06-2

Acknowledgments

A simple "thanks" is an inadequate expression of appreciation for the people who made this book a reality. The only thing more inadequate, however, would be for me to fail to acknowledge their intellect, enthusiasm, integrity, and energy. Gretchen Knapp and Suzanne Kraszewski transformed our drafts into finished chapters, and all of my fellow authors join me in thanking them. My colleague Cathy Shulkin edited every word of my contributions to this volume, and magically transformed my rant (composed at 33,000 feet in a middle seat) into comprehensible prose. Cathy, Gretchen, and Suzanne taught me the meaning of Stephen King's dictum that "to write is human; to edit, divine."

Jeff Jones, the president of Solution Tree, would prefer no doubt to be acknowledged not as a great publisher and transformational influence on education, but as a parent whose interest in education is intensely personal. His children and mine depend upon the quality of our work. Jeff's vision, commitment, and unflagging personal integrity are qualities I have learned cannot be taken for granted.

My fellow authors are exceptionally busy and could have thought of a thousand excuses not to participate in this project or put up with my editorial suggestions. Each of them could have written a book on this subject with their name in lights. It takes an exceptional degree of professional integrity and personal confidence to collaborate on a project like this, and therefore I extend my deepest appreciation to Larry Ainsworth, Lisa Almeida, Anne Davies,

Richard DuFour, Linda Gregg, Thomas Guskey, Robert Marzano, Ken O'Connor, Rick Stiggins, Stephen White, and Dylan Wiliam.

Every hour I devote to writing and editing is an hour I failed to spend with my own family, and to them I owe the greatest debt of acknowledgment. I am the son and grandson of teachers, and my greatest wish for James, Julia, Alex, and Brooks is that whatever their professional future, they find the time to nurture, encourage, love, and teach children.

—Douglas Reeves

Table of Contents

About the Editor vii

Introduction From the Bell Curve to the Mountain:
A New Vision for Achievement, Assessment,
and Equity
Douglas Reeves 1

SECTION 1 **Classroom Assessment**

Chapter 1 Using Assessments to Improve Teaching
and Learning
Thomas R. Guskey 15

Chapter 2 Involving Students in the Classroom
Assessment Process
Anne Davies 31

Chapter 3 Assessment *for* Learning: An Essential
Foundation of Productive Instruction
Rick Stiggins 59

SECTION 2 **System-Level Assessment**

Chapter 4 Common Formative Assessments:
The Centerpiece of an Integrated
Standards-Based Assessment System
Larry Ainsworth 79

Chapter 5   Designing a Comprehensive Approach to Classroom Assessment
Robert J. Marzano 103

Chapter 6   The Last Frontier: Tackling the Grading Dilemma
Ken O'Connor 127

SECTION 3   **Assessment Challenges**

Chapter 7   The Journey Toward Effective Assessment for English Language Learners
Lisa Almeida 147

Chapter 8   Crossing the Canyon: Helping Students With Special Needs Achieve Proficiency
Linda A. Gregg 165

SECTION 4   **Assessment Leadership**

Chapter 9   Content *Then* Process: Teacher Learning Communities in the Service of Formative Assessment
Dylan Wiliam 183

Chapter 10   Data on Purpose: Due Diligence to Increase Student Achievement
Stephen White 207

Chapter 11   Challenges and Choices: The Role of Educational Leaders in Effective Assessment
Douglas Reeves 227

Epilogue   Once Upon a Time: A Tale of Excellence in Assessment
Richard DuFour 253

About the Editor

Douglas Reeves

Douglas Reeves, Ph.D., is founder of The Leadership and Learning Center (formerly the Center for Performance Assessment), an international organization dedicated to improving student achievement and educational equity. Through its long-term relationships with school systems, The Leadership and Learning Center helps educators and school leaders improve student achievement through practical and constructive approaches to standards, assessment, and accountability. Dr. Reeves is also a frequent keynote speaker in the United States and abroad for education, government, and business organizations.

Dr. Reeves is the author of many articles and more than 20 books, including *The Learning Leader: How to Focus School Improvement for Better Results* (ASCD, 2006), as well as the best-selling *Making Standards Work: How to Implement Standards-Based Assessments in the Classroom, School, and District*, now in its third edition. Other titles include *Assessing Educational Leaders: Evaluating Performance for Improved Individual and Organizational Results* (Corwin Press, 2004); *Accountability for Learning: How Teachers and School Leaders Can Take Charge* (ASCD, 2004); *Accountability in Action: A Blueprint for Learning Organizations, Second Edition* (Advanced Learning Press, 2005); *The Daily Disciplines of Leadership: How to Improve Student Achievement, Staff Motivation, and Personal Organization* (Jossey-Bass, 2002); *The Leader's Guide to Standards: A Blueprint for Educational Equity and Excellence* (Jossey-Bass, 2002); and *Reason to Write: Help Your Child Succeed in School and in Life Through Better Reasoning and Clear Communication* (Simon & Schuster, 2002).

Dr. Reeves was twice selected for the Harvard Distinguished Authors Series. He won the Parent's Choice Award for his writing for children and parents and was named the 2006 Brock International Laureate, one of the most significant education awards in the world. His work appears in numerous national journals, magazines, and newspapers, including a monthly column titled "Leading to Change" in *Educational Leadership,* the world's largest educational leadership journal.

Beyond his work in large-scale assessment and research, Dr. Reeves has devoted many years to classroom teaching with students of all ages. His family includes four children, all of whom have attended public schools, and his wife, Shelley Sackett, an attorney, mediator, and school board member. Dr. Reeves lives near Boston.

For more information about research conducted by Dr. Reeves, please visit www.LeadandLearn.com.

Introduction

From the Bell Curve to the Mountain: A New Vision for Achievement, Assessment, and Equity

Douglas Reeves

As educators, school leaders, and policymakers, we exist in a world where too often assessment equals high-stakes tests. This is a very limited view of assessment. The chapters in this book present a broader view. But *Ahead of the Curve* is neither a diatribe against tests nor a wistful call for the return to the mythical test-free days that never were. Rather, the contributors to this volume call for a redirection of assessment to its fundamental purpose: the improvement of student achievement, teaching practice, and leadership decision-making. The stakes could not be higher. We have two alternatives before us: Either we heed the clarion call of Schmoker (2006) that there is an unprecedented opportunity for achieving results now, or we succumb to the complaints of those who claim that schools, educators, and leaders are impotent compared to the magnitude of the challenge before them.

These challenges are both external and internal. While the external challenges—poverty, housing, nutrition, and pervasive inequities of opportunity—are apparent and well-recognized, educators and school leaders must be equally candid when addressing internal challenges, including long-held traditions that elevate personal preference over evidence. The chapters that follow presume a culture in which the most important criterion for educational decision-making is the evidence. We embrace explicitly the proposition that effective practice and popular practice are very likely two different things.

While external challenges are relevant, the evidence is clear that they are not determinative. When we focus exclusively on external challenges, educators are victims who wait for the impact of outside forces to exert their will on us. We stand by helplessly. When we focus on internal challenges—and that is the essential mission of this book—we consider a new vision of achievement, assessment, and equity.

The fundamental premise of this new vision is a rejection of the determinism inherent in the bell curve and the embrace of the essential truth that teachers and school leaders make a difference. When we take this perspective, we stand on the shoulders of giants, including John Goodlad (1984, 1990, 1994), Linda Darling-Hammond (1997, 1999), Kati Haycock (1998), and a legion of scholars who believe that teaching is not merely the act of transmitting knowledge, but an inherently collaborative, interactive, and relationship-based enterprise. When we embrace the power of teaching and leadership, we reject demographic determinism. In the following pages, you will read not theory and ideals, but practice and practicality. Let us briefly explore the primary themes of *Ahead of the Curve*.

The Bell Curve: No Place in Classroom Assessment

The normal distribution, or bell curve as it is popularly known, has a place in some forms of statistical analysis. It has no place as the central organizing framework for classroom assessment, however, as it compares student performance to the performance of other students, rather than to an objective standard. The bell curve

sits in stark contrast to the very essence of standards-based education, in which the fundamental purpose of assessment is not to rate,
rank, sort, and humiliate students, but rather to provide meaningful
feedback that leads to improved performance. The authors of this
volume consistently echo the admonition of Rick Stiggins that
assessment is most productive when its purpose is *for* learning.

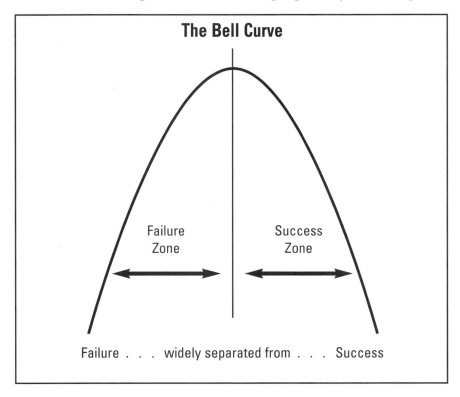

The underlying logic of the bell curve structure is simply the
wrong model for evaluating educational achievement. It is the worst
of all possible worlds: It fails to acknowledge good performance and
gives unearned accolades to poor performance. Those who fail to
"beat" their neighbors are labeled inferior, even when proficient, and
those who do beat their neighbors are labeled superior, no matter
how inadequate their performance. Its impact is as insidious for
poor, disadvantaged, and minority students as for historically advan-
taged students.

When bell curve defenders assert, "The bell curve is reality—get over it," I gently remind them of the many instances in the real world in which we have explicitly rejected the bell curve and embraced an approach based on standards, and therefore a distinctly nonsymmetrical distribution. For example, the next time you board an aircraft, ask yourself before you turn off your electronic devices and buckle your seat belt if you want the pilot to be on a bell-shaped distribution in which half of the pilots are deemed acceptable not because they can land the airplane correctly, but because they "beat" the pilots on the left side of the curve. Or consider the case of teenage drivers: We do not award them licenses based upon performance that is marginally less scary than that of their classmates. The requirement is not that the successful teen drivers beat someone else, but rather that most of the time they can differentiate between the accelerator and brake pedal. Brain surgeons, cooks, astronauts, and computer programmers—and their professional counterparts from nearly every field—do not evaluate themselves based on the bell curve, but rather against an established standard of performance. If the "real world" is our standard, then by that criterion alone we would reject the bell curve.

If we reject the bell curve, then what is the alternative? The "mountain curve" shows a distribution of achievement that is, in statistical parlance, skewed to the right. In practical terms, it means that rather than dividing students into winners and losers, as the bell curve does, we have a distribution of student achievement that acknowledges differences, but also that those differences occur within a zone of success. There are other characteristics of the mountain curve that are worthy of examination.

While the bell curve offers a wide separation between students on the right and left sides, the mountain curve offers a much narrower distinction. Why? Because in schools committed to the mountain curve, the focus is exclusively on achievement. Much of the

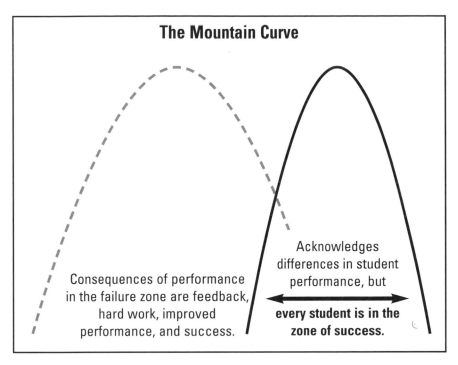

The Mountain Curve

Consequences of performance in the failure zone are feedback, hard work, improved performance, and success.

Acknowledges differences in student performance, but **every student is in the zone of success.**

differences among students in bell-curve schools can be accounted for by factors other than achievement, including speed of learning, parental assistance with homework, time management, and personal organization.

When we follow the advice of contributor Thomas Guskey to use data to influence instructional decisions and Ken O'Connor's suggestions to improve grading systems, and when we consider Lisa Almeida's and Linda Gregg's focus on providing opportunities for success for English language learners and special-education students, then we will find a growing number of student performances that are "ahead of the curve" and thus are better described by the mountain than the bell. Chapters by Dylan Wiliam and Rick Stiggins convey the message that we do not need to use classroom assessment to sort and select students and conform to the bell curve. Larry Ainsworth's contribution suggests that successful assessment combines classroom practice with a systemic focus on common expectations. While the authors of this volume represent a wide variety of perspectives, they coalesce around a consistent theme: Rather than manipulate student results to fit the normal curve, we must instead change the curve itself from a bell to a mountain.

Such a transformation entails deep implementation of the teaching strategies presented here by Robert Marzano, the data analysis of Stephen White, and the classroom practices contributed by Anne Davies. In the final chapter, Rick DuFour describes the importance of transcending the gulf between intention and reality with interventions, assessments, and collaboration that come together to form professional learning communities.

The Imperative of Practical Application

Stanford researchers Pfeffer and Sutton (2006) provide substantial evidence that it is more important to hear true things than to say smart things. They remind us that eloquence without practical application is useless. While the displacement of the bell curve from classroom practice may strike some as esoteric, the real-world dilemmas confronted by the authors in the pages of this book are relentlessly practical. Teachers, parents, students, and educational leaders want to know, in the words of one of the best book titles I have ever seen, "How's my kid doing?" (Guskey, 2002). The imperative of practicality, therefore, leads us to consider grading strategies, the needs of special-education students and English language learners, and the daily conundrums of classroom assessment. To transform the ideas in this book into reality, schools must ask with relentless persistence:

- Are our professional practices leading to improved achievement?
- If so, how can we replicate these practices?
- If not, how will we change them immediately?

- What is the evidence that we have to justify continuation of current practice?

- What is the risk of trying new practice?

- What is the risk of continuing current practice?

The last question is particularly salient. Too frequently, improvements in teaching and leadership are stopped cold by the cynical demand, "Show me proof that this will work!" Of course, even the most rigorous scientific research can yield inconsistent results. For example, vaccinations will, for some children, induce the disease that they were administered to prevent. Chemotherapy prescribed after many clinical trials may be successful or may yield toxic side-effects and fail to cure the cancer. Bridges built with scientific precision may fail. Unsinkable ships designed by the best engineers will encounter icebergs. People who watch their diet and exercise regularly have heart attacks while others who smoke like chimneys become centenarians. Demands for perfect proof are nothing but smoke screens designed to prevent any change. Every change has risk. The essential question is not, "What is the proof?" but rather, "What is the risk if we engage in this change compared to the risk of continuing our present practice?"

Consider the example of a school system I visited not long ago. Incontrovertible evidence showed that the elementary and secondary schools that devoted more time to literacy—in some cases 180 minutes per day—experienced significantly higher levels of student success than schools that devoted only the typical 60 to 90 minutes to literacy. Nevertheless, the resistance to a prospective schedule change was pervasive. Fear of change created an impenetrable barrier to the opportunity for improvement. Because a few schools that devoted extra time to literacy had failed to make progress, the resisters had all the ammunition that they needed. They relied upon the presumption that if evidence is conflicting and the advocates of change lacked perfect proof, then change should be forestalled.

But again, the critical question is: "What is the risk of changing compared to the risk of not changing?" In the case of student literacy, the risks of not changing are stark: higher dropout rates, failures in multiple subjects, enormous social costs, and lifetime risks for both the students, their descendants, and society. And what is the risk, to students and society, of changing? Excessively literate children who are overly well-prepared for school? Even in the absence of perfect evidence, any rational consideration of the alternatives in this case suggests that the risk of change is minimal compared to the risk of blind adherence to the status quo.

Assessment Is a Leadership Issue

For too long, the siren song of "close the door and let me teach" has led to a chasm between classroom practice and educational leadership. The boundaries between teaching and administration were clear: Instruction, assessment, feedback, grading, and almost every interaction between teacher and student—with the possible exception of discipline—were private matters that excluded school leaders. When we say that assessment is a leadership issue, we are not advocating micromanagement. Rather, we are recognizing an ethical imperative. Assessment is a reflection of values. Our assessment policies put into action our beliefs about the ability of all students to succeed. Our assessment practices reflect our beliefs about the use of feedback to improve instruction.

Beliefs and values in any system are not matters for idiosyncratic application. For example, police officers have enormous discretion to make on-the-spot decisions to protect public safety, but they do not have the discretion to abrogate human rights. Great chefs have the discretion to create fun, exciting, intriguing, and delicious entrees, but they do not have the discretion to get creative with health and safety standards in the kitchen. They follow the boundaries set by law, policy, and social contracts, and it is the responsibility of school leaders and policymakers to establish similar boundaries in our schools. Leaders must establish assessment boundaries of accuracy, fairness, and effectiveness. This does not constitute micromanagement; policy and daily classroom assessment practice that fail to meet these criteria are not reflections of professional creativity. They are simply out of bounds.

Parker Palmer writes eloquently of *The Courage to Teach* (1998). Courage is also required to lead. Those who implement changes in assessment, grading, and professional practices and policies risk not only confrontation, but also unpopularity, social isolation, public humiliation, and ultimately, even their livelihoods. I have witnessed friends and colleagues learn too late that although some school systems talk a good game about improved achievement for students, they are willing to pursue that goal only as long as the process does not cause discomfort for adults. Visiting senior leaders who have seen with their own eyes how the professional practices explored in this book improve school equity and excellence have said to me, "But we could never do that in our system. The culture just won't allow it." The problem goes beyond culture, however. Such statements reveal an all-too-common lack of courage in the leaders, board members, and citizens who decide every day if they will give primacy to the interests of adults or to the children they serve.

The Collaboration Imperative

The final theme of the book is that effective assessment practice is inherently collaborative. The Leading Edge series unites education authorities from around the globe and asks them to confront the important issues that affect teachers and administrators. Just as the first book in the series, *On Common Ground,* brought together leading educators and researchers to address the imperative of professional learning communities, *Ahead of the Curve* brings an illustrious group of thinkers, researchers, teachers, and writers to wrestle with assessment issues. We do not agree on every element of pedagogy and assessment, but we are committed to reasoning together to find a sustainable approach to assessment that is not dependent upon political winds or transient legislative mandates. The professional practices and policies we suggest transcend time, borders, and cultures. Our focus is on the enduring commitment we share with every reader, the commitment for improved opportunity and performance—for students, teachers, and leaders.

The history of education is littered with short-lived reforms that briefly showed promise and then soon faded away (Ravitch, 2000). Indeed, the vast majority of claims of "new" reforms can be traced to previous decades, if not to Socrates and the Lyceum. Before he took his draught of hemlock, we must remember, Plato's teacher invented Socratic dialogue, though it seems that some 21st-century professional developers believe that they invented the concept. Education of the "whole child" was suggested by Rousseau two centuries before it was announced with breathless enthusiasm at conferences in the 21st century.

Robert Marzano and his colleagues (Marzano, Pickering, & Pollock, 2001; Marzano, 2003; Marzano, Waters, & McNulty, 2005) have described the state of education research as "the best of times and the worst of times": Thanks to an abundance of research and documented practice, we know what to do. A heavy burden falls on the authors of this book to say that the 21st century really will be different. They must persuade you that their ideas provide an enduring framework that helps students find success and helps educators find meaning, purpose, and collegiality in a profession that has been beset by fragmentation and isolation. *Ahead of the Curve* provides a comprehensive view of the challenges of assessment. Section 1 explores the issues of classroom assessment. Section 2 considers the challenges of system-level assessment. Section 3 considers specific assessment challenges for English language learners and special-education students. Section 4 addresses the issues of assessment leadership. And the epilogue presents a powerful example of assessment excellence in action.

This book is a journey and not a destination, and many readers will conclude their study with questions, challenges, and most importantly, success stories of their own that will add context and practical application to the ideas in these pages. Therefore, we introduce a novel concept: a "Section 5" to this book to which you and your colleagues are collaborative contributors. Solution Tree, our publisher, has created www.allthingsassessment.info, a commercial-free website, to provide a continuously updated source of new information about successful professional practices in educational assessment. The Leadership and Learning Center has created a commercial-free interactive website, www.wikiassessments.com, where you can contribute your own ideas about best practices in assessment. Your insights, examples, and successes can be part of a continuing effort to improve not only assessment practice, but our entire commitment to teaching and learning.

References

Darling-Hammond, L. (1997). *The right to learn: A blueprint for creating schools that work.* San Francisco: Jossey-Bass.

Darling-Hammond, L. D., & Sykes, G. (1999). *Teaching as the learning profession: Handbook of policy and practice.* San Francisco: Jossey-Bass.

Goodlad, J. I. (1984). *A place called school.* New York: McGraw-Hill.

Goodlad, J. I. (1990). *Teachers for our nation's schools.* San Francisco: Jossey-Bass.

Goodlad, J. I. (1994). *Educational renewal: Better teachers, better schools.* San Francisco: Jossey-Bass.

Guskey, T. R. (2002). *How's my kid doing? A parents' guide to grades, marks, and report cards.* San Francisco: Jossey-Bass.

Haycock, K. (1998, Summer). Good teaching matters...a lot. *Thinking K–16: A Publication of the Education Trust, 3*(2), 3–14.

Herrnstein, R. J., & Murray, C. (1996). *The bell curve: Intelligence and class structure in American life.* New York: Simon & Schuster.

Kozol, J. (2005). *The shame of the nation: The restoration of apartheid schooling in America.* New York: Crown Publishers.

Marzano, R. J. (2003). *What works in schools: Translating research into action.* Alexandria, VA: Association for Supervision and Curriculum Development.

Marzano, R. J., Pickering, D., & Pollock, J. E. (2001). *Classroom instruction that works: Research-based strategies for increasing student achievement.* Alexandria, VA: Association for Supervision and Curriculum Development.

Marzano, R. J., Waters, T., & McNulty, B. A. (2005). *School leadership that works: From research to results.* Alexandria, VA: Association for Supervision and Curriculum Development.

Palmer, P. J. (1998). *The courage to teach.* San Francisco: Jossey-Bass.

Perkins, D. N. (1995). *Outsmarting IQ: The emerging science of learnable intelligence.* New York: Free Press.

Pfeffer, J., & Sutton, R. I. (2006). *Hard facts, dangerous half-truths and total nonsense: Profiting from evidence-based management.* Boston: Harvard Business School.

Ravitch, D. (2000). *Left back: A century of failed school reforms.* New York: Simon & Schuster.

Schmoker, M. (2006). *Results now: How we can achieve unprecedented improvements in teaching and learning.* Alexandria, VA: Association for Supervision and Curriculum Development.

Thomas R. Guskey

Dr. Thomas R. Guskey is distinguished service professor of educational assessment and evaluation at Georgetown College in Georgetown, Kentucky. Formerly with the University of Kentucky, he served as director of research and development for the Chicago Public Schools, and was the first director of the Center for the Improvement of Teaching and Learning. Dr. Guskey coedits the *Experts in Assessment* series (Corwin Press) and was featured on the National Public Radio program *Talk of the Nation.* His books have won numerous awards, and his articles have appeared in prominent research journals, as well as *Educational Leadership*, *Kappan*, and *The School Administrator.* He served on the policy research team of the National Commission on Teaching and America's Future, on the task force to develop the *National Standards for Staff Development*, and recently was honored by the American Educational Research Association for his work relating research to practice.

In this chapter, Dr. Guskey addresses the complex question, "How do we make assessment results useful?" Data from large-scale assessments are usually used to rank-order schools and students for the purpose of accountability. But do these assessments succeed in improving student learning? The author argues that assessments must become an integral part of the instructional process to help teachers improve their instruction or modify their approach to individual students. The assessments best suited to guide improvements in instruction and student learning are the quizzes, tests, writing assignments, and other assessments teachers administer on a regular basis in their classrooms. Dr. Guskey highlights three important ways teachers need to change their approach to assessment to improve student learning: Use assessments as sources of information for both students and teachers; follow assessments with high-quality, corrective instruction; and give students second chances to demonstrate success.

Dr. Thomas R. Guskey can be reached at Guskey@uky.edu.

Chapter 1

Using Assessments to Improve Teaching *and* Learning

Thomas R. Guskey

Large-scale assessment programs provide the foundation for nearly every modern education reform initiative. Policymakers and legislators at the state and national levels see assessments as essential for change. They believe that good data on student performance drawn from large-scale assessments will help focus educators' attention and guarantee success, especially if consequences are attached to the assessment results; however, large-scale assessments, like all assessments, are designed for a specific purpose—to rank-order schools and students for the purposes of accountability, and some do that fairly well. But assessments designed for ranking are generally not good instruments for helping teachers to improve their instruction or modify their approach to individual students. Students take these assessments at the end of the school year, when most instructional activities are near completion. Teachers do not receive the results until many months later, and by that time their students have usually moved on to other classrooms with different teachers. Finally, the results teachers receive usually lack the level of detail needed to target specific improvements (Barton, 2002; Hattie & Timperley, 2007; Kifer, 2001).

The assessments best suited to guide improvements in instruction and student learning are the quizzes, tests, writing assignments, and other assessments teachers administer on a regular basis in their classrooms. Teachers trust the results from these assessments because they relate directly to instructional goals in the classroom (see Guskey, 2007). Plus, results are immediate, relevant, and easy to analyze at the individual student level. However, to use classroom assessment to make improvements, teachers must change both the way they view assessment and the way they interpret results. Specifically, they need to see their assessments as an integral part of the instructional process and as an essential element in their efforts to help students learn.

Despite the importance of assessments in education today, few teachers receive much formal training in assessment design or analysis. A survey by Stiggins (1999) showed, for example, that less than half the states require competence in assessment for licensure as a teacher. Lacking specific training, teachers often do what they recall their own teachers doing: They rely heavily on the assessments offered by the publishers of their textbooks or instructional materials. When no suitable assessments are available, they construct their own in a haphazard way, with questions and essay prompts similar to those their teachers used. They treat assessments strictly as evaluation devices, administering them when instructional activities are completed and using them primarily to gather information for assigning students' grades.

Making Assessments Useful

For assessments to become an integral part of the instructional process, teachers need to change their approach in three important ways: They must 1) use assessments as sources of information for both students and teachers, 2) follow assessments with high-quality corrective instruction, and 3) give students second chances to demonstrate success.

What makes these changes in approach so difficult, however, is that each change compels teachers to depart significantly from the practices they experienced as students. In other words, teachers must think about and use assessments differently than their teachers did.

Use Assessments as Sources of Information for Both Students and Teachers

Nearly every student has suffered the experience of spending hours preparing for a major assessment, only to discover that the material he or she studied was different from what the teacher chose to emphasize on the assessment (see Guskey, 2006). This experience teaches students two unfortunate lessons: First, they discover that hard work and effort often do not pay off in school because the time and energy they spent in preparation for the assessment had little or no influence on the results. And second, they learn that they cannot trust teachers (Guskey, 2000b). These are hardly the lessons responsible teachers want their students to learn.

Nevertheless, this experience is a common one for students because many teachers still mistakenly believe that they must keep their assessments secret. As a result, students come to regard assessments as guessing games, especially from the middle grades on. They come to believe that their success in school depends largely on how well they can guess what their teachers will ask on quizzes, tests, and other types of assessments. Some teachers even take pride in their ability to out-guess students. They include questions about isolated concepts or obscure facts just to see if students are reading carefully. Generally, teachers do not include such "gotcha" questions maliciously, but rather they do so often unconsciously because such questions were asked of them when they were students.

Classroom assessments that serve as meaningful sources of information do not surprise students. Instead, they are well aligned extensions of the teacher's instructional activities. Such assessments reflect the concepts and skills the teacher emphasized in class, along with the criteria the teacher provided for how he or she would judge student performance. Ideally these concepts, skills, and criteria are also aligned with state, provincial, or district standards. Students see these types of assessments as fair measures of important learning goals. The results of the assessments facilitate learning by providing essential feedback on students' learning progress and by helping to identify learning problems (Bloom, Madaus, & Hastings, 1981; Stiggins, 2002).

Critics sometimes contend that this approach to assessment is "teaching to the test," but this is not necessarily the case. We have to ask, "What determines the content and methods of teaching?" If a test is the primary determinant of what teachers teach and how they teach it, then they are indeed teaching to the test. This occurs frequently today in schools and districts where student performance, as well as that of teachers, is judged by the results of a single large-scale assessment.

However, if desired learning goals or standards are the foundation of students' instructional experiences, then assessments of student learning are simply extensions of those same goals and standards. Instead of teaching to the test, teachers are more accurately "testing or assessing what they teach." They recognize that if a particular concept or skill is important enough to assess, then it should be important enough to teach. And if it is not important enough to teach, then there is little justification for including it in the assessment.

The best classroom assessments also serve as meaningful sources of information for teachers. Assessments provide teachers with specific guidance in their efforts to improve the quality of their teaching by helping identify what they taught well and what needs work. Gathering this vital information does not require sophisticated statistical analysis of assessment results. Teachers need only make a simple tally of how many students missed each item on the assessment or failed to meet a specific criterion. Figure 1 shows an example of this type of assessment analysis.

Item	Errors		Problem #1	Errors
1.	I		Criterion 1	
2.	III		Criterion 2	卌 卌 卌 III
3.			Criterion 3	II
4.	II		Criterion 4	卌
5.	IIII			
6.	I			
7.	卌 卌 IIII		Problem #2	Errors
8.	卌 卌 卌		Criterion 1	I
9.	III		Criterion 2	I
10.	II		Criterion 3	II
11.	I		Criterion 4	卌 II
12.	卌			

Figure 1: Sample Tally of Student Errors on a Classroom Assessment

State assessment results sometimes provide similar item-by-item information, but concerns about content security and the cost of developing new questions each year often make assessment developers reluctant to offer such detailed information. Once teachers have tallied their students' results, they can pay special attention to trouble spots where large numbers of students made errors (in the example in Figure 1, items 7 and 8, and criterion 2 of problem #1).

When reviewing results, the teacher must first consider the quality of the item or criterion. In other words, is the problem with the instruction or is it with the assessment? Perhaps the question is ambiguously worded or the criterion is unclear. Perhaps students misinterpreted the question or the instructions. Whatever the case, teachers must determine whether or not these items and criteria adequately address the knowledge, understanding, or skill they were intended to measure.

If teachers find no obvious problems with the item or criterion, then they must turn their attention to their teaching. When as many as half the students in a class answer a clear question incorrectly or fail to meet a particular criterion, it is not a student learning problem—it is a teaching problem. Whatever strategy the teacher used, whatever examples were employed, or whatever explanation was offered, it simply did not work.

Analyzing assessment results in this way means setting aside some very powerful ego issues. Many teachers may initially say, "I taught them. They just didn't learn it!" But with further reflection, most recognize that effectiveness in teaching is not defined on the basis of what they do as teachers. Rather, it is defined by what their students are able to do. If few students learned what was taught, can it be said that the teaching was effective? Can effective teaching take place in the absence of learning? Certainly not.

Some argue that such a perspective puts too much responsibility on teachers and not enough on the students. Occasionally teachers respond, "Don't students have significant responsibilities in this process? Shouldn't students be expected to display initiative and personal accountability? And besides, if they don't get it, that's their fault, not mine. I'm here to teach, and they're here to learn."

Indeed, teachers and students share responsibility for learning. Even with valiant teaching efforts, we cannot guarantee that all students will learn everything excellently. In fact, only rarely do teachers find items or assessment criteria that every student has answered correctly. There are always a few students who are unwilling to put forth the necessary effort, but these students tend to be the exception, not the rule. If a teacher is reaching less than half of the students in the class, the teacher's method of instruction needs to improve. And teachers need this kind of evidence to help target their instructional improvement efforts.

Follow Assessments With High-Quality Corrective Instruction

If assessments provide vital information for both students and teachers, then it makes sense that they do not mark the end of learning. Assessments must be followed by high-quality corrective instruction designed to help students remedy whatever learning errors identified with the assessment (see Guskey, 1997). To charge ahead knowing that certain concepts or skills have not been learned well would be foolish. Teachers must therefore follow their assessments with instructional alternatives that present those concepts in new ways and engage students in different and more appropriate learning experiences.

Using high-quality corrective instruction is not the same as re-teaching, which often consists simply of restating the original explanations louder and more slowly. Instead, the teacher must use approaches that accommodate differences in students' learning styles and intelligences (Sternberg, 1994). Although teachers generally try to incorporate different approaches when they plan their lessons, corrective instruction extends and strengthens that work. Students who have few or no learning errors to correct should also participate in enrichment or extension activities to help broaden and expand their learning. Materials designed for gifted and talented students are an excellent resource for such activities.

Developing ideas for high-quality corrective instruction and enrichment activities can be difficult, especially if teachers believe they must do it alone. Fortunately, they do not have to. Colleagues are some of the best resources for developing teaching strategies. Structured professional development opportunities can help teachers share strategies and collaborate on teaching techniques (Guskey, 1998, 2000a). Faculty meetings devoted to examining classroom assessment results and developing alternative strategies can be highly effective. District-level personnel and collaborative partnerships with local colleges and universities are valuable resources for ideas and practical advice.

Occasionally, teachers express concern that if they take class time to offer corrective instruction, they will need to sacrifice curriculum coverage. But this need not be the case. Initially, corrective work *must* be done in class, under the teacher's direction. Efforts to involve students in corrective instruction once per week or during special study sessions conducted before or after school rarely succeed (see Guskey, 1997). In addition, teachers who ask students to complete corrective work independently, outside of class, generally find that those students who most need to spend time on corrective work are the least likely to do so. For these reasons, early instructional units will require more time, typically an extra class period or two.

However, as students become accustomed to this process and realize the personal benefits it offers, the teacher can drastically reduce the amount of class time allocated to corrective work and accomplish much of it during review sessions or with homework assignments. By not allowing minor errors to become major learning problems, teachers better prepare students for subsequent learning tasks, and thus less time is required for corrective work (Whiting, Van Burgh, & Render, 1995). For this reason, instruction in later learning units usually can proceed at a more rapid pace. By pacing their instructional units more flexibly, most teachers find that they need not sacrifice curriculum coverage to offer students the benefits of high-quality corrective instruction.

Give Students Second Chances to Demonstrate Success

To become an integral part of the instructional process, assessments cannot be a one-shot, "do-or-die" experience for students. Instead, assessments must be part of an ongoing effort to help students learn. If teachers follow assessments with high-quality corrective instruction, then students should have a second chance to demonstrate their new level of competence and understanding. This second chance determines the effectiveness of the corrective process while also giving students another opportunity to experience success in learning, thus providing them with additional motivation.

Writing teachers have long recognized the many benefits of a second chance. They know that students rarely write well in their initial attempt. So these teachers build into the writing process several opportunities for students to gain feedback on early drafts and then to use that feedback to revise and improve their writing. Teachers of other subjects frequently balk at the idea—mostly because it differs from their personal learning experiences.

Some teachers express concern about the fairness of giving students a second chance and point out that, "Life isn't like that." They describe how a surgeon does not get a second chance to perform an operation successfully and a pilot does not get a second chance to land a jumbo jet safely. Because of the very high stakes involved, each must get it right the first time.

But how did these highly skilled professionals learn their craft? The first operation performed by that surgeon was on a cadaver, which clearly allows a lot of latitude for mistakes. Similarly, the pilot spent many hours in a flight simulator before ever attempting a landing from the cockpit. Such experiences allowed these professionals to learn from their mistakes and improve their performance. Similar instructional techniques are used in nearly every professional endeavor. Only in schools do students face the prospect of one-shot, do-or-die assessments, with no chance to demonstrate what they learned from previous mistakes.

All educators strive to help their students become lifelong learners, and to develop learning-to-learn skills. What better learning-to-learn skill is there than learning from one's mistakes? Mistakes should not mark the end of learning; rather, they can be the beginning. Some assessment experts argue, in fact, that students learn nothing from a successful performance. Instead, they learn when their performance is less than successful, for then they can gain direction about how to improve (Wiggins, 1998).

Other teachers suggest that it is unfair to offer the same privileges and high grades to students who require a second chance as we offer to those students who demonstrate a high level of learning on the initial assessment. After all, these students may simply have failed to take responsibility or prepare appropriately for the assessment. Certainly we should recognize students who do well on the initial assessment and provide opportunities for them to extend their learning through enrichment activities. But those students who do well on a second assessment have also learned well. More important, their poor performance on the first assessment may not have been their fault. Maybe the teaching strategies used during the initial instruction were inappropriate for these students, but the corrective instruction proved more effective. If we determine grades and give special privileges (for example, honor roll membership) on the basis of performance and these students have performed at the same high level, then they certainly deserve the same grades and privileges as those students who scored well on their first try.

A comparable example is the driver's license examination. Many individuals do not pass this examination on the first attempt. On the second or third try, however, they reach the same high level of performance as others did on their first attempt. Should these drivers be penalized for not showing appropriate responsibility or being inadequately prepared? Should they, for example, be restricted to driving in fair weather only? Should they be required to pull their car over in inclement weather and park until the weather clears? Of course not, because they eventually met the same high performance standards as those who passed on their first attempt. The same should hold true for students who show that they, too, have learned well.

The critical issue is this: What is the purpose of a grade? Is the purpose to punish students for not providing the teacher with precisely what was expected on the first try? If so, then a low grade due to inadequate performance in an initial attempt may be justifiable. If this is indeed the case, however, then the teacher must make this purpose clear and must be prepared to defend this purpose to everyone involved—students, parents, school officials, and others. On the other hand, if the purpose of the grade is to provide an accurate description of how well students have learned, then a different outlook is required. In this case, what students know and are able to do become the basis of the grade, rather than how or when they learned the information. From an educational perspective based on what is most helpful to students, this is clearly a more sound, defendable, and equitable position.

A Familiar Process

Using assessments as sources of information, following assessments with corrective instruction, and giving students second chances to demonstrate their learning may seem unfamiliar at first, but most teachers already do these things when they tutor individual students. If the student makes a mistake, the teacher stops and points out the mistake, then he or she provides the student with immediate feedback on the error. The teacher then re-explains the concept or understanding in a different way to help the student remedy the mistake. Finally, the teacher asks another question or poses a similar problem to ensure the student understands before moving on. The challenge for teachers is to use their classroom assessments in similar ways to provide all students with this sort of individualized assistance.

Successful coaches use exactly the same process. Immediately following a gymnast's performance on the balance beam, for example, the coach explains to her what she did correctly and what could be improved. The coach then offers specific strategies for improvement and encourages her to try again. As the athlete repeats her performance, the coach watches carefully to ensure that she has corrected the problem. Teachers who see their classroom assessments as the same type of demonstration of learning can help their students use the results to likewise improve their performance.

Successful students typically know how to take corrective action on their own. They save their assessments and review the items or criteria they missed. They rework problems, look up answers in their textbooks or other resource materials, and ask the teacher about ideas or concepts they do not understand. Less successful students rarely take such initiative. After looking at their grades, they typically crumple up their assessments and deposit them in the trash can as they leave the classroom. Teachers who use classroom assessments as part of the instructional process help *all* of their students do exactly what the most successful students have learned to do for themselves.

A Vital Component

Using classroom assessment to improve both teaching *and* student learning is not a new idea. Nearly 40 years ago, Benjamin Bloom showed how to conduct this process in practical and highly effective ways when he described the practice of mastery learning (Bloom, 1968, 1971). And despite the relatively modest change required to implement the process, extensive research demonstrates that it can have exceptionally positive effects on student learning. A study by Whiting, Van Burgh, and Render (1995) representing 18 years of data gathered from over 7,000 high-school students showed mastery learning to have a remarkably positive influence on students' test scores and grade-point averages, as well as on their attitudes toward school and learning. Another field experiment conducted in elementary- and middle-school classrooms showed that the implementation of mastery learning led to significantly positive increases in students' academic achievement and self-confidence (Anderson et al., 1992). Even more impressive, a comprehensive, meta-analysis of the research on mastery learning concluded:

> Few educational treatments of any sort were consistently associated with achievement effects as large as those produced by mastery learning. . . . In evaluation after evaluation, mastery programs have produced impressive gains. (Kulik, Kulik, & Bangert-Drowns, 1990, p. 292)

Some researchers even suggest that the superiority of Japanese students in international comparisons of achievement in mathematics operations and problem-solving may be due largely to Japan's widespread use of instructional practices similar to mastery learning (Nakajima, 2006; Waddington, 1995). Research evidence also shows that the positive effects of mastery learning are not limited to cognitive or achievement outcomes. The process yields improvements in students' confidence in learning situations, school attendance rates, involvement in class sessions, attitudes toward learning, and a variety of other affective measures (Guskey & Pigott, 1988). This multidimensional impact has been referred to as mastery learning's "multiplier effect," which makes it an especially powerful tool in school-improvement efforts.

Assessments are a vital component in our efforts to reform and improve education. But as long as we use them only as a means to rank schools and students, we will miss out on their most powerful benefits. We must focus instead on viewing assessments in a different way, considering assessments for a broader array of purposes, and changing the way we use assessment results. As teachers, we must improve the quality of our classroom assessments to ensure that they are well-aligned with valued learning goals and state or district standards. When teachers' classroom assessments become an integral part of the instructional process and a central ingredient in efforts to help students learn, the benefits of assessment for both teachers and students will be boundless.

References

Anderson, S., Barrett, C., Huston, M., Lay, L., Myr, G., Sexton, D., & Watson, B. (1992). *A mastery learning experiment* (Technical Report). Yale, MI: Yale Public Schools.

Barton, P. E. (2002). *Staying on course in education reform.* Princeton, NJ: Statistics & Research Division, Policy Information Center, Educational Testing Service.

Bloom, B. S. (1968). Learning for mastery. *Evaluation Comment* (UCLA-CSIEP), *1*(2), 1–12.

Bloom, B. S. (1971). Mastery learning. In J. H. Block (Ed.), *Mastery learning: Theory and practice.* New York: Holt, Rinehart & Winston.

Bloom, B. S., Madaus, G. F., & Hastings, J. T. (1981). *Evaluation to improve learning.* New York: McGraw-Hill.

Guskey, T. R. (1997). *Implementing mastery learning* (2nd ed.). Belmont, CA: Wadsworth.

Guskey, T. R. (1998). Making time to train your staff. *The School Administrator, 55*(7), 35–37.

Guskey, T. R. (2000a). *Evaluating professional development.* Thousand Oaks, CA: Corwin Press.

Guskey, T. R. (2000b). Twenty questions? Twenty tools for better teaching. *Principal Leadership, 1*(3), 5–7.

Guskey, T. R. (2006). *It wasn't fair! Educators' recollections of their experiences as students with grading.* Paper presented at the annual meeting of the American Educational Research Association, San Francisco.

Guskey, T. R. (2007). Multiple sources of evidence: An analysis of stakeholders' perceptions of various indicators of student learning. *Educational Measurement: Issues and Practice, 26*(1), 19–27.

Guskey, T. R., & Pigott, T. D. (1988). Research on group-based mastery learning programs: A meta-analysis. *Journal of Educational Research, 81*(4), 197–216.

Hattie, J., & Timperley, H. (2007). The power of feedback. *Review of Educational Research, 77*(1), 81–112.

Kifer, E. (2001). *Large-scale assessment: Dimensions, dilemmas, and policies.* Thousand Oaks, CA: Corwin Press.

Kulik, J. A., & Kulik, C. C. (1989). Meta-analysis in education. *International Journal of Educational Research, 13*(2), 221–340.

Kulik, C. C., Kulik, J. A., & Bangert-Drowns, R. L. (1990). Effectiveness of mastery learning programs: A meta-analysis. *Review of Educational Research, 60*(2), 265–299.

Nakajima, A. (2006). A powerful influence on Japanese education. In T. R. Guskey (Ed.), *Benjamin S. Bloom: Portraits of an educator* (pp. 109–111). Lanham, MD: Rowman & Littlefield Education.

Sternberg, R. J. (1994). Allowing for thinking styles. *Educational Leadership, 52*(3), 36–40.

Stiggins, R. J. (1999). Evaluating classroom assessment training in teacher education programs. *Educational Measurement: Issues and Practice, 18*(1), 23–27.

Stiggins, R. J. (2002). Assessment crisis: The absence of assessment *for* learning. *Phi Delta Kappan, 83*(10), 758–765.

Waddington, T. (1995). *Why mastery matters.* Paper presented at the annual meeting of the American Educational Research Association, San Francisco.

Whiting, B., Van Burgh, J. W., & Render, G. F. (1995). *Mastery learning in the classroom.* Paper presented at the annual meeting of the American Educational Research Association, San Francisco.

Wiggins, G. (1998). *Educative assessment.* San Francisco: Jossey-Bass.

Anne Davies

Dr. Anne Davies is an author, consultant, and researcher who applies her expert knowledge of developing quality classroom assessments to her mission to increase the possibility of learning for all students. Educators at every grade level in Canada, the United States, and elsewhere have benefited from the high-touch support she provides during professional development events and multiyear projects. A world-renowned keynote presenter and professional development consultant, Dr. Davies' genuine care and commitment to supporting educators and their important work make her an approachable and insightful specialist. Dr. Davies is the author and coauthor of more than 24 books and multimedia resources as well as numerous chapters and articles.

In this chapter, Dr. Davies explores the four research-based cornerstones for thoughtfully and deliberately involving students in the classroom assessment process to support learning:

- Formative classroom assessment
- Feedback
- Motivation
- Summative evaluation

Dr. Davies then examines four specific strategies in depth, using real school examples to illustrate how educators can:

- Define learning destinations so that students understand their achievement goals.
- Involve students as partners in co-constructing criteria.
- Multiply the amount of feedback students receive to "feed-forward" their learning.
- Engage students in collecting, selecting, reflecting on, and presenting evidence of their learning.

For more information about Dr. Anne Davies, visit www.annedavies.ca.

Chapter 2

Involving Students in the Classroom Assessment Process

Anne Davies

Teachers want to teach engaged, enthusiastic students who learn and achieve at high levels and produce quality evidence of their learning. Research and best practice tell us what some teachers have known for a while: When students are involved in the classroom assessment process, they are more engaged and motivated, and they learn more. This deep student involvement is essential if students are to learn and achieve at high levels. Four cornerstones (Davies, in press) derived from the research provide a foundation for thoughtfully and deliberately involving students in the classroom assessment process: formative classroom assessment, feedback, motivation, and summative evaluation.

Cornerstone 1: Formative Classroom Assessment

Research shows that when students are involved in the assessment process—by co-constructing the criteria by which they are assessed, self-assessing in relation to the criteria, giving themselves information to guide (or "feed-forward" their learning), collecting and presenting evidence of their learning, and reflecting on their strengths and needs—they learn more, achieve at higher levels, and are more motivated. They are also better able to set informed, appropriate learning goals to further improve their learning (see Crooks, 1988; Black & Wiliam, 1998; Davies, 2004; Stiggins, 1996). This is called "formative" assessment because the assessment is used to impact learning—not merely as a measure of what was learned. Using assessment in this way leads to greater socioeconomic, professional, and personal success for students (Dweck, 2000; Sternberg, 1996). The gains in achievement for students who use this type of assessment are so considerable that Black and Wiliam (1998) found it to be "amongst the largest ever reported for educational interventions" (p. 61).

Cornerstone 2: Quality Feedback for Learning

There are two general categories of feedback: specific, descriptive feedback and evaluative feedback (Gipps & Stobart, 1993). Each has a different impact on learning (Butler 1987, 1988).

Specific, Descriptive Feedback

Specific, descriptive feedback is needed both during and after the learning. It is formative. In this kind of feedback, student work is compared to criteria, rubrics, models, exemplars, samples, or descriptions of excellence. Students learn what elements of their work (products, processes, or presentations) meet quality expectations and where they need to learn more and improve their work. Students understand this feedback more readily because it relates directly to their learning. Less effective feedback merely judges the learning (for example, "Good job!" or "Needs work!"), while specific, descriptive feedback related to the criteria informs learners about what they have done well and what they need to do differently. For example: "In your paragraph, you have a clear lead sentence. That's great. You need to add more details in support of the lead sentence." This kind of feedback "feeds-forward" student learning; it propels the learning forward.

Evaluative Feedback

This second type of feedback needs to come at the end of the learning. It is summative. It tells the learner how she or he has performed compared to others (norm-referenced) or in relation to what was to be learned (criterion-referenced). Evaluative feedback is communicated using letters, numbers, checks, or other symbols; it is encoded. Students who receive evaluative feedback usually understand whether or not they need to improve. However, unless students can decode the evaluative feedback, they may not have enough information to understand how to improve.

Researchers report that letter grades and other symbols that communicate evaluative feedback can have a negative effect on learning for all students. These negative effects are most pronounced with low-achieving students. Students with poor marks are more likely to see themselves as failures, and students who see themselves as failures are less likely to succeed as learners (Black & Wiliam, 1998; Butler 1987, 1988; Crooks, 1988; Dweck, 2000; Hattie, 1992, 2005; Kamii, 1984; Lepper & Greene, 1978; Phillips, 1995; Shepard & Smith, 1986, 1987). Poor marks, grades, and negative comments may result in these struggling students becoming unmotivated, unengaged, and less willing to take the risks necessary for learning (Deci, Koestner, & Ryan, 1999; Dweck, 2000; Covington, 1992; Harlen & Deakin-Crick, 2003; Lepper & Greene, 1978). They experience greater potential for interruptions to their learning, and as a result, they learn less and achieve less. This makes sense considering what brain research has shown: When we are threatened or perceive ourselves to be threatened, our brains are too busy defending themselves to engage in learning (Jensen, 1998; Le Doux, 1996; Pert, 1999; Pinker, 1997). When evaluative feedback is decreased, and specific, descriptive feedback is increased, students learn more.

Cornerstone 3: Motivation

The way teachers assess and evaluate student work impacts students' motivation for learning. Educators report and research confirms (Harlen & Deakin-Crick, 2003) that when students are involved in the assessment process they:

- Develop a sense of ownership and commitment to their learning.

- Make choices about what to focus on next in their learning.

- Engage in learning.

- Experience fewer discipline problems.

When teachers emphasize learning and performance, rather than competition and grades, students are more likely to be intrinsically motivated and encouraged to take risks that challenge and expand their learning. And when feedback is more specific and descriptive, students are more likely to remain focused on learning and make informed choices about what to do next. For example, when students are asked to write a better paragraph, they may not know what is lacking in their previous work and therefore will not know what to do differently. When the feedback is more specific—"In your paragraph, you have a clear lead sentence. That's great. You need to add more details in support of the lead sentence"—students know what to do differently: Add more details.

When students make choices about their learning, their engagement and achievement increase. When they have no choices, their engagement and learning decrease (Davies, 2004; Harlen & Deakin-Crick, 2003; Hayden et al., 2007; Jensen, 1998).

Rewards are a form of evaluative feedback. They are sometimes used as a way to motivate, but they do not provide specific feedback. Some researchers have concluded that marks, grades, and other rewards may demotivate students, interfere with learning, and potentially disrupt relationships among teachers and students in the learning environment (Butler, 1987; 1988; Deci, Koestner, & Ryan, 1999; Harlen & Deakin-Crick, 2003).

Cornerstone 4: Summative Evaluation of Student Evidence

Summative evaluation is an essential cornerstone because evaluation requires sufficient evidence that students have achieved the intended learning. In the past, there was an assumption that such evaluation was best done externally, with tests and other forms of evaluation created and monitored by outside sources. Assessment Reform Group's research (2006) has revealed, however, that when a teacher's professional judgment regarding the quality of student work is based on knowledge arising from the conscientious development and application of consistent criteria for summative evaluation, the teacher's judgments are likely to be more valid and reliable than the results of external tests. It is essential that evidence of learning be triangulated (collected from multiple sources and in multiple forms) and collected over time. And when teachers work together and develop clearly specified criteria that describe progressive levels of competence and procedures for using criteria to evaluate student work, they are more able to reliably assess and evaluate a greater range of classroom work. Looking at a greater range of student work (including both qualitative and quantitative evidence) as they learn to apply shared criteria can increase the validity of teachers' judgments and limits the need for external evaluation. This process helps teachers become more confident and better able to make independent judgments (Assessment Reform Group, 2006; Sadler, 1989).

Involving Learners in Assessment

These four cornerstones have significant implications for involving students at a deep level in classroom-assessment practices. As the first cornerstone suggests, it is essential that we increase the amount and quality of formative assessment in our classrooms if we are to promote deep student involvement. The second cornerstone tells us that the quality and amount of feedback is significant to student learning. Intentionally involving students in the feedback process will not only help improve their learning, but also involve them at a deeper level.

Motivation, the third cornerstone, is an integral part of an assessment process in which students play a significant role. Students are highly motivated when they have more choice during the learning process and receive more quality feedback. They can collect evidence of their own learning from a variety of sources. This has benefits for educators as well, as it leads to more differentiation of assessment and better quality evidence of learning.

The final research cornerstone—summative evaluation of student evidence—gives educators the confidence they need to move forward in their plans to involve students deeply in the assessment process. Involving students in this way can increase the reliability and validity of summative evaluation by increasing the range of qualitative and quantitative evidence used to document student success.

The rest of this chapter describes specific strategies educators can use to involve students in the assessment process as supported by these essential research cornerstones:

- Defining learning destinations so students understand the goals they seek to achieve

- Involving students as partners in co-constructing criteria

- Multiplying the amount of feedback students receive to "feed-forward" their learning

- Engaging students in collecting, selecting, reflecting on, and presenting evidence of their learning

Defining the Learning Destination

Chelsie Ruiz, a kindergarten teacher at Kekaha Elementary School in Kekaha, Kauai, Hawaii, has summarized the standards for each subject area into simple language her students and their parents understand. When students meet with her to select samples of their work, she shows them the list of standards and explains that they need to show evidence of what they have been learning. Then they select evidence, or proof of learning, and put it in their portfolios. When parents review the portfolios during conference time, they can see how the evidence relates to the standards for these students.

Students learn more when they understand the goals they are expected to achieve—when the learning destination is clear and defined. In the words of Rick Stiggins (2007), "Students can hit any target that they know about and that holds still for them" (p. 1). When teachers inform students of the focus for learning (the standards they must achieve), students have a chance to engage, bring their prior knowledge to the learning, feel a sense of ownership, and become more effective partners in the learning-assessment process. To do this, teachers can analyze the standards or learning outcomes that they are responsible for teaching and summarize them in simple language that students can easily understand. This makes it possible for students to begin self-monitoring their way to success.

Research has shown that when athletes picture themselves exercising, their brains register the exercise, even though their bodies have not physically moved (see Jeannerod, 1995). Likewise, students have more opportunities for success when they understand what success looks like, consider what they need to do to become successful learners, and mentally prepare themselves for success. Teachers can facilitate this process by sharing, analyzing, and discussing samples with students so they understand the essential components of quality work. Students feed-forward their learning when they match their work to samples, self-assess, or work with peers to make their products of better quality. Teachers support this learning by helping students determine their next steps so they can eventually learn how to get to the learning destination themselves.

As a result of understanding the learning destination and appreciating what quality work and success look like, students:

- Begin to learn the language of assessment. This means students learn to talk about and reflect on their own work using the language of criteria and learning destinations. Later, this is the language they will use as they give themselves and others specific feedback to feed their learning forward.

- Gain the knowledge they need to make decisions that help close the gap between where they are in their learning and where they need to be.

Merely explaining to students what they will be learning and what this learning might look like is not enough. Teachers need to go further and involve students as partners in the classroom assessment process by working with them to co-construct criteria, give and receive feedback for learning, and collect, select, reflect on, and present evidence of learning to determine the next steps to feed their learning forward (goal-setting). Informal goal-setting takes place the moment students decide to do something different—the moment they determine next steps for their learning. Formal and informal goal-setting can take place at any time. When it occurs depends on the students and the teacher. These strategies are supported by our second cornerstone: providing quality feedback for learning.

Involving Students as Partners in the Process

Early in the school year, Mr. W., a social-studies teacher, showed the class two maps—one that met quality criteria and one that did not. Students analyzed the two maps, with Mr. W.'s support, and co-constructed criteria that described the characteristics of the effective map. Then students made their own maps of the same area. During the year, as they made maps of different places, they returned to the same samples to revisit, review, and refine criteria. The first map samples provided a lot of support early in their learning. Later in their learning, the samples provided reminders of attributes of quality maps (Gregory, Cameron, & Davies, 1997).

Partners in Co-Constructing Criteria

Good teaching decisions depend on quality information. Teachers need good data to support learning, and students need it even more. Students make many critical decisions that impact the steps they take in the learning process. Sometimes those decisions are uninformed or based on incomplete information because students do not understand what they are expected to learn and how they can best show that they have learned it. Teachers can begin by sharing the overall learning destination with students; next, they can deepen students' understanding by involving them as partners in co-constructing criteria. This process helps each student understand the essential characteristics of success and quality work.

Criteria enable students to demonstrate their learning and achievement in relation to particular processes or products. Criteria define quality work. They do so by describing important attributes of the process or product. When we involve students in co-constructing criteria, they grasp important ideas more readily because they are translating expectations into language that they understand. In the process, teachers learn what students already know (or do not know). Students have an opportunity to confirm their knowledge, consolidate their learning (move from believing they know it, to knowing it, and then to knowing they know it), integrate new knowledge, and make better choices for the next steps in their learning process.

For example, when teachers co-construct criteria by defining with students what is important in creating a map, writing a story, doing a research report, or presenting to a small group, students have the opportunity to share their ideas and check their own theories. Sometimes students do not know enough to set good criteria, so teachers inform the criteria-setting process by showing samples or models or by waiting until later in the learning process to co-construct criteria.

This criteria-setting process helps keep students motivated, engaged, involved, and informed while building ownership and helping teachers identify the needs of the group so they can tailor their instruction. Phil Divinsky, a secondary teacher who works with students who have special needs, involves his students in criteria-setting to establish a class agreement regarding how they will act towards one another, as well as how they will go about their learning (Divinsky, 2007). Lisa McCluskey, a kindergarten teacher, involves students in co-constructing criteria early in the year to help students understand what is important during group meetings or snack time (Davies, 2003). Debbie Jamieson, a teacher in a seventh- and eighth-grade classroom where every student has a laptop computer, asks students to talk about what is important when giving a slide-show presentation. She then uses their ideas to set criteria to guide their work (Davies, 2004).

Using Samples to Strengthen Learning

Samples of student work at various stages in the learning process are key tools for setting criteria for success. Students are more likely to understand what success looks like for a project or a process when they can examine samples of work. These samples help students understand:

- How learning develops over time

- Different ways to show or represent learning

- The attributes of quality the teacher expects to find as evidence that learning has occurred

Samples that show successive changes in quality help students understand how learning develops over time. Teachers may share several samples from the same student that show the student's initial ideas, early drafts, and the finished piece. When teachers want students to see the different ways they can represent their learning, they may choose a variety of samples in different forms (such as written pieces, oral presentations, multimedia projects, dramatizations, physical models, and so on) that show a high level of quality. When students must show what they know in a certain way—for example, by writing a lab report for science class—teachers can either provide a format for the assignment or involve students in creating a common framework for the project using samples of previous student work. This sharing of work helps students understand what it means to meet the quality expectations represented in the co-constructed criteria.

Samples are particularly important for students who struggle to learn. They act as a road map for producing quality work. Sample selection should be carefully linked to the purpose of the learning and the learning needs of students. If samples show work that is more advanced than what students are actually able to do, students may become frustrated. If samples are limited to what students already know and can do, they may fail to inspire new learning.

The Impact of Co-Constructing Criteria

Some educators who have spent time trying to create criteria and rubrics in student-accessible language without the help of students think, "This is too hard to do well!" Co-constructing criteria *with* students is a far more powerful strategy because it begins with student ideas. Sometimes teachers hesitate to involve students in co-constructing criteria. They may wonder if their students are qualified to participate in the process. As a result, they never find out what students know and understand about quality products or processes. Students do have ideas about quality work. They are able to contribute to defining the criteria against which they are assessed. Gregory, Cameron, and Davies (1997, p. 7) describe a step-by-step process for co-constructing criteria with students:

- Brainstorm a list of ideas with students. For example, students might consider "What is important for a quality book report?" Students might decide that a quality book report must make sense; contain interesting information; have a beginning, middle, and end; be neat; use paragraphs; use descriptive language; include details; and have correct spelling, punctuation, and capitalization, among other things.

- Guide students to sort, group, and label the brainstormed ideas and determine essential attributes. After reviewing the brainstormed list, students might decide to group the information into three categories: Information that makes the book report interesting to the audience, content that makes the report easy to follow, and content that makes the report easy to read.

- Make and post a T-chart. Figure 1 shows a sample T-chart for a quality book report using the three categories.

- Use the criteria to guide student work. The specific details in the T-chart help students understand what their quality work should look like. Then, as students learn more, they continue to revisit and revise the criteria.

Co-constructing criteria changes the teaching and learning environment. Having criteria means more students are engaged and learning at higher levels. To illustrate, a high-school science teacher assigned a major project worth 40% of the final grade to her students every year. Some students—as many as 60% some years—would not even bother to turn it in. After she learned this simple four-step process for co-constructing criteria, she immediately began to involve her students in setting criteria for a successful project. Like

CRITERIA FOR A QUALITY BOOK REPORT	SPECIFICS/DETAILS
Interesting to Audience	* interesting information * descriptive language * has humor, drama, emotion * practice reading it out loud * grab the reader's attention * add details * remember your audience
Easy to Follow	* makes sense * has beginning, middle, & end * use paragraphs * correct spelling * practice reading it aloud * neat
Easy to Read	* neat * indent paragraphs * correct punctuation * capitals * correct spelling * remember your audience

Figure 1: Sample T-Chart for "What Is Important for a Quality Book Report?" (Elementary Level)

many of her colleagues, she did not think her students would know enough or be engaged enough to do a good job of co-constructing criteria. The teacher was amazed by the results:

> It was the only thing I did differently. I was so surprised. The students were so thoughtful and respectful. Their criteria were really good. One class set the very same criteria I had set in previous years. Guess what? This year *every* student turned in their project.

What made the difference for students? Was it the respect they felt from their teacher, the choices they made, their feelings of ownership of the process, a greater understanding of the material? The answer might be different for every learner, but the important thing is they made the choice to do the work, and increased learning appears to be related to students' active engagement through choice (Langer, 1989, 1997; Schlechtly, 2002). This is a clear research trend: When students are involved in assessment, more learning takes place (see Black & Wiliam, 1998; Crooks, 1988).

Giving and Receiving Feedback for Learning

William Grindell's tenth-grade students at Farrington High School in Honolulu, Hawaii, were studying the relationship between cultural traditions of particular religions in relation to the larger societies in which their members exist. Toward the end of the unit, the students were asked to create a brochure. Together they fine-tuned the rubric for the brochure, and then students got started. When the brochure was almost complete, he explained to the students that their work could be even better if they got feedback from themselves and from others. Mr. Grindell gave everyone a photocopy of a sample brochure. They analyzed it using the criteria they developed earlier. He gave a list of examples of feedback and asked the students to determine which examples were of good quality. They talked about how they would feel if they were given that kind of feedback and what kind of feedback would help them do better. Once they discussed the different kinds of feedback and came to an agreement about what good quality feedback looked (and sounded) like, he explained that when they gave each other feedback, it had to be specific and descriptive so others would know what to do better next time. Working in teams, they exchanged brochures, highlighted the sections on the rubric that applied, and gave each other specific, descriptive feedback in relation to the criteria.

Specific feedback is important for learning. Think about how digital cameras provide us with instant feedback we can use to choose our next steps: We take a picture, review it, analyze it, maybe ask for someone else's opinion, and then decide our next step—do we take another picture, and how will it be different than the first? Each time students reflect on their learning using co-constructed criteria, they practice articulating what they have learned. When they practice articulating important ideas, they become better able to give themselves and others specific, descriptive feedback that will feed-forward the learning.

The quality of feedback increases dramatically when informed by clear criteria and samples of excellent work. Specific, descriptive feedback, particularly when given in relation to co-constructed criteria, provides students with the opportunity to improve. To increase the amount of specific, descriptive feedback for students, teachers should seek sources of feedback for students beyond themselves. Consider these examples:

- Students analyze what worked and what did not as they review each other's writing assignments (Davies, 2006).

- Students invite their parents to view their portfolios online and provide feedback (Sueoka, 2007).

- Young children listen to each other read and note on a list of criteria what they do and what they need to do (Davies, 2000).

These simple practices are ways to multiply the feedback effect. Consider the teacher who tries to give students a lot of timely feedback. Over the course of a week, he or she manages to give every student specific, descriptive feedback four times (see Figure 2a).

Now imagine the teacher has involved students in co-constructing criteria. Before asking students to turn in their work for feedback, she asks students to self-assess using co-constructed criteria (give themselves feedback). Without the teacher working any harder, the students receive twice the amount of feedback to feed their learning forward (see Figure 2b). Now imagine the classroom is a place where everyone understands quality because they have set criteria and have been using the language of the criteria to describe and assess their work in progress. This time the teacher asks students to give their work to someone else to assess using the criteria. Their job is to review another student's work and find evidence of two things that meet the criteria, and select one thing from the criteria that needs to be improved (see Figure 2c). Next, students are asked to apply the feedback they have received, self-assess, and give themselves specific, descriptive feedback. The teacher then receives the work, and gives the students specific, descriptive feedback that also feeds the learning forward. Again, students are receiving more feedback without the teacher working any harder. Rather, the teacher is working differently. And what about the classroom where every student has access to email and the Internet (see Figure 2d)? Could students send their work to other people in other places and get even more feedback to feed-forward the learning? Absolutely! Research shows students seek feedback when it is easily available and when their work can be improved (Davies, 2004, in press).

The second research cornerstone shows us that the learning brain needs continuous feedback. In the example in Figure 2a–d, students have received at least triple the amount of feedback to feed-forward their learning because the teacher has engaged students as partners in the classroom assessment process. When teachers are the only source of quality feedback in the classroom, students will receive

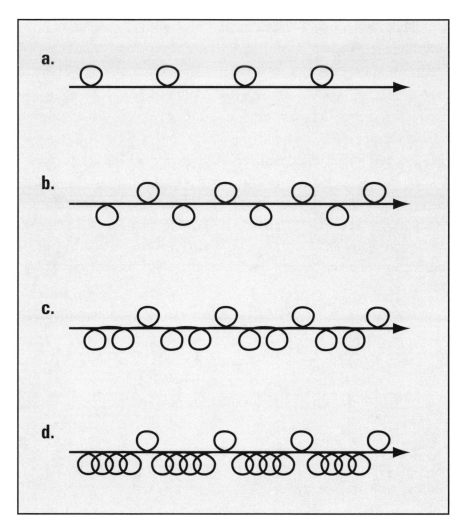

Figure 2a–d: Multiplying Feedback
(Special thanks to Doug Snow for his assistance with this figure.)

less specific, descriptive feedback. As a result, they are likely to learn less. Students can learn to give powerful and effective feedback to themselves and others. They do this by examining their work in relation to the co-constructed criteria, specifically determining whether or not they have met the quality expectations and clarifying how they can improve their work even further.

Collecting, Selecting, Reflecting, and Presenting Evidence of Learning

Ms. L. teaches high school mathematics. She asks students to collect evidence of their learning in a portfolio. While they need to show they are proficient in the course as demonstrated through work samples, tests, quizzes, and assignments, they also have to find evidence that they are improving their mathematical "habits of mind" (Costa & Kallick, 2000). They can draw evidence from any aspect of their learning inside or outside of class. This past year the portfolio categories were persistence, questioning, drawing on past knowledge and experience, and precision of thought and language. Each year the categories change as she emphasizes different aspects of being a mathematician (Labbe, 2007).

Think about the typical classrooms of your youth. Students did the work. The teacher decided what was important. The teacher marked and graded the work. Students did some more work. Students periodically turned in cumulative assignments and wrote tests. The teacher based the summative evaluation on certain predetermined pieces of evidence—usually a combination of completed student assessment tasks and tests in this classroom. Today we are questioning whether these practices are appropriate. After all, would this be enough evidence for a driver's license? Probably not. Someone seeking a driver's license needs to pass a written test *and* demonstrate good driving skills as well as articulate the expertise and knowledge needed to drive safely. The evidence is triangulated (collected from multiple sources). Given today's learning expectations, teachers also need higher quality evidence collected over time from multiple sources.

In today's classrooms, students generate a wide range of evidence of their learning. It is essential that teachers plan to collect evidence in relation to standards (or long-term learning destinations). Anything a student says, does, or creates is potential evidence of learning. Teachers engaged in quality classroom assessment collect this evidence of student learning over time, looking for patterns and trends and evaluating on the basis of co-constructed criteria and learning goals. This process makes it possible for students to show what they know in a variety of ways. Collecting a wide range of evidence over a long period of time increases the reliability and validity of the classroom assessment findings.

Students come from varying backgrounds with differing experiences, knowledge, and skills (both inherent and learned). They require different kinds of input and levels of support to learn. Often students need to take divergent learning paths, and as a result, create unique evidence of their learning along the way. Many factors, such as learning needs, learning styles, and multiple intelligences, lead students to produce these varying types of evidence. For example, one student might have an Individual Education Plan (IEP) because he has difficulty writing. His collection of evidence may contain fewer writing pieces and more drawings, maps, and audio tapes. Another student's learning difficulty may not be severe enough to qualify for an IEP, however, given the child's learning needs, the teacher may encourage her to build on her strengths while compensating for her weaknesses. This results in a collection of evidence of learning that is different from the first student's. Yet both students have collected evidence of their learning in relation to the standards or learning outcomes. Potentially every student could have a different collection of evidence because every student has taken a different learning journey towards the same standards or outcomes. This is the result of differentiated assessment and student involvement in the assessment process.

Teachers can collect evidence of student learning through work folders, portfolios that showcase chosen work, progress folios, websites, or any format that shows the extent to which students have succeeded in reaching the learning destination. But when students are involved in collecting, evaluating, reflecting on, organizing, and presenting this evidence of their learning, teachers gain more information about students and their learning.

Once students collect evidence of their learning, a natural next step is showing this evidence to others. Like a performance review in the workplace, communicating evidence of learning to others compels students to step back, reflect, and assess their efforts. The audience—often parents—reviews the evidence and gives feedback. In this situation, both the learner and the audience have the chance to gain a deeper understanding of the learning, and the audience can support the learner's needs in the future. Involving parents and others in the assessment process supports learning because:

- Students learn to articulate what they have learned and what they still need to work on.

- Students learn more as they reflect and select evidence of learning to show others.

- When students show evidence of learning to an audience, they receive feedback and recognition for their learning.

- When parents are involved in talking about learning with their children, students achieve more.

In addition, when students present evidence to someone whose opinion they care about, they prepare themselves more thoroughly and are more likely to assume responsibility for their learning. More involved parents equals higher student achievement levels (Henderson & Berla, 1995).

Presenting or sharing student evidence of learning can be done in several ways. Students might take their work samples home in portfolios or demonstrate their learning at home. For example, they might show their skills in physical education, cook a recipe, play an instrument, solve a problem, read a book, or show a slide-show presentation of their latest research project. The possibilities are endless. Students and their parents might participate in goal-setting conferences early in the term. Or students and parents might meet at school to review the evidence of learning in a parent-student conference. Teachers may choose to join the parent-student conference to clarify questions or to help set goals. No matter what the venue for sharing, it is important that students identify what they have learned, what the evidence of learning shows in terms of meeting the standards or outcomes, and ask for specific feedback that can support their next learning steps.

Involving students in the collection of evidence of learning in this way ties back into the fourth research cornerstone—summative evaluation of student evidence. This deep student involvement in assessment creates a broad picture of what students know and are able to do. Showing evidence of learning in this way helps teachers and families understand what students know, what needs to be learned, and what quality looks like, and also helps families understand more clearly the summative evaluation information contained in their student's report card.

Feeding the Learning Forward by Setting Goals

Kari Nye, a teacher at Glacier View Elementary School in Courtenay, British Columbia, co-constructed criteria with her elementary class for their current-events presentations. Students took turns presenting their current events, and after each presentation, the students and Ms. Nye talked about what made the presentation effective and added each item to their list of "What makes an effective current events presentation?" As students became more aware of the criteria, they began to take turns providing specific, descriptive feedback to one another using the frame of two strengths and one idea for improvement. This one idea for improvement became a goal area—a feed-forward suggestion for improvement. Over time, the criteria list grew, their understandings of what was important for a quality current-events presentation deepened, their speaking and presentation skills improved, and the goals became more specific next steps to improvement.

When students co-construct criteria and self-assess using those criteria, they are able to identify next steps to take in their learning: This is feedback that feeds-forward to further learning. When students examine what they are doing well and what they need to improve in relation to co-constructed criteria, they are setting their own goals for learning. The most powerful goals are those that reflect steps along the way—not just the final outcome. By taking small steps, students can self-monitor their way to success. These small goals are more realistic and manageable for students, even more so when they involve co-constructed criteria expressed in terms students understand. Research indicates that moving closer to achieving a goal triggers a part of the brain linked to motivation (Csikszentmihalyi, 1997). Students involved in this kind of self-assessment and goal-setting are motivated to learn more because they can continue to assess their work against co-constructed criteria during the learning process. When students have a clear understanding of the learning destination and apply knowledge of their current strengths and needs gained through specific, descriptive feedback, they are able to set appropriate and realistic learning goals. As we learned in the four research cornerstones, goals such as these help students focus and accomplish more.

A Strong Foundation of Deep Involvement

With the growing emphasis on high-stakes evaluation, it is imperative that classroom teachers do even more formative classroom assessment with deep student involvement to ensure that students learn. Students need to know the destination for their learning. They need to understand what quality work is and what success might look like. Ongoing formative assessment with student involvement is one of the best ways to help students self-monitor their way to success. The research is clear: Students learn and achieve more when they are deeply involved in the process of classroom assessment, and teachers who use quality classroom assessment practices have more students learning and achieving at high levels. It is worth the investment to learn how to involve students in the assessment process, because after all, in the end it is what students learn that truly matters. If you want more students to learn and achieve, put your energy where it counts: Involve every student deeply in the classroom assessment process.

Acknowledgments

I would like to thank the many teachers who have welcomed me into their classrooms and given me permission to share their classroom assessment stories of learning for the benefit of our students.

References

Assessment Reform Group. (2006). *The role of teachers in the assessment* of *learning.* Cambridge: Author. Available at: http://k1.ioe.ac.uk/tlrp/arg/publications.html.

Black, P., & Wiliam, D. (1998). Assessment and classroom learning. *Assessment in Education, 5*(1), 7–75.

Brookhart, S. (2001). Successful students' formative and summative uses of assessment information. *Assessment in Education, 8*(2), 153–169.

Butler, R. (1987). Task-involving and ego-involving properties of evaluation: Effects of different feedback conditions on motivational perceptions, interest and performance. *Journal of Educational Psychology, 79*(4), 474–482.

Butler, R. (1988). Enhancing and undermining intrinsic motivation: The effects of task-involving and ego-involving evaluation on interest and performance. *British Journal of Educational Psychology, 58*(1), 1–14.

Catlin, K., Lewan, G., and Perignon, B. (1999). Increasing student engagement through goal setting, cooperative learning and student choice. ED433100. Unpublished thesis.

Costa, A. L., & Kallick, B. (Eds.) (2000). *Assessing and reporting on habits of mind.* Alexandria, VA: Association for Supervision and Curriculum Development.

Covington, M. V. (1992). *Making the grade: A self-worth perspective on motivation and school reform.* Cambridge, UK: Cambridge University Press.

Crooks, T. (1988). The impact of classroom evaluation on students. *Review of Educational Research, 58*(4), 438–481.

Csikszentmihalyi, M. (1997). *Finding flow.* Basic Books: New York.

Davies, A. (2000). Feed back . . . feed forward: Using assessment to boost literacy learning. *Primary Leadership, 2*(3), 53–55.

Davies, A. (2003). *A facilitator's guide to making classroom assessment work: The middle years.* Courtenay, BC: Connections Publishing.

Davies. A. (2004). *Finding proof of learning in a one-to-one computing classroom.* Courtenay, BC: Connections Publishing.

Davies, A. (2005). *A facilitator's guide to making classroom assessment work K–12* (Rev. ed.). Courtenay, BC: Connections Publishing.

Davies, A. (2006). *Classroom assessment presenters' kit—A video resource.* Courtenay, BC: Connections Publishing.

Davies, A. (2007). *Making classroom assessment work* (2nd ed.). Courtenay, BC: Connections Publishing.

Davies, A. (in press). Assessment and professional learning: An essential partnership. In *Encyclopedia of Education,* 3rd Edition. New York: Macmillan.

Deci, E. L., Koestner, R., & Ryan, R. M. (1999). A meta-analytic review of experiments examining the effects of extrinsic rewards on intrinsic motivation. *Psychological Bulletin, 125*(6), 627–668.

Divinsky, P. (2007). Creating the classroom culture. In A. Davies and K. Busick (Eds.), *Classroom assessment: What's working in high school.* Courtenay, BC: Connections Publishing.

Dweck, C. (2000). *Self-theories: Their role in motivation, personality, and development.* Philadelphia: Psychology Press.

Elbow, P. (1986). *Embracing contraries: Explorations in learning and teaching.* New York: Oxford University Press.

Gipps, C., & Stobart, G. (1993). *Assessment: A teacher's guide to the issues* (2nd ed.). Oxford: Hodder and Stoughton.

Gregory, K., Cameron, C., & Davies, A. (1997). *Knowing what counts: Setting and using criteria.* Courtenay, BC: Connections Publishing.

Harlen, W., & Deakin-Crick, R. (2003). Testing and motivation for learning. *Assessment in Education, 10*(2), 169–208.

Hattie, J. (1992). Measuring the effects of schooling. *Australian Journal of Education, 36*(1), 5–13.

Hattie, J. (2005, August 7–9). What is the nature of evidence that makes a difference to learning? Presentation made at the Australian Council for Educational Research Conference, Melbourne, Australia.

Hattie, J., & Timperley, H. (2005). *The power of feedback.* Unpublished manuscript, University of Auckland, New Zealand.

Hayden, J., Sakai, K., Rees, G., Gilbert, S., Frith, C., & Passingham, R. (2007). Reading hidden intentions in the human brain. *Current Biology, 17*(4), 323–328.

Henderson, A., & Berla, N. (1995). *A new generation of evidence: The family is critical to student achievement.* Washington, DC: Center for Law and Education.

Jeannerod, M. (1995). Mental imagery in the motor context. *Neuropsychologia, 33*(11), 1419–1432.

Jensen, E. (1998). *Teaching with the brain in mind.* Alexandria, VA: Association for Supervision and Curriculum Development.

Kamii, C. (1984). Autonomy: The aim of education envisioned by Piaget. *Phi Delta Kappan, 65*(6), 410–415.

Labbe, M. (2007). Reflective assessment in mathematics. In A. Davies & K. Busick (Eds.), *Classroom assessment: What's working in high school.* Courtenay, BC: Connections Publishing.

Langer, E. (1989). *Mindfulness: Choice and control in everyday life.* Reading, MA: Addison Wesley.

Langer, E. (1997). *The power of mindful learning.* Reading, MA: Addison Wesley.

Le Doux, J. (1996). *The emotional brain.* New York: Simon & Schuster.

Lepper, M. R., & Greene, D. (Eds.). (1978). *The hidden costs of rewards: New perspectives on the psychology of human motivation.* Hillsdale, NJ: Lawrence Erlbaum.

Meisels, S., Atkins-Burnett, S., Xue, Y., & Bicket, D. D. (2003). Creating a system of accountability: The impact of instructional assessment on elementary children's achievement scores. *Educational Policy Analysis Archives, 11*(9). Available at: http://epaa.asu.edu/ epaa/v11n9/

Noack, M. (2007). Action research and the power of peer feedback. In A. Davies & K. Busick (Eds.), *Classroom assessment: What's working in high school.* Courtenay, BC: Connections Publishing.

Pert, C. (1999). *Molecules of emotion: The science behind mind-body medicine.* New York: Scribner.

Pinker, S. (1997). *How the mind works.* New York: HarperCollins.

Phillips, D. C. (1995). The good, the bad, and the ugly: The many faces of constructivism. *Educational Researcher, 2*(7), 5–12.

Rodriguez, M. C. (2004). The role of classroom assessment in students' performance on TIMSS. *Applied Measurement in Education, 17*(1), 1–24.

Sadler, D. R. (1989). Formative assessment and the design of instructional systems. *Instructional Science, 16*(2), 119–144.

Schlechtly, P. C. (2002). *Working on the work: An action plan for teachers, principals, and superintendents.* San Francisco: Jossey-Bass.

Senge, P. (1990). *The fifth discipline: The art and practice of the learning organization.* New York: Doubleday.

Shepard, L. A., & Smith, M. L. (1986). *Flunking grades: Research and policies on retention.* New York: The Falmer Press.

Shepard, L. A., & Smith, M. L. (1987). What doesn't work: Explaining policies of retention in the early grades. *Phi Delta Kappan, 69,* 129–134.

Sternberg, R. (1996). *Successful intelligence: How practical and creative intelligence determines success in life.* New York: Simon & Schuster.

Stiggins, R. (1996). *Student centered classroom assessment.* Columbus, OH: Merrill.

Stiggins, R. J. (2007). *Introduction to student-involved assessment FOR learning* (5th ed.). Columbia, OH: Pearson Prentice Hall.

Sueoka, L. (2007). A culture of learning: Building a community of shared learning through student online portfolios. In A. Davies & K. Busick (Eds.), *Classroom assessment: What's working in high school.* Courtenay, BC: Connections Publishing.

Wolfe, P. (2001). *Brain matters: Translating research into classroom practice.* Alexandria, VA: Association for Supervision and Curriculum Development.

Rick Stiggins

Dr. Rick Stiggins is founder and executive director of the ETS Assessment Training Institute in Portland, Oregon. Since 1992, the Institute's professional learning programs have helped teachers and school leaders understand how to use the assessment process and its results to benefit (not merely monitor) student learning. The hallmark of these programs has been their focus on the use of student-involved assessment to maximize their confidence, motivation, and learning. The flagship program, Classroom Assessment FOR Student Learning, provides a multimedia, collaborative, and hands-on way for teachers to become competent, confident classroom assessors. Dr. Stiggins has served on the faculties of Michigan State University, the University of Minnesota, and Lewis and Clark College, Portland, as well as on the research and development staffs of ACT and the Northwest Regional Educational Laboratory.

Dr. Stiggins believes that while classroom assessment certainly can and should serve accountability purposes by providing evidence for report-card grading, we can and should take advantage of the process to help us accomplish far more than that: Classroom assessment can serve to promote student success.

In this chapter, Dr. Stiggins argues that truly productive assessment cannot merely be about qualities of instruments and their resulting scores. Rather, it must also be about the impact of the score *on the learner.* He first describes what it means to assess accurately using the four keys to assessment quality: clear purpose, clear targets, accurate assessment, and effective communication. He then describes the effective use of the assessment process and its results to help students advance their learning with enthusiasm so they feel in control of their learning as they attain new levels of proficiency: assessment *for* learning.

For more information about Dr. Rick Stiggins, visit www.ets.org/ati.

Chapter 3

Assessment *for* Learning: An Essential Foundation of Productive Instruction

Rick Stiggins

Years ago during my graduate studies in educational measurement, I learned that my job was to assure the dependability (validity and reliability) of the scores resulting from the assessment process. My studies of classical and modern psychometrics focused my attention on the attributes of the resulting scores. I was taught how to design and develop instruments that consistently produced scores that accurately reflected the learning target.

In the past decade, I have experienced a profound transformation in my understanding of the keys to productive assessment. I continue to honor my professional heritage: I believe more strongly than ever that assessment results must be accurate in all contexts. Inaccurate data leads to counterproductive instructional decisions, and thus it is harmful to students. However, I have come to realize that truly productive assessment cannot merely be about qualities of instruments and the attributes of their resulting scores. Rather, it must also be about the impact of that score *on the learner*. In other words, I have come to see that students also read, interpret, and, most importantly, act on the data we generate with our assessments about their achievement. They make crucial decisions based on those data. In fact, I have come to understand that the decisions they make as users of assessment results exert far greater influence on their success as learners than do the decisions made by the adults—the parents, teachers, administrators, and policymakers—around them.

This transformation in my thinking about the dynamics of assessment came neither from my work in measurement research nor from my knowledge of professional literature, but rather from my experiences as a father. As our daughter grew, I had a chance to see firsthand the emotional and learning benefits that came from using effective assessment to support her learning. Unfortunately, I also had a front-row seat from which to observe the immense and long-lasting harm that can be done when assessment is clumsy, inept, or used in counterproductive ways.

For these reasons, I have built this chapter around two basic assessment lessons: First, we must assess accurately. I will describe exactly what this means. Second, we must use the assessment process and its results productively: to keep students believing in themselves as capable learners who make sound decisions that will lead them to greater levels of achievement. I will provide specific guidelines for how to do this as well.

In professional learning communities, faculties team up to create assessments and to gather and interpret evidence of student learning in order to make program improvement decisions that will enhance that learning and make schools more effective (DuFour, 2005). Obviously, we all believe decisions that are based on sound evidence will support student learning, while decisions based on inaccurate evidence or no evidence at all can harm that learning. Therefore, sound assessment practices represent a key foundation of effective schools. In this chapter, we will explore the keys to quality common assessments within professional learning communities.

But professional learning communities cannot be merely about teachers making decisions based on common assessment data. Students must be partners in the community, too. Assessment must encourage and support them in their pursuit of excellence. Historically, we have done this by using the threat of a pending assessment in an attempt to drive students to study. This worked for some, but not for others. More recently, however, we have come to understand that students who believe they are capable learners experience greater success in school than students who have lost faith in themselves. In other words, we can replace the emotional dynamics of fear and vulnerability with those of academic self-efficacy and eagerness to learn as the driving emotions for academic success. But we can do this only if we expand our sense of professional learning communities to include our students as instructional decision-makers, and if we provide faculties with the opportunity to learn to use assessment in ways that involve students. I will show you how to tap these emotional dynamics of assessment to help all students succeed.

The Keys to Assessment Quality

We have established that accuracy is necessary, but not sufficient, for productive assessment. There are three key factors to consider in assuring assessment accuracy. To create quality assessments, educators must do the following:

- Start with a clear *purpose* for assessment—a sense of why we are assessing.

- Include a clear achievement *target*—a vision of what we need to assess.

- Design an assessment that accurately *reflects* the target and *satisfies* the purpose.

- *Communicate* results effectively to the intended user(s).

If we fail to attend to any of these features, we risk the quality of the data we gather, and therefore we risk harm to learners. Let us consider each in greater detail.

Key 1: Clear Purpose

If we assess, in part, to gather evidence to inform instructional decisions, then in any specific assessment context, the assessor needs to start the process with answers to these questions:

- What are the instructional decisions we hope to make?
- Who is making them?
- What information will be helpful?

The answers to these questions will vary profoundly across contexts, from the classroom to the institutional and policy-making levels.

As instruction unfolds daily in the classroom, the key question to be answered with data is this: "What comes next in the learning?" The decision-makers are students and teachers. The information these decision-makers need is continuous evidence of how each individual student is doing on her or his learning journey towards each standard. Both student and teacher must know where the learner is now, how that compares to ultimate learning success, and how to close the gap between the two. Students must not be wondering *if* they will succeed—only *when* they will succeed. Obviously, this is the domain of day-to-day classroom assessment.

At the program level of decision-making, on the other hand, we need to know which achievement standards students are and are not mastering—which of our programs are working and which need adjustment. Those who will plan and implement those adjustments are teachers (often working in teams), principals, and curriculum personnel. The evidence they need must reveal who is and is not meeting standards—in terms that are comparable across classrooms so data can be aggregated at the program level to affirm effectiveness or reveal potential changes. This, then, is the purview of the interim, benchmark, short-cycle assessment—the common assessment in the professional learning community context.

Note that both classroom and program levels of decision-making are important, but they are different. The former focuses on each student's journey to each standard, while the latter centers on group mastery of the standards themselves. Classroom assessment must be continuous, while program assessment can be periodic. The classroom level informs students and teachers as they make immediate instructional decisions, while the program level informs teacher teams and school leaders as they make intermittent program adjustments. Both must be done well for students to prosper.

Finally, there is the institutional or policy level of assessment use which, these days, requires that school and community leaders determine if enough students are meeting standards. They need evidence of student mastery of state standards that is comparable across classrooms and schools once each year to be accountable to the community and to allocate resources for program improvement. This, then, is the purview of our annual large-scale accountability tests.

When it comes to assessment results, the users and their information needs are different at each level. This is why assessors in any context must start with a clear sense of purpose: They must know who their assessment should help, and how it should help, in order to design it properly.

Key 2: Clear Targets

The second key to quality assessment is the clear, complete, and appropriate articulation of the achievement target(s) to be mastered. We cannot dependably assess that which we have not defined. These days, we start target definitions with state standards or local adaptations of those standards. When these standards are organized in a logical manner to unfold properly within and across grade levels, they can be the focus of both interim/benchmark/common assessments and the annual accountability tests that help us know if students are on track to success.

However, our thinking about clear targets cannot stop here. We have yet to account for the classroom level, where we need to help students ascend through the levels of proficiency leading to mastery of each standard. Every standard must be deconstructed into the scaffolding that students must climb on their journey to success. These continuously unfolding classroom targets, then, become the focus of day-to-day formative assessments (assessments used to guide learning).

To accomplish this deconstruction, faculties can work in teams to organize standards and build the scaffolding for each standard. They can start by asking specific questions for each standard. Following is an example of this process for the standard, "Learn to write proficiently." The specific questions are followed by sample answers (oversimplified here for the purpose of demonstration).

- What must our students *know and understand* when the time comes for them to demonstrate that they have met this standard? What are the foundations of knowledge that underpin success here? In our example, the student must master the vocabulary, syntactic structure, and mechanics needed to communicate ideas, and, in addition, must bring knowledge about the subject to his or her writing.

- What patterns of *reasoning*, if any, must students have mastered to be ready to demonstrate that they have met this standard? Must they be prepared to use their knowledge to reason productively in this case? In our example, the student must infer what words, sentence structures, and organizational principles will lead to the clearest communication of the ideas to be shared in the writing. He or she must also be able to evaluate the quality of the writing as it is being composed using appropriate quality criteria and make adjustments as needed to improve communication.

- What *performance skills,* if any, does this standard assume our students will master on their journey to competence? Do we expect achievement-related behaviors? In our example, the student must have mastered either the penmanship or keyboarding skills needed to record ideas for others to see.

- What *products,* if any, must our students learn to create to be judged competent in terms of this standard? In our example, the student must be able to compose an actual sample of his or her own original text that satisfies standards of word choice, sentence fluency, and organization.

The answers to these questions determine the progression of learning that will help students climb the scaffolding to meet each standard. These, then, will need to be the focus of day-to-day classroom assessment to inform the question, "What comes next in the learning?"

Key 3: Accurate Assessment

Given the need to provide information to assessment users about student mastery of specific targets in various contexts, the assessor must be prepared to design and build or select quality assessments for many different kinds of assessment circumstances. While this does not include the institutional or policy level where state assessments rule, it can include the interim level with common assessments, and it certainly does include the classroom level. To create an accurate assessment, the developer must do the following:

- Select a proper assessment *method,* such as selected response, written response, performance assessment, or personal communication.

- Build each assessment out of quality *ingredients,* whether they are test items, performance or essay tasks, or scoring guides.

- Include enough items to *sample* appropriately student knowledge so as to gather enough evidence to lead to a confident conclusion about achievement without wasting time gathering too much.

- Anticipate all relevant sources of *bias* that can distort results, such as wording in items that gives members of one cultural subgroup an advantage over another (perhaps due to differences in language or social experience); these must be avoided or eliminated if they creep into the assessment.

Assessment developers who cannot follow these guidelines place students in harm's way with the possibility of mismeasuring their achievement. Now let us consider each of these items in greater detail.

Proper methods. There is a variety of assessment methods to choose from: selected response formats (multiple choice, true/false, matching), written response or essay, performance assessment (observation and judgment), and direct personal interaction with our students (talking to them). These methods are not interchangeable. We cannot have a "favorite" method that we use every time. The assessment method must fit the context.

In education today, we continue to rely far too heavily on multiple-choice tests. It is simply not possible to obtain a comprehensive portrait of student achievement with only a multiple-choice test. That method is both efficient and powerful in a very limited array of contexts. But like the other methods, it is a formula for disaster in the hands of an incompetent user or common-assessment team. If they are used in a context (for a purpose or with a target) where they cannot provide a quality portrait of achievement, the result will be a misrepresentation of student learning and counterproductive instructional decisions.

No assessment method is inherently superior to others in all contexts. Assessment methods must be chosen carefully to reflect the achievement target(s) in question and to provide the information needed by the intended user(s). (See Stiggins, Arter, Chappuis, and Chappuis [2004] for specific guidance on choosing proper assessment methods.)

Quality ingredients. Once a method is selected, the assessment must be built of quality items, tasks, exercises, and scoring schemes. This is crucial. Performance assessments must be constructed of high-quality performance tasks and scoring rubrics; multiple-choice tests must be constructed of high-quality questions. Developers must understand the difference. This too may require some time spent in professional learning, depending on the developers' assessment backgrounds.

Quality sample. A quality assessment gathers enough information to lead to a confident conclusion, but it does not gather too much information. So how much is enough evidence? How many test items? How many performance tasks or essay exercises? The context determines the answers to these questions. The higher the stakes, the more certain we must be, and the more data we must gather. The more complex the target, the more evidence we may need. The more evidence a task provides, the fewer tasks we need. Each assessment method brings with it a set of rules for use that maximize sampling efficiency. One must take advantage of professional learning opportunities to master those sampling rules.

Minimizing bias. Even if we select a proper method, use high-quality ingredients, and sample appropriately, there are many things that can go wrong and distort results. For example, emotional upsets can keep students from providing dependable information about their achievement, and distractions during the administration of an assessment can keep them from showing their true level of attainment. If students are not disposed to let us know how much they have achieved, our assessments will not provide dependable evidence of their learning. Bias can also arise in the scoring process when scoring is subjective, as it is in essay or performance assessment. For example, bias has crept into the assessment when the scorer's knowledge of a student's ethnic background inappropriately influences judgments of proficiency. If we fail to eliminate these sources of bias, our evidence will be inaccurate.

Key 4: Effective Communication

Once the information needs of assessment users have been identified, achievement expectations are in place, and accurate assessments are being used, the foundation is laid for gathering good data. But note that all of this work is wasted if procedures are not also in place to deliver the assessment results into the user's hands in a timely and understandable form.

For communication to be effective in the context of formative assessment, it needs to inform the learner about how to do better the next time; that is, it must be descriptive rather than judgmental. Feedback is most helpful when it focuses on attributes of the student's work ("Change your writing in this way . . . "), not when it focuses on the student's learning ("Try harder"). It must provide sufficient detail to inform without overwhelming, and it must arrive in time to help the learner.

These characteristics of effective communication are satisfied most easily when all involved parties agree in advance about the important achievement expectations, or learning targets. A lack of understanding about what success looks like is a barrier to understanding the true meaning and implications of assessment results.

Effective communication also depends on the availability of accurate information about each student's achievement (see Key 3). Inaccurate or inaccessible information serves no one well, as it can lead to counterproductive instructional decisions. To ensure the effective transmission of information from one person to another, both parties must understand the meaning of the symbols involved, whether they are grades, test scores, work samples, or verbal descriptions of achievement. For example, miscommunication will occur if it is assumed that a report-card grade indicates a student's level of achievement when, in fact, the teacher has woven achievement, effort, attitude, compliance with rules, attendance, and other nonachievement characteristics into the grade.

Whether administering daily classroom assessments, common assessments in a professional learning community, or state assessments for accountability, the foundations of productive assessment are the same: We need accurate information about student learning, effectively communicated. A quality assessment arises from a clear knowledge of the information needs of the intended user and a clear vision of the achievement target to be assessed. With these in hand, we can design an accurate assessment—one that relies on a proper assessment method, includes high-quality items or exercises, samples appropriately, and eliminates all relevant sources of bias.

Using Assessment to Encourage and Support Learning

In the opening to this chapter, I argued that quality assessment represents a necessary but insufficient condition for productive assessment. I hope it is clear now specifically what we mean by quality, and how to achieve it. The second active ingredient in productivity is the effective use of the assessment process and its results to help students advance their learning with enthusiasm and feel in control of their learning as they attain new levels of proficiency.

While classroom assessment certainly can and should serve accountability purposes by providing evidence for report-card grading, we can and should take advantage of the process to help us accomplish far more than that: It can serve to promote student success. Traditionally, we think of assessment as an index of student attainment, but it also can serve as the cause of achievement. In our work at the ETS Assessment Training Institute (ETS), we refer to these two purposes as assessment *of* learning and assessment *for* learning. With assessment *for* learning, all students can experience the ongoing joy and optimism that comes from expecting to succeed and living up to that expectation.

Connecting Assessment *of* and *for* Learning

Traditionally, we have used assessments to discover how much our students have learned up to a particular point in time. Evidence from these assessments, according to our effective schools models, must be fed to the adults in the system so they can make informed instructional decisions to help students. This certainly makes sense in terms of school improvement under certain conditions. At ETS Assessment Training Institute, we call this assessment *of* learning.

But what if we supplement it with assessment *for* learning by asking, "How can we use the assessment process to cause students to learn more; that is, to increase achievement in the future?" To accomplish this, we use assessment to inform students about themselves. If assessments *of* learning check to see if our students are meeting standards (state, district, or classroom), assessments *for* learning ask if our students are making progress toward meeting those standards (day to day in the classroom—during the learning). One is for accountability, while the other is used to support learning. Both are important, but they are different because they serve fundamentally different purposes. The key to our collective success as educators is to balance the two—to find the synergy between them.

Examples of assessments *of* learning arise from our accountability legacy: externally imposed standardized tests like college admissions tests, state assessments, district-wide tests, and so on. They also include classroom assessments used to assign report-card grades such as unit tests, final exams, and the like. These are assessments conducted after a unit or class is finished to determine if learning has occurred. They inform multiple levels of accountability and instructional decisions and, therefore, are important.

Examples of assessments *for* learning are those that we use to diagnose student needs, support students' practice, or help students watch themselves improving over time. In all cases, we seek to provide teachers and students with the kinds of information they need to make decisions that promote continued learning. Assessments *for* learning occur while the learning is still happening and throughout the learning process. So early in the learning, students' scores will not be high. This is not failure—it simply represents where students are now in their ongoing journey to ultimate success.

For example, when an elementary student is beginning to write, his or her emergent writer proficiencies—such as word choice, sentence structure, and organization of ideas—may be lacking. If the faculty has teamed up to map the learning progressions that lead to proficiency in writing, and then discovers which learning strategies are working for the student, they can provide the student with descriptive feedback that will help him or her understand how to do better the next time. The careful management of this kind of assessment and feedback, within and across grade levels in ways that involve students as partners over the long haul, will result in competent writers.

The teacher's role in assessment *of* learning is as it always has been: to administer accurate assessments and use sound grading practices. But in assessment *for* learning, this role changes. The teacher's role in this case is to carry out the following sequence:

1. Become a confident, competent master of the standard our students are expected to master.

2. Deconstruct each standard into the enabling classroom achievement targets that form the scaffolding leading up to the standard.

3. Create a student-friendly version of those targets to share with students from the beginning of the learning.

4. Create high-quality classroom assessments that reflect those targets.

5. Use those assessments (in collaboration with students) to track improvement over time.

The student's role in assessment *of* learning is as it always has been: to study hard and strive for the highest scores and grades; that is, demonstrate competence. But in assessment *for* learning, the student's role is to strive to understand what success looks like and to use each assessment to try to understand how to do better the next time. In other words, students seek to understand what good writing looks like so they can assess where they are currently and then close the gap between the two.

This leads to a fundamental redefinition of the relationship between assessment and student motivation. Rather than relying on assessment as the source of information used to decide who gets rewarded and punished—that is, for sorting winners from losers—we use assessment as a road map to ultimate success, with signposts along the way for both students and their teachers. Success at making progress (at learning) becomes its own reward, promoting confidence and persistence. This changes the emotional dynamics of the assessment experience in immensely productive ways for all students, especially for those who have not yet met standards. Students become good writers not to earn a good grade, but because they believe they can, and it is that belief that motivates them.

The Foundations of Assessment *for* Learning

We know that the consistent application of principles of assessment *for* learning enhances student learning, and we understand why. The evidence that it works in promoting greater achievement has been summarized by Black and Wiliam (1998). Based on results of dozens of studies conducted around the world, we know that students experience profound gains in their achievement with the largest gains accruing for perennial low achievers. The Black and Wiliam synthesis instructs us that the keys to maximizing these gains are to increase:

- The accuracy of classroom assessments
- Student access to descriptive (versus judgmental) feedback
- Student involvement in assessment, record-keeping, and communication

It should be self-evident that accurate assessments lead to better instructional decisions than do inaccurate assessments. Descriptive feedback provided to students who understand the target will power them toward success far more productively than will judgmental feedback in the form of grades, for example. This is especially true for struggling learners.

These practices enhance the learner's sense of control of his or her academic success or academic self-efficacy. Albert Bandura (1994/ 1998) has described the psychology that, in effect, can be interpreted to underpin assessment *for* learning as I am defining it:

A strong sense of efficacy enhances human accomplishment and personal well-being in many ways. People with high assurance in their capabilities approach difficult tasks as challenges to be mastered rather than as threats to be avoided. Such an efficacious outlook fosters intrinsic interest and deep engrossment in activities. They set themselves challenging goals and maintain strong commitment to them. They heighten and sustain their efforts in the face of failure. They quickly recover their sense of efficacy after failures or setbacks. They attribute failure to insufficient effort or deficient knowledge and skills which are acquirable. They approach threatening situations with assurance that they can exercise control over them. . . .

In contrast, people who doubt their capabilities shy away from difficult tasks which they view as personal threats. They have low aspirations and weak commitment to the goals they choose to pursue. When faced with difficult tasks, they dwell on their personal deficiencies, on the obstacles they will encounter, and all kinds of adverse outcomes rather than concentrate on how to perform successfully. They slacken their efforts and give up quickly in the face of difficulties. They are slow to recover their sense of efficacy following failure or setbacks. Because they view insufficient performance as deficient aptitude it does not require much failure for them to lose faith in their capabilities. (pp. 1–2)

These two paragraphs capture the essence of what differentiates the productive and counterproductive emotional dynamics of assessment. Productive assessment leaves students feeling in control and optimistic, even if they do not perform well. Counterproductive assessment robs students of that sense of control, resulting in a pervasive sense of hopelessness.

How do we help students remain optimistic about their potential success at learning? One way is to help them understand from the beginning of the learning what success will look like when they get there (Sadler, 1989). We do this by starting instruction with a student-friendly version of the learning targets. We accompany this with actual samples of student work that illustrate the continuum of achievement students will travel on their journey to success. This gives students a frame of reference from which to track their own progress.

Another way is to help students know where they are now in relation to that vision of excellence (Sadler, 1989). We do this by providing them with continuous access to descriptive feedback that shows them how to do better the next time. And we help them learn to self-assess so that, over time, they can learn to generate their own descriptive feedback. When we do these things, we bring our students to a place where they can become partners with us, their teachers, in setting goals for what comes next in the learning. This builds a strong sense of academic self-efficacy.

Finally, we help our students become increasingly efficacious when we show them how to close the gap between where they are now and where we want them to be in their learning (Sadler, 1989). We do this when we help them learn to improve the quality of their work one key attribute at a time, when we help them learn to see and keep track of changes in their own capabilities, and when we help them reflect on the relationship between those improvements and their own actions.

All of these strategies manifest specific ways to use assessment *for* learning. Making these strategies operational in the classroom requires in-depth professional development (see Stiggins, Arter, Chappuis, & Chappuis, 2004 for further details). These strategies are most obviously and easily applied at the classroom level. However, they also represent productive options in the development and use of common assessments for program evaluation and improvement. Imagine a professional learning community in which students become members of teams to design, conduct, and interpret common assessments. Students can collaborate to deconstruct standards, transform classroom targets into student-friendly language, devise assessment exercises, score schemes and assessments, and interpret results with an eye toward their own self-interest. Obviously, they would need careful guidance from their teachers, each of whom must understand the principles of productive assessment from the outset. But I believe a vision of partnership at this level of assessment holds immense promise.

References

Bandura, A. (1998). Self-efficacy. In H. Friedman (Ed.), *Encyclopedia of mental health*. San Diego: Academic Press. (Reprinted from *Encyclopedia of human behavior,* Vol. 4, pp. 71–81, by V. S. Ramachaudran, Ed., 1994, New York: Academic Press.)

Black, P., & Wiliam, D. (1998). Assessment and classroom learning. *Educational Assessment: Principles, Policy and Practice, 5*(1), 7–74. Also summarized in Black, P., & Wiliam, D., (1998), Inside the black box: Raising standards through classroom assessment. *Phi Delta Kappan, 80*(2), 139–148.

DuFour, R. (2005). What is a professional learning community? In R. DuFour, R. Eaker, & R. DuFour (Eds.), *On common ground: The power of professional learning communities* (pp. 31–43). Bloomington, IN: Solution Tree (formerly National Educational Service).

Sadler, R. (1989). Formative assessment and the design of instructional systems. *Instructional Science, 18,* 119–144.

Stiggins, R. J., Arter, J., Chappuis, J., & Chappuis, S. (2004). *Classroom assessment FOR student learning: Doing it right—Using it well.* Portland, OR: ETS Assessment Training Institute.

Larry Ainsworth

Larry Ainsworth is the executive director of professional development at The Leadership and Learning Center (formerly the Center for Performance Assessment) in Englewood, Colorado. He travels widely throughout the United States to assist school systems in implementing best practices related to standards, assessment, and accountability across all grades and content areas. With 24 years experience as an upper elementary and middle-school classroom teacher in demographically diverse schools, Mr. Ainsworth brings a wide range of professional experiences to each of his presentations. The author or coauthor of eight books, he has delivered keynote addresses nationwide and conducted breakout sessions at national and regional conferences throughout the United States. His primary motivation is to assist educators and leaders in helping all students succeed by taking the mystery out of the instruction, learning, and assessment process.

In this chapter, Mr. Ainsworth first considers the roadblocks to effective assessments and describes how common formative assessments can become much more that just one more thing to squeeze into the school day. He then emphasizes the need for an *aligned set* of assessments, from the classroom level to the state level, so that educators can gain "predictive value" from the assessments they administer. Next, he provides a further description of common formative assessments and details three powerful practices that are foundational to their effective use: Power Standards, "unwrapping" the standards, and data teams.

Then he presents the "big picture" of an integrated standards-based instruction and assessment system followed by a recommended sequence for designing common formative assessments. The chapter highlights the major benefits of using common formative assessments regularly and concludes with key recommendations for getting started.

For more information about Larry Ainsworth, visit www.LeadandLearn. com.

Chapter 4

Common Formative Assessments: The Centerpiece of an Integrated Standards-Based Assessment System

Larry Ainsworth

Educators today are awash in assessments, from those required by their states for the No Child Left Behind legislation to the quarterly district assessments that benchmark students' progress toward proficiency of the state standards—and the assessment deluge does not stop there! Teachers also struggle with the numerous school-based assessments they must administer throughout the school year. The continual pressure to administer these regularly scheduled tests looms large in the classroom, establishing a pace of instruction that is often too fast for students. Given this, how can we suggest that busy teachers consider adding yet another regular assessment to the mix? Even the idea of it can understandably create resistance.

Classroom assessment requires time. With so many standards to teach, and with so many diverse student learning needs to meet, instructional time is becoming increasingly precious. Robert

Marzano (2003) reported that the instructional hours during each school day that are actually devoted to instruction vary widely from a low of 21% to a high of 69%. How, then, can we urge educators and leaders to consider adding yet another type of assessment that will take even more time away from instruction? We must first determine the actual impact of existing assessments on instruction and student learning by determining the real worth of each of those assessments. Once this is accomplished, educators are in a much stronger position to decide whether to continue administering assessments that consume precious instructional time without yielding the kind of valuable feedback on student learning that can be used to adjust instruction.

There is also the question of the frequency of assessments: How often should educators assess to determine student learning? Assessment experts (Marzano, Stiggins, Black, Wiliam, Popham, and Reeves) agree that numerous short assessments given over time provide a better indication of a student's learning than one or two large assessments given in the middle and at the end of the grading period (Ainsworth & Viegut, 2006). The true value of assessment is its ability to help educators make accurate and timely inferences about student progress so that they can modify instruction accordingly.

And finally, what to do with all the data we are collecting? Without a systematic process to analyze assessment data for the explicit purpose of informing instruction (Ainsworth & Viegut, 2006), the valuable information that could be gleaned from such an analysis remains untapped. Douglas Reeves (2004) refers to this dilemma as the "over-testing and under-assessing" of students (p. 71). Richard DuFour (2005) has aptly named this the DRIP syndrome: Schools have become "data rich but information poor" (p. 40). School systems across the country are realizing the need for a definite process to analyze assessment results and use that data to inform instruction.

Common formative assessments—assessments *for* learning that are collaboratively designed, administered, scored, and analyzed by team members—provide the answers to these key questions. This chapter first considers the roadblocks to effective assessments and describes how common formative assessments can become much more that just one more thing to squeeze into the school day. It then emphasizes the need for an *aligned set* of assessments, from the classroom level to the state level so that educators can gain "predictive value" from the assessments they administer. Next, it provides a further description of common formative assessments and details three powerful practices that are foundational to their effective use. It then presents the "big picture" of an integrated standards-based instruction and assessment system followed by a recommended sequence for designing common formative assessments. The chapter then highlights the major benefits of using common formative assessments regularly and concludes with key recommendations for getting started.

Aligning Assessments *of* and *for* Learning

Each year, schools administer the large-scale external assessments created by their state to gauge student progress toward attainment of the standards. The results of these assessments are used to determine whether or not schools have met "adequate yearly progress" (AYP) as required by No Child Left Behind. By analyzing large-scale assessment results, educators and leaders can make important changes in curriculum content and delivery as well as enhance individual classroom assessments (Sargent, 2004). However, the usefulness of such data is limited for several reasons:

1. Looked at in isolation, the results from state assessments have only minimal impact on an individual child's academic growth (Popham, 2001).

2. The time that elapses between the administration of the state tests and the receipt of results greatly limits the assessment's relevancy to ongoing instructional decision-making.

3. State test data focus on comparisons between groups of students, rather than on individual student gains from one assessment to the next.

4. The feedback from most state assessments is not specific enough to pinpoint the unique learning needs of individual students.

5. Even though state test results provide a "snapshot" of student understanding, when looked at in isolation, they do not provide the "photo album" of student understanding (gathered over time) that can truly represent what students know and are able to do.

To compensate for these inherent limitations of external assessments, educators need a dynamic, in-school assessment system that includes common formative assessments. By combining large-scale summative assessments *of* student learning with smaller in-school formative assessments *for* learning, educators can create a more comprehensive representation of student progress (Stiggins, Arter, Chappuis, & Chappuis, 2004).

This is not to minimize the role of external assessments in favor of internal assessments only. Both assessments *of* and *for* learning are important (Stiggins, 2002), and "while they are not interchangeable, they must be compatible" (NEA, 2003, p. 7). The key to maximizing the usefulness of both types is to intentionally align assessments *of* and *for* learning so that they are measuring the same student progress. If educators begin administering shorter assessments *for* learning aligned to their district and state assessments periodically throughout the school year, and then use the resulting data to adjust instruction accordingly, they will very likely see corresponding results on their assessments *of* learning and realize assessment's dual purpose: "as an *instructional tool* for use while learning is occurring and as an *accountability tool* to determine if learning has occurred" (NEA, 2003, p. 3).

Predictive Value

As educators strive to deliberately align their formative and summative assessments, the formative assessment results will provide them with credible evidence of how students are likely to do on the summative assessments—in time for them to make instructional changes. By collaboratively designing the summative assessment *before* any actual instruction takes place, educators are "beginning with the end in mind." Knowing—in advance—what the students will need to know and be able to do on the summative assessment will most definitely impact instruction. To measure student progress along the way, educators can administer *shorter* formative assessments that are closely aligned to their summative assessment. The formative assessment results, when analyzed carefully, will provide the educators with "predictive value" as to how their students are likely to do on the subsequent assessments. The results will allow them to more accurately diagnose student learning needs to determine what instructional modifications are needed.

This underscores the need for collaborative teams of educators to regularly meet to analyze the results of their formative assessments, to set a short-term goal for student achievement, and then to decide together the most effective instructional strategies they will use to accomplish their goal. This is the important work of grade-level and department data teams. The information gained from this kind of focused collaboration can become a powerful means for differentiating instruction and designing appropriate lessons and learning activities for small, flexible groups of students with specific learning needs. Educators can identify and provide appropriate interventions for students whose assessment results indicate they will have difficulty achieving proficiency by the end of the instructional cycle. Educators can identify and provide accelerated instruction for those students who already demonstrate proficiency on the formative assessment. Special educators and special-area teachers can use these formative assessment results diagnostically to help students prepare for upcoming summative assessments during their instructional time with them.

School systems often administer quarterly assessments in targeted content areas for specific grade levels so district and school administrators can "benchmark" student progress *across* the district. If the district benchmark assessments are designed to reflect the format and rigor of the state assessments (including selected- and constructed-response formats with proper standards terminology), the assessment results can "forecast" how students are likely to do on the state assessments, again in time to make instructional changes. Deliberately matching in-school formative assessments to district benchmark assessments will extend the alignment—and the benefits—even further.

What *Are* Common Formative Assessments?

Formative assessment is not a new concept to educators. *Classroom* formative assessments—often referred to as "pretests" or "pre-assessments" and given to students before the start of instruction—can determine to what degree students already know (or do not know) the learning objectives before they are taught. These informal pre-assessments are not used to assign grades, but rather strictly to help educators learn where to focus their instruction. *Common* formative assessments serve many of the same functions as classroom formative assessments, but with two key distinctions:

1. They are collaboratively designed and administered by grade-level or course teams to *all* students several times during the quarter, semester, trimester, or school year.

2. They are intentionally created to gauge student understanding of the most essential (power) standards *only* (described later in this chapter).

These assessments *for* learning are designed as matching pre- and post-assessments to ensure a same-assessment to same-assessment comparison of individual student growth. They are similar in design and format to district and state assessments so that students have opportunities throughout the year to practice responding to items that match in type, terminology, and rigor the items they will encounter on the state assessments.

Common formative assessment items typically represent a blend of item types, including selected response (multiple choice, true/false, matching, and fill-in items where students select an answer choice from a provided list) and constructed response (both short-response and/or extended response) where students must "construct" their response to an item and reveal the extent to which they can apply the targeted concepts and skills.

Student responses from *both* types of assessments allow educators to make more accurate inferences about student understanding than they can from the results of one type of assessment format only. Educators create answer keys to score the selected-response items and scoring guides (rubrics) to score the constructed-response items. The length of the assessment is kept short to facilitate quick scoring, either collaboratively or independently. Educators analyze the results in data teams to guide instructional planning and thus better meet the learning needs of *all* students prior to the administration of the next common formative assessment. The common formative assessment process shows how assessment actually informs instruction.

Powerful Practices

There are three powerful instruction and assessment practices that, when deliberately connected, work together to significantly improve student achievement. These key practices—identifying "Powers Standards," "unwrapping" the standards, and using data teams—are an integral part of the big picture of an integrated standards and assessment system.

Power Standards

Power Standards (Ainsworth, 2003; Reeves, 2001, 2002) are a subset of the entire list of grade-specific or course-specific learning outcomes described in the content standards for a given content area. These high-impact standards represent what students must know and be able to do by the end of a particular grade level or course. Power Standards reflect the collective wisdom of educators who first use their professional judgment and experience to select those specific standards they consider critical for students to fully understand and be able to demonstrate. They then cross-reference those initial selections with their state assessment data and state assessment guidelines to make sure their choices match those standards emphasized the most on the state assessment. After making any needed revisions, the proposed Power Standards are vertically aligned (pre-kindergarten to grade 12) so that there is a "flow" of priority standards from one grade to the next. The first drafts are reviewed and revised by all staff and then published and distributed across the system to promote consistency and focus.

Power Standards are not all that we teach; rather, they represent those *prioritized* learning outcomes that are absolutely essential for all students to know and be able to do. The following metaphor, contributed by Rich Quinn of East Hartford, Connecticut, may prove helpful when considering the prioritization of standards: Think of a fence that is made up of both fence posts and rails. The Power Standards are the fence posts, and the supporting standards are the rails. Like fence posts, Power Standards provide the curricular focus teachers need to "dig deeper" and assure student competency. Like fence rails, supporting standards are those curricular standards that *connect to and support* the Power Standards.

W. James Popham (2003) endorses the need for "powering" the standards: "Teachers need to prioritize a set of content standards so they can identify the content standards at which they will devote powerful, thoroughgoing instruction, and then they need to *formally and systematically* assess student mastery of only those high-priority content standards" (p. 36). The Power Standards thus become the primary purpose for creating common formative assessments—to measure throughout the year student attainment of those standards that have been identified as critical for student success in school, in life, and on all high-stakes tests.

"Unwrapping" the Standards

Educators use a four-step process to analyze the wording of standards in order to identify the key concepts and skills that students need to know and be able to do (Ainsworth, 2003b).

1. First, they "unwrap" the standard. In this step, educators analyze the wording of the targeted standards in order to pinpoint exactly what the students need to know (key concepts) and be able to do (key skills). They unwrap by underlining the key concepts (represented as nouns or noun phrases) and circling the skills (represented as verbs).

2. Then they organize the concepts and skills on a graphic organizer of their choice (an outline, bulleted list, or concept map) and determine for each skill an approximate level corresponding to Bloom's Taxonomy (Anderson & Krathwohl, 2001; Bloom, 1956; Marzano & Kendall, 2006), such as recall (level 1), understand (level 2), apply (level 3), interpret (level 4), synthesize (level 5), and create (level 6).

3. Next, educators determine the "big ideas" (main ideas or foundational understandings directly related to the unwrapped

standards) that students will eventually discover and state in their own words in response to essential questions (unit-based guiding questions introduced to them at the beginning of an instructional unit).

4. The value of unwrapping Power Standards becomes evident when educators then write common formative assessment items (in both selected- and constructed-response formats) that are directly matched to the level of Bloom's Taxonomy for each unwrapped skill. By writing items reflective of the rigor of the skills in the standards, educators will be better able to accurately predict their students' ability to respond to state assessment items written at different levels of cognitive demand.

Interested readers will find more than 85 examples of unwrapped standards in grades K–12 from a variety of content areas in *"Unwrapping" the Standards* (Ainsworth, 2003b).

Data Teams

These teams serve a specific function: to analyze common formative assessment data that can be used to target and implement instructional strategies aimed at improving student performance between the pre- and post-assessments. The data team process (from The Leadership and Learning Center, formerly the Center for Performance Assessment) includes five main steps:

1. Collect and chart the student performance data.

2. Analyze strengths and obstacles.

3. Set a short-term goal for student improvement.

4. Select effective instructional strategies (both experience-based and research-based) to meet that goal.

5. Determine results indicators to gauge the effectiveness of the selected teaching strategies.

Grade-level or department data teams (including special educators and special-area educators) plan how to deliver interventions and accelerated learning to meet the diverse needs of their students as they work through each of the five data team steps. They write an action plan to guide the implementation of their data-driven steps, and then they meet formally and informally between the pre- and post-assessments to monitor and adjust their instruction as needed.

The feature box below (and continued on page 90) shows an example using the five data team steps.

The Data Team Process

Step 1: Collect and Chart Data Results

Grade 5 Math Teachers	Number of Students	Number Proficient and Higher	Number Below Proficient	Percent Proficient and Higher
Betty	25	3	22	12%
Tom	27	5	22	19%
Susan	25	5	20	20%
TOTALS	**77**	**13**	**64**	**17%**

Step 2: Analyze Strengths and Obstacles

- List the strengths of students who were proficient and higher *by examining student work.*

- List the obstacles, or reasons, why students did not achieve a level of proficiency. Where were the errors? Is there a trend? Were there common errors? What is preventing students from being proficient? Are there misconceptions about concepts or skills?

(continued)

The Data Team Process (continued)

Step 3: Set a Goal for Student Improvement

The percentage of Grade 5 students scoring at proficiency or higher in math problem-solving will increase from 17% to 75% by October 30 (in 4 weeks) as measured by a teacher-created assessment administered on October 29.

Step 4: Select Instructional Strategies

- Teachers will select one or more of the following 10 research-based strategies for classroom instruction: similarities and differences; summarizing and note-taking; effort and recognition; homework and practice; nonlinguistic representation; cooperative learning; setting objectives; providing feedback; generating and testing hypotheses; and cues, questions, and advance organizers (Marzano, Pickering, & Pollock, 2001).

- To achieve their goal, teachers will use a graphic organizer to help students show how to solve a multi-step word problem using computation and graphic representation.

- In addition, teachers will help students improve their ability to solve multi-step word problems by practicing at home the process they learn in school.

Step 5: Determine Results Indicators

By emphasizing graphic organizers and focused homework/practice, more students will:

- Be proficient (meet or exceed the instructional goal).

- Understand how to solve a multi-step word problem.

- Be able to write a short constructed-response that includes correct process steps and a correct explanation.

From The Leadership and Learning Center's Common Data Team Seminar. Reprinted with permission from The Leadership and Learning Center, formerly the Center for Performance Assessment. Copyright © 2007.

The Big Picture: Powerful Practices

The diagram in Figure 1 (page 92) represents the connections between each of these powerful practices and showcases common formative assessments as the centerpiece of an integrated standards-based instruction and assessment system (for more information, see Ainsworth and Viegut, 2006).

The flow of the arrows indicates that the entire process is built upon the foundation of the Power Standards, which are then unwrapped to pinpoint the particular concepts and skills contained within them. Big ideas and corresponding essential questions focus both instruction and assessment. Once this foundation is in place, the instruction-assessment cycle begins with the common formative pre-assessment, the results of which are analyzed in data teams. Teachers then plan and deliver units of instruction, which often include hands-on learning and classroom performance tasks with accompanying scoring guides or rubrics (Reeves, 1996–2004). These serve as "learning vehicles" for students to acquire understanding of the targeted unwrapped standards *prior to* taking the common formative post-assessment.

By aligning each of these key assessments—classroom to school, school to district, and district to state—the results at each level of assessment provide educators with predictive value for how students are likely to do at the next level of assessment in time to make instructional changes. In this context, all assessments *for* learning administered within the individual school are considered formative. Those administered at the district level may be regarded as either formative or summative (thus the double-headed arrow), whereas common end-of-course assessments and state assessments are summative only (as indicated by the single arrow).

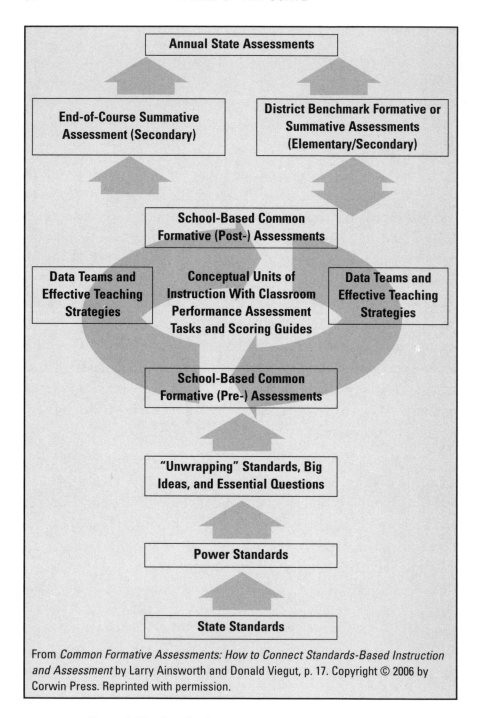

Annual State Assessments

End-of-Course Summative Assessment (Secondary)

District Benchmark Formative or Summative Assessments (Elementary/Secondary)

School-Based Common Formative (Post-) Assessments

Data Teams and Effective Teaching Strategies

Conceptual Units of Instruction With Classroom Performance Assessment Tasks and Scoring Guides

Data Teams and Effective Teaching Strategies

School-Based Common Formative (Pre-) Assessments

"Unwrapping" Standards, Big Ideas, and Essential Questions

Power Standards

State Standards

From *Common Formative Assessments: How to Connect Standards-Based Instruction and Assessment* by Larry Ainsworth and Donald Viegut, p. 17. Copyright © 2006 by Corwin Press. Reprinted with permission.

Figure 1: The Standards-Assessment Alignment Diagram

A Sequence for Designing Common Formative Assessments

The following is a sequence for designing and administering high-quality common formative assessments for those schools or districts interested in creating a closely aligned standards-based instruction and assessment system.

1. Identify the prioritized Power Standards for each grade level and course in selected content areas by using professional judgment and by referencing school and district state assessment data and state assessment requirements. Then vertically align the Power Standards from pre-kindergarten through grade 12.

2. Select an agreed-upon instructional topic of importance to assess through the common formative assessment process within a particular grade level or course, such as phonemic awareness, reading strategies, expository writing, subtraction with regrouping, linear equations, scientific inquiry, colonization of the New World, and so on.

3. Unwrap the Power Standards that match that targeted instructional topic. Create a graphic organizer that represents the unwrapped concepts and skills. Identify the approximate level of Bloom's Taxonomy for each of the skills. Determine the big ideas and essential questions to focus instruction and assessment for the selected topic during the corresponding instructional cycle.

4. Collaboratively design common formative pre- and post-assessments—aligned to one another—in grade-level and department data teams.

5. Administer and score the common formative pre-assessments, either collaboratively or independently.

6. Analyze pre-assessment results in data teams following the five-step process: chart the data; analyze the data; write a

short-term instructional goal; select effective teaching strategies; and determine the results indicators.

7. Plan and teach the instructional unit in each individual classroom, guided by the unwrapped Power Standards, the big ideas, essential questions, and the common formative post-assessment requirements.

8. Administer and score the common formative post-assessments, either collaboratively or independently.

9. Analyze the post-assessment results in data teams: Compare the pre-assessment results to the post-assessment results, celebrate successes, plan further intervention strategies for students who have not reached proficiency, reflect on the process, and select the instructional focus for the next instruction-assessment cycle.

To connect this in-school common formative assessment process to the district and state assessments, and to any common end-of-course assessments, continue with the following steps:

10. Align common formative assessments with quarterly or trimester district benchmark assessments (elementary and secondary) and any common end-of-course assessments (high school).

11. Administer and score quarterly district benchmark assessments and common end-of-course assessments; analyze those results (whether formative or summative) in data teams.

12. Align quarterly district benchmark and common end-of-course assessments with the annual state assessments.

To ensure deliberate alignment between in-school common assessments and district, end-of-course, and state assessments, try to create this alignment as early as possible in the sequence of steps. The most effective way to accomplish this is to review state assessment requirements. Refer also to current year and prior year school and district state assessment data along with released state assessment items from prior years. This will assist educators in writing common formative assessment items that resemble the format, rigor, and wording of what students will experience on the state assessments.

Intentionally aligning in-school common formative assessments to district, end-of-course, and state assessments should not be misconstrued as teaching to the test, but regarded instead as sound and fair instructional practice. The process is much like that of a coach who understands both the rules and strategies necessary to win a game and then helps his or her players learn those strategies during practice sessions before each big game. When grade-level or course data team members collaboratively design a matching set of common formative pre- and post-assessments—aligned to external district and state assessments—they will know in advance exactly what those assessments require of students in terms of content, skills, and difficulty. To meet this "cognitive demand," educators do not teach to the test, but rather they *teach to the skills* that their students will need to be successful (Popham, 2003).

The Benefits of Using Common Formative Assessments

Educators who invest the time in this process will enjoy many benefits. First and foremost, they will receive regular and timely feedback regarding student attainment of the most critical standards. As a result, they can better meet the diverse learning needs of all students. In addition, providing students with "multiple-measure assessments" (assessments that include a combination of both selected- and constructed-response items) allows students to demonstrate their understanding in a variety of formats. The common formative assessment process promotes ongoing collaboration opportunities for grade-level, course, and department educators to meet regularly to discuss and share effective instructional practices that they can implement immediately in their classrooms.

Common formative assessments also foster consistent expectations and priorities within a grade level, course, and department regarding standards, instruction, and assessment. This includes the establishment of agreed-upon criteria for student proficiency within each individual classroom, grade level, school, and across the district. Understanding the big picture of how each powerful practice connects with all of the others promotes the deliberate alignment of classroom, school, district, and state assessments to better prepare students for achieving success at each level. Most importantly, common formative assessment results enable educators to diagnose student learning needs accurately *in time to make instructional modifications.* In addition, common formative assessments provide students with timely feedback regarding their current level of understanding so that they can identify for themselves what they already know and what they have yet to learn. In these ways, both educators and students are able to utilize common formative assessment results to their maximum potential.

Administrators can support educators in using quality common formative assessments by first understanding the role these assessments *for* learning play in an interdependent instruction and assessment system, and then helping grade-level or course/department teams *find the time to meet on a regular basis.* This will most certainly require creative scheduling, but the importance of establishing time structures to allow for collaboration cannot be overemphasized. Implementing common formative assessments—including the design, administration, scoring, and analysis of assessment results—requires considerable time and commitment on the part of everyone involved. Educators benefit greatly when administrators rearrange teaching schedules and student supervision responsibilities in order to make regular collaboration possible. In this way, they are helping their school become a true professional learning community (DuFour, DuFour, & Eaker, 2005; DuFour & Eaker, 1998).

Recommendations for Getting Started

Placing educators at the center of the process is critical to the success of implementing common formative assessments. Without direct involvement by those who will be expected to carry out the work, there is limited ownership and "buy-in." Educators need to develop their own assessment literacy by attending professional development sessions that allow them to experience writing assessment items matched to the unwrapped concepts and skills they are targeting. Creating quality assessment items is a stimulating challenge and demanding work. Once educators understand the process through hands-on experience, they inevitably discuss among themselves ways to accelerate the item-writing part of the process. Busy as they are, they realize the value of "working smarter, not harder" by looking for assessment items from outside sources.

W. James Popham (2006) cautions educators and leaders interested in using formative assessments to beware of commercially produced assessments that may claim to be formative, but really are just old tests dressed up in desirable new names (such as "formative," "benchmark," or "interim"): "Educators need to realize that the research rationale for formative assessment is based on short-cycle assessments (a term attributed to British researchers Dylan Wiliam and Paul Black).... If the results don't get back in time for teachers to adjust instruction for the students being assessed, then it's not formative assessment" (2006, p. 86). Educators need to know in advance if any commercially produced assessments will provide them with timely results. Again, a key benefit of common formative assessments is that they can be quickly scored and the results made available to educators soon after administration. Remember also that these assessments need to meet the criteria for valuable assessments described earlier in the chapter (high impact on student learning, aligned to unwrapped Power Standards, and so on). Commercially produced items need to pass the criteria for well-constructed, reliable, and bias-free items if they are to be useful in the context of common formative assessment.

There are, however, definite time-saving devices that educators can utilize. School systems are recognizing the value of establishing their own teacher-created "banks" of common formative assessment items. Once educators learn how to write quality assessment questions that meet the criteria for well-written items, they can "deposit" those items into the school or district bank as they continue creating them or adapting them from other sources. Some of the best sources for such items are state education websites that post released assessment items from prior state assessments. These items can be useful for studying formatting, standards vocabulary, and the varying levels of rigor found within the assessments. Another source that may prove helpful is the assessment or evaluation component of the school- or district-adopted textbook series. Once educators have improved their individual and collective assessment literacy by understanding the criteria for well-written assessment items, they are in a much better position to select or modify items from external sources to meet their specific purposes. (For more information on writing quality assessment items, see Haladyna, 1997; Popham, 2003; Stiggins, 1997; Stiggins, Arter, Chappuis, & Chappuis, 2004.)

A Powerful Process

Educators who take an active role in creating common formative assessments to gauge student understanding of high-priority standards will experience firsthand the power of this process. When introducing this new practice, realize that it may be initially perceived as just "one more thing" to do. Leaders should first show and explain the connections between the interdependent practices so that everyone understands the big picture of an integrated standards-based instruction and assessment system. Leaders should emphasize the importance of common formative assessments as the way to connect all these key practices in a truly meaningful way. It helps to keep in mind at the onset that this is a *process to be completed over time,* not a singular event. To implement each of these practices effectively, they should be gradually incorporated into the existing culture, one by one. It helps to keep everyone focused on these powerful practices that, over time, will truly improve instruction and achievement for *all* students.

The evidence is in: common formative assessments produce results. "Persuasive empirical evidence shows that these [properly formulated formative classroom assessments] work; clearly, teachers should use them to improve both teaching and learning" (Popham, 2006, p. 87). Once educators implement this process with fidelity in their own schools and districts, they will be able to attest to the truth of this statement themselves.

References

Ainsworth, L. (2003a). *Power Standards: Identifying the standards that matter the most.* Englewood, CO: Advanced Learning Press.

Ainsworth, L. (2003b). *"Unwrapping" the standards: A simple process to make standards manageable.* Englewood, CO: Advanced Learning Press.

Ainsworth, L., & Viegut, D. (2006). *Common formative assessments: How to connect standards-based instruction and assessment.* Thousand Oaks, CA: Corwin Press.

Anderson, L. W., & Krathwohl, D. (Eds.). (2001). *A taxonomy for learning, teaching, and assessing: A revision of Bloom's Taxonomy of educational objectives.* New York: Longman.

Bloom, B. S. (Ed.). (1956). *The taxonomy of educational objectives: Handbook I, cognitive domain.* New York: David McKay.

DuFour, R., & Eaker, R. (1998). *Professional learning communities at work: Best practices for enhancing student achievement.* Bloomington, IN: Solution Tree (formerly National Educational Service).

DuFour, R., DuFour, R., & Eaker, R. (Eds.). (2005). *On common ground: The power of professional learning communities.* Bloomington, IN: Solution Tree (formerly National Educational Service).

Haladyna, T. M. (1997). *Writing test items to evaluate higher-order thinking.* Boston: Allyn & Bacon.

Marzano, R. J. (2003). *What works in schools.* Alexandria, VA: Association for Supervision and Curriculum Development.

Marzano, R. J., & Kendall, J. S. (2006). *The new taxonomy of educational objectives* (2nd ed.). Thousand Oaks, CA: Corwin Press.

Marzano, R. J., Pickering, D. J., & Pollock, J. E. (2001). *Classroom instruction that works: Research-based strategies for increasing student achievement.* Alexandria, VA: Association for Supervision and Curriculum Development.

National Education Association. (2003). *Balanced assessment: The key to accountability and improved student learning.* Washington, DC: National Education Association.

Popham, W. J. (2001). *The truth about testing: An educator's call to action.* Alexandria, VA: Association for Supervision and Curriculum Development.

Popham, W. J. (2003). *Test better, teach better: The instructional role of assessment.* Alexandria, VA: Association for Supervision and Curriculum Development.

Popham, W. J. (2006). Phony formative assessments: Buyer beware! *Educational Leadership, 64*(3), 86–87.

Reeves, D. B. (1996–2004). *Making standards work: How to implement standards-based assessments in the classroom, school, and district* (3rd ed.). Englewood, CO: Advanced Learning Press.

Reeves, D. B. (2001). *101 questions & answers about standards, assessment, and accountability.* Denver: Advanced Learning Press.

Reeves, D. B. (2002). *The leader's guide to standards: A blueprint for educational equity and excellence.* San Francisco: Jossey-Bass.

Reeves, D. B. (2004). *Accountability for learning: How teachers and school leaders can take charge.* Alexandria, VA: Association for Supervision and Curriculum Development.

Sargent, J. (2004). *Data retreat workbook.* Green Bay, WI: Cooperative Educational Service Agency #7.

Stiggins, R. J. (1997). *Student-centered classroom assessment* (2nd ed.). Upper Saddle River, NJ: Prentice Hall.

Stiggins, R. J. (2002). Assessment crisis: The absence of assessment FOR learning. *Phi Delta Kappan, 83*(10), 758–765.

Stiggins, R. J., Arter, J. A., Chappuis, J., & Chappuis, S. (2004). *Classroom assessment* for *student learning: Doing it right—using it well.* Portland, OR: ETS Assessment Training Institute.

Robert J. Marzano

Dr. Robert J. Marzano is president of Marzano & Associates in Centennial, Colorado, senior scholar at Mid-continent Research for Education and Learning in Aurora, Colorado, and associate professor at Cardinal Stritch University in Milwaukee, Wisconsin. He is the author of 25 books, 150 articles and chapters, and 100 sets of curriculum materials for teachers and students in grades K–12. During his 35 years in public education, Dr. Marzano has worked in every state in the U.S. multiple times, as well as in many countries in Europe and Asia. The central theme in his work has been translating research and theory into practical programs and tools for K–12 teachers and administrators.

Effective classroom assessment has the potential to dramatically enhance student academic achievement, but how do school leaders set out to design a comprehensive approach to classroom assessment? This chapter describes how a school or district might do just that. It begins with four research-based findings regarding effective classroom assessment. These findings form the basis of a five-step process for designing a comprehensive system of classroom assessment:

- Reconstitute state and national standards.
- Design a scale that measures learning over time, and rewrite the standards according to the scale.
- Teachers design formal and informal formative assessments using the scale.
- Use a "value added" approach to judging student performance.
- Redesign report cards.

For more information about Dr. Robert J. Marzano and his work, visit www.marzanoandassociates.com.

Chapter 5

Designing a Comprehensive Approach to Classroom Assessment

Robert J. Marzano

This chapter makes the case that effective classroom assessment has the potential to dramatically enhance student academic achievement. It also describes how a school or district might go about designing a comprehensive approach to classroom assessment. It begins with four research-based findings regarding effective classroom assessment (see Marzano, 2006). These findings form the basis of a five-step process for designing a comprehensive system of classroom assessment.

Finding 1: Classroom Assessment Feedback Should Provide Students With a Clear Picture of Their Progress on Learning Goals and How They Might Improve

Classroom assessment is a form of feedback students receive about their progress, and it stands to reason that feedback will enhance learning. Indeed, as a result of reviewing almost 8,000 studies, Hattie (1992) found that "the most powerful single modification that enhances achievement is feedback. The simplest prescription for improving education must be 'dollops of feedback'" (p. 9). More recently, Hattie and Timperley (2007) updated and extended this

review of the research on feedback and came to the same basic conclusion. Unfortunately, not all forms of feedback are equally effective. A meta-analysis by Bangert-Drowns, Kulik, Kulik, and Morgan
(1991) that reviewed findings from 40 studies on classroom assessment found that simply *telling* students they were correct or incorrect in their answers had a negative effect on their learning, whereas
explaining the correct answer and/or asking students to continue to
refine their answers was associated with a gain in achievement of 20
percentile points.

Displaying the results of students' classroom assessments graphically also appears to enhance student learning. It can also help
teachers more accurately judge students' levels of understanding
and skill. In fact, a meta-analysis by Fuchs and Fuchs (1986) that
examined the findings from 21 studies found that displaying students' assessment results graphically is associated with a gain of 26
percentile points in student achievement. Presumably, seeing a
graphic representation of students' scores provides teachers with a
more precise and specific frame of reference from which to make
decisions about next instructional steps. Fuchs and Fuchs also noted
that if assessment results are interpreted by a set of "rules" (explicit
criteria), student achievement is enhanced by 32 percentile points.

Finding 2: Feedback on Classroom Assessments Should Encourage Students to Improve

One of the more perplexing findings from the research is that
the manner in which feedback is communicated to students greatly
affects whether it has a positive or negative effect on student achievement. After analyzing 607 experimental/control comparisons involving some 23,000 students, Kluger and DeNisi (1996) found that in
33% of the studies they examined, feedback had a negative impact
on achievement. One cause they identified for this paradoxical effect
is whether feedback encourages or discourages students. Kluger and
DeNisi found that when assessment feedback is discouraging to

students, their achievement decreases by 5.5 percentile points. This leads to a critical question: What constitutes encouraging versus discouraging feedback? Kluger and DeNisi warn that there are no simple answers to this question, but there is some strong guidance from the research.

In a review of the research on drive theory and attribution theory, I identified two characteristics of encouraging feedback (Marzano, 2006). First, feedback must provide students with a way to interpret even low scores in a manner that does not imply failure. If it does not, students who are fearful of failure will continually be discouraged when they do not receive high scores. Second, feedback must help students realize that effort on their part results in more learning (as evidenced by higher scores).

Finding 3: Classroom Assessment Should Be Formative

Conventional wisdom holds that formative assessment occurs while students are in the process of learning new knowledge, and summative assessment occurs at the end of a learning episode. Although formative and summative assessment have both been widely addressed in the literature on classroom assessment, formative assessment has received much more attention. Specifically, formative classroom assessment has been the focus of almost every major attempt to synthesize the research on classroom assessment. After analyzing more than 250 studies on formative assessment, Black and Wiliam (1998) concluded that formative assessment done well results in student achievement gains of about 26 percentile points.

Unfortunately, formative assessment is not defined consistently within the research literature. As Black and Wiliam (1998) note, "Formative assessment does not have a tightly defined and widely accepted meaning" (p. 7). Fortunately, their definition is both comprehensive and useful. They define formative assessments as "all those activities undertaken by teachers and/or by students which provide information to be used as feedback to modify the teaching and learning activities in which they engage" (pp. 7–8). This definition casts a wide net both in terms of types of activities that qualify as assessments and the timing of those activities. By definition, then, formative classroom assessment can and should begin immediately within a learning episode and span its entire duration. Additionally, formative classroom assessment can take a wide variety of formal and informal formats.

Finding 4: Formative Classroom Assessments Should Be Frequent

One of the strongest findings from the research is that the frequency of assessments is related to student academic achievement. This was dramatically demonstrated in the meta-analysis of 29 studies on the frequency of assessments by Bangert-Drowns, Kulik, and Kulik (1991). Based on the study, one can conclude that if an educator gives five assessments, there will be a gain in student achievement of 20 percentile points. If he or she administers 25 assessments, the gain will be 28.5 percentile points. The researchers comment on a number of aspects of this finding: First, they emphasize the relatively strong effect of a single assessment: a 13.5-percentile-point increase in achievement. Second, they highlight the fact that over time, the effect of assessment frequency tapers off. Their recommendation is that teachers should systematically use classroom assessments as a form of feedback. Indeed, they found a positive trend for assessment—even up to 30 assessments in a 15-week period of time. This same phenomenon was reported by Fuchs and Fuchs (1986) in their meta-analysis of 21 controlled studies. They reported that providing two assessments per week results in a percentile gain of 30 points.

While there is no set number of assessments that should be administered during a unit of instruction or a grading period, the message from the research is clear: Systematic use of classroom assessments—weekly or even more frequently—can have a strong positive effect on student achievement.

Since research is typically conducted in highly controlled situations, translating these research findings into classroom practice requires interpretation and adaptation. Following is a five-step process based on these findings for designing and implementing a comprehensive approach to classroom assessment.

1. Reconstitute state and national standards.

2. Design a scale that measures learning over time, and rewrite the standards according to the scale.

3. Teachers design formal and informal formative assessments using the scale.

4. Use a "value added" approach to judging student performance.

5. Redesign report cards.

Step 1: Reconstitute State and National Standards

The first finding from the research speaks to the need for assessments to provide a clear picture of student progress on learning. While it might not be evident initially, state standards as they are currently formatted are a major impediment to the implementation of this finding. One reason is that state and national standards simply articulate too much. A study conducted by researchers at Mid-continent Research for Education and Learning (McREL) found that teachers need 71% more instructional time than is currently available to address the content in state and national standards (Marzano, Kendall, & Gaddy, 1999).

Another critical problem with state and national standards is that they do not isolate specific dimensions or traits. Measurement theory is based on the principle that an assessment for which only one score is provided for student achievement measures a single dimension or trait of that achievement (Hattie, 1984, 1985; Lord, 1959). State and national standards are not designed with this measurement principle in mind. Consider the following science benchmark from *National Science Education Standards* (National Research Council, 1996, p. 127):

- Light travels in a straight line until it strikes an object. Light can be reflected by a mirror, refracted by a lens, or absorbed by the object.

- Heat can be produced in many ways, such as burning, rubbing, or mixing one substance with another. Heat can move from one object to another by conduction.

- Electricity in circuits can produce light, heat, sound, and magnetic effects.

- Electrical circuits require a complete loop through which an electrical current can pass.

- Magnets attract and repel each other and certain kinds of other materials.

This benchmark for kindergarten through grade four clearly addresses multiple dimensions of student achievement. Depending on how the information is presented, it might involve as many as five dimensions, one for each of the bullets. The same problem is evident in the national health standards as articulated in *National Health Education Standards: Achieving Health Literacy* (Joint Committee on National Health Education Standards, 1995). Consider the elements listed for grades five through eight for the standard of "demonstrating the ability to practice health-enhancing behaviors and reduce health risks" (p. 32).

- Explain the importance of assuming responsibility for personal health behaviors.

- Analyze a personal health assessment to determine health strengths and weaknesses.

- Distinguish between safe and risky or harmful behaviors in relationships.

- Demonstrate strategies to improve or maintain personal and family health.

- Develop injury-prevention and injury-management strategies for personal and family health.

- Demonstrate ways to avoid and reduce threatening situations.

- Demonstrate strategies to manage stress.

These examples are drawn from national standards documents. The same problems are found in state standards documents (see Marzano, 2006). Clearly, standards documents as they are currently written mix multiple dimensions or traits in their descriptions of what students should know and be able to do. To remedy this situation, standards documents can be reconstituted to articulate a small number of "measurement topics" that address single dimensions, or dimensions that are closely related in terms of student understanding. Consider Figure 1 (pages 110–111), which contains sample measurement topics for language arts, mathematics, science, and social studies.

Notice there are 10 language-arts measurement topics (organized into three broad categories), 12 science topics (organized into four broad categories), 12 mathematics measurement topics (organized into six broad categories), and 10 social-studies topics (organized into five broad categories). Articulating measurement topics in this way—as small sets of uni-dimensional topics involving closely related dimensions—will require states (or districts adapting state standards) to focus on a more manageable set of content from the state documents.

LANGUAGE ARTS

Reading:

1. Word recognition and vocabulary
2. Reading comprehension
3. Literary analysis

Writing:

4. Spelling
5. Language mechanics and conventions

6. Research and technology
7. Evaluation and revision

Listening and Speaking:

8. Listening comprehension
9. Analysis and evaluation of oral media
10. Speaking applications

SCIENCE

Nature of Science:

1. Nature of scientific knowledge and inquiry
2. Scientific enterprise

Physical Sciences:

3. Structure and properties of matter
4. Sources and properties of energy
5. Forces and motion

Life Sciences:

6. Biological evolution and diversity of life

7. Principles of heredity and related concepts
8. Structure and function of cells and organisms
9. Relationships among organisms and their physical environment

Earth and Space Sciences:

10. Atmospheric processes and the water cycle
11. Composition and structure of the Earth
12. Composition and structure of the Universe and the Earth's place in it

Figure 1: Sample Measurement Topics

MATHEMATICS

Numbers and Operations:

1. Number sense and number systems
2. Operations and estimation

Computation:

3. Addition and subtraction
4. Multiplication and division

Algebra and Functions:

5. Patterns, relations, and functions
6. Algebraic representations and mathematical models

Geometry:

7. Lines, angles, and geometric objects
8. Transformations, congruency, and similarity

Measurement:

9. Measurement systems
10. Perimeter, area, and volume

Data Analysis and Probability:

11. Data organization and interpretation
12. Probability

SOCIAL STUDIES

Citizenship, Government, and Democracy:

1. Rights, responsibilities, and participation in the political process
2. The U.S. and state constitutions
3. The civil and criminal legal systems

Culture and Cultural Diversity:

4. The nature and influence of culture

Economics:

5. The nature and function of economic systems
6. Economics throughout the world
7. Personal economics

History:

8. Significant individuals and events
9. Current events and the modern world

Geography:

10. Spatial thinking and the use of charts, maps, and graphs

Figure 1: Sample Measurement Topics (continued)

Step 2: Design a Scale That Measures Learning Over Time, and Rewrite the Standards According to the Scale

This step responds to the first and second findings: Feedback should provide students with information about how to improve their progress on learning goals and encourage students to improve. Once measurement topics have been identified, construct a scale that is sensitive to learning over time. It has been demonstrated both empirically and conceptually that scoring assessments using a 100-point or percentage scale typically is not sensitive to learning over time (Marzano, 2002, 2006). Specifically, when teachers design their assessments using the 100-point scale, they construct and weigh items on different tests in highly subjective ways. Consequently, a student who receives a score of 80 on one test and 90 on another has not necessarily gained 10 points in terms of knowledge. That gain might be a simple artifact of the teacher changing his or her scheme for constructing and weighing test items. Figure 2 shows a scale that is sensitive to learning over time.

To illustrate the scale shown in Figure 2, consider the topic of probability in mathematics. The lowest score value on the scale is a 0.0, which represents no knowledge of the topic. Even with help, the student demonstrates no understanding or skill relative to the topic of probability. A score of 1.0 indicates that *with help* the student shows partial knowledge of the simpler details and processes as well as the more complex ideas and processes. To be assigned a score of 2.0, the student independently demonstrates understanding of and skill at the simpler details and processes, but not of the more complex ideas and processes. A score of 3.0 indicates that the student demonstrates skill and understanding of all the content—simple and complex—*that was taught in class*. A score of 4.0 indicates that the student demonstrates inferences and applications that *go beyond what was taught in class*.

Score 4.0	In addition to Score 3.0 performance, the student demonstrates in-depth inferences and applications that go beyond what was taught.
Score 3.5	In addition to Score 3.0 performance, the student demonstrates partial success at inferences and applications that go beyond what was taught.
Score 3.0	There are no major errors or omissions regarding any of the information and/or processes (simple or complex) that were explicitly taught.
Score 2.5	There are no major errors or omissions regarding the simpler details and processes, and partial knowledge of the more complex ideas and processes.
Score 2.0	There are no major errors or omissions regarding the simpler details and processes, but there are major errors or omissions regarding the more complex ideas and processes.
Score 1.5	The student demonstrates partial knowledge of the simpler details and processes, but there are major errors or omissions regarding the more complex ideas and processes.
Score 1.0	With help, the student demonstrates a partial understanding of some of the simpler details and processes and some of the more complex ideas and processes.
Score 0.5	With help, the student demonstrates a partial understanding of some of the simpler details and processes, but not of the more complex ideas and processes.
Score 0.0	Even with help, the student demonstrates no understanding or skill.

Figure 2: Sample Scale for Measuring Learning Over Time

All measurement topics at every grade level should be constructed using the scale format. Figure 3 (pages 116–117) shows how knowledge of atmospheric processes and the water cycle would be measured for eighth-grade students using the scale format.

It is possible to design similar scales for kindergarten through seventh grade and for courses at the high-school level. Note that there are specific learning objectives for levels 3.0 and 2.0 in the scale. This provides teachers with guidance for instruction of specific elements within each topic and identifies the simple versus the more complex elements of those topics.

Step 3: Teachers Design Formal and Informal Formative Assessments Using the Scale

This step incorporates the third finding: Classroom assessment should be formative. With measurement topics stated in scale format as shown in Figure 3, teachers have strong guidance for designing and scoring formative assessments. Specifically, each formative assessment must have items or tasks that students must learn for level 2.0, level 3.0, and level 4.0 of the scale. Level 2.0 and level 3.0 elements are explicitly stated in the scale. For example, assume an eighth-grade science teacher wished to design a formative assessment for the topic of atmospheric processes and the water cycle (shown in Figure 3). She might construct the following level 2.0 items, which are typically short-answer (fill in the blank) and forced choice (true/false, multiple choice, matching):

- Briefly define each of the following terms: climatic pattern, atmospheric layers, stratosphere.

- Identify whether each of the following statements is true or false.

  - The thermosphere is between the troposphere and the stratosphere.

- The Earth's atmosphere helps protect life on Earth by absorbing ultraviolet solar radiation.

- The temperature of the Earth's atmosphere varies with altitude.

The teacher might construct the following level 3.0 items, which are typically constructive response and involve articulating and describing generalizations and principles:

- Explain how evaporation affects the climatic pattern in areas around large bodies of water, like the shoreline communities of Lake Michigan.

- Assume that a weather balloon traveled up into the stratosphere. Explain what would happen as it progresses through the various layers of the atmosphere.

In Figure 3, the level 4.0 elements are not explicitly identified for teachers. Although they could be, many schools simply provide teachers with general guidance about how they might design level 4.0 tasks. For example, teachers might be instructed to create level 4.0 tasks using the following mental processes:

- **Comparing** is the process of identifying similarities and differences among or between things or ideas. (Technically speaking, *comparing* refers to identifying similarities, and *contrasting* refers to identifying difference. However, many educators use the term "comparing" to refer to both.)

- **Classifying** is the process of grouping things that are alike into categories based on their characteristics.

- **Creating metaphors** is the process of identifying a general or basic pattern that connects information that is not related at the surface or literal level.

Level 4.0	In addition to Level 3.0 performance, the student makes in-depth inferences and applications that go beyond what was taught in class.
Level 3.5	In addition to Level 3.0 performance, the student makes in-depth inferences and applications with partial success.
Level 3.0	While engaged in tasks that address atmospheric processes and the water cycle, the student demonstrates an understanding of important information, such as: • How the water cycle processes (condensation, precipitation, surface run-off, percolation, and evaporation) impact climatic patterns • The effects of temperature and pressure in different layers of the Earth's atmosphere The student exhibits no major errors or omissions.
Level 2.5	The student demonstrates partial knowledge of the more complex ideas and processes stated in level 3.0, and there are no major errors or omissions regarding the simpler details and processes stated in level 2.0.

Level 2.0	There are no major errors or omissions regarding the simpler details and processes, such as:
	• Recognizing or recalling specific terminology, including:
	  – Climate/climatic pattern
	  – Atmospheric layers
	  – Troposphere
	  – Stratosphere
	  – Mesosphere
	  – Thermosphere

**Figure 3: Sample Science Measurement Topic—
Atmospheric Processes and the Water Cycle, Grade Eight**

Level 2.0 (cont.)	• Recognizing or recalling isolated details, such as:
	  – Precipitation is one of the processes of the water cycle.
	  – The troposphere is the lowest portion of Earth's atmosphere.
	
	However, the student exhibits major errors or omissions regarding the more complex ideas and processes stated in level 3.0.

Level 1.5	The student demonstrates partial knowledge of the simpler details and processes stated in level 2.0, but there are major errors or omissions regarding the more complex ideas and processes stated in level 3.0.
Level 1.0	With help, the student shows partial understanding of some of the simpler details and processes stated in level 2.0 and some of the more complex ideas and processes stated in level 3.0.
Level 0.5	With help, the student demonstrates partial understanding of some of the simpler details and processes stated in level 2.0, but no understanding of the more complex ideas and processes stated in level 3.0.
Level 0.0	Even with help, the student demonstrates no understanding or skill.

Figure 3: Sample Science Measurement Topic—
Atmospheric Processes and the Water Cycle, Grade Eight (continued)

- **Creating analogies** is the process of identifying the relationship between two sets of items—in other words, identifying the relationship between relationships.

- **Analyzing errors** is the process of identifying and correcting errors in the way information is presented or applied.

Using these guidelines, an eighth-grade science teacher might construct the following level 4.0 task to include in the assessment:

Complete the following analogy and explain why it is accurate: condensation is to *evaporation* as _____ is to _____.

The items in this assessment can be easily scored using the scale in Figure 2. If students answer all items correctly, they receive a score of 4.0. If they answer all level 3.0 and 2.0 items correctly, and get partial credit on the level 4.0 item, they receive a score of 3.5. If students answer all level 3.0 and 2.0 items but miss the level 4.0 item, they receive a score of 3.0. If students answer all level 2.0 items correctly, receive partial credit for the level 3.0 items, but do not answer the level 4.0 items correctly, they receive a score of 2.5, and so on.

Step 4: Use a "Value Added" Approach to Judging Student Performance

This step incorporates the fourth finding regarding frequency of formative assessments, as well as the second finding about encouraging students to improve. At the beginning of a grading period, students will most likely receive low scores on formative assessments like the one described in the previous section. That is, most students would probably not answer level 3.0 and level 4.0 items correctly. However, by the end of a grading period, students should show growth in their scores. This is the heart of formative assessment: examining the gradual increase in knowledge for specific learning goals throughout a unit.

Since formative assessments are designed to provide a view of students' learning over time, one useful activity is to have students chart their own progress on each learning goal. To do so, the teacher provides a blank chart for each learning goal like the sample in Figure 4.

The first column in Figure 4 represents an assessment the teacher gave on October 5. This student received a score of 1.5 on that assessment. The second column represents the assessment on October 12. This student received a score of 2.0 on that assessment. The third column represents the assessment on October 20, and so on. Asking students to keep track of their scores on learning goals in this way provides them with a visual map of their progress. It also allows for powerful discussions between teacher and students. The teacher can discuss progress on each learning goal with each student. Also, in a tracking system like this, the student and teacher are better able to communicate with parents about their child's progress in specific areas of information and skill.

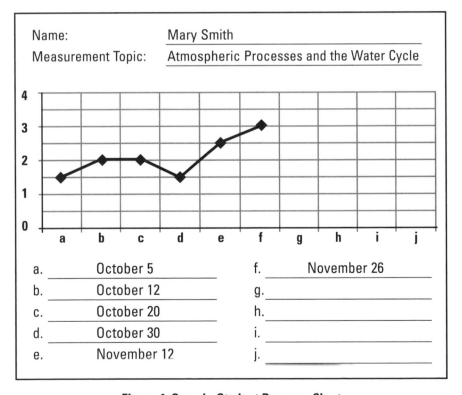

Figure 4: Sample Student Progress Chart

One of the most powerful aspects of formative assessment is that it allows students to see their progress over time. In a system like this, virtually every student will "succeed" in the sense that each student will increase his or her knowledge relative to specific learning goals. One student might have started with a score of 2.0 on a specific learning goal and then increased to a score of 3.5; another student might have started with a 1.0 and increased to a 2.5. Both of these students have learned. "Knowledge gain," then, is the currency of student success in an assessment system that is formative in design. Focusing on knowledge gain is also a legitimate way to recognize and celebrate success.

Step 5: Redesign Report Cards

The final step in designing a comprehensive system of assessment based on the research findings is to redesign report cards to better represent student performance. Such a report card is shown in Figure 5 (pages 121–123).

This is an example report card for fourth grade, but it can be easily adapted for kindergarten through grade 12. For the purposes of this discussion, we will assume that the school is departmentalized for each subject. That is, different teachers are responsible for each subject area (as opposed to self-contained classrooms where one teacher addresses all subject areas). In this grading period, five subject areas have been addressed: language arts, mathematics, science, social studies, and art. Final topic scores appear in each subject area. Note that each subject area includes both academic and life-skills topics. Life-skills topics include participation, work completion, behavior, and working in groups. Also note that traditional letter grades are not included in the report card. Rather, an overall scale (or rubric) score for each subject area is computed by averaging overall topic scores for the subject area. Thus, the overall score for math is an average of the final topic scores for number systems, estimation, and so on (for alternatives to averaging see Marzano,

Name: John Mark

Address: 123 Some Street

City: Anytown, CO 80000

Grade Level: 4

Homeroom: Ms. Smith

Language Arts	2.46	Participation	3.40
Mathematics	2.50	Work Completion	2.90
Science	2.20	Behavior	3.40
Social Studies	3.10	Working in Groups	2.70
Art	3.00		

Language Arts

Reading

Word Recognition and Vocabulary	2.5
Reading for Main Idea	1.5
Literary Analysis	2.0

Writing

Language Conventions	3.5
Organization and Focus	2.5
Research and Technology	1.0
Evaluation and Revision	2.5
Writing Applications	3.0

Listening and Speaking

Comprehension	3.0
Organization and Delivery	3.0
Analysis and Evaluation of Oral Media	2.5
Speaking Applications	2.5

Life Skills

Participation	4.0
Work Completion	3.5
Behavior	3.5
Working in Groups	3.0

Average for Language Arts   2.46

Figure 5: Sample Report Card

Mathematics

Number Systems	3.5	
Estimation	3.0	
Addition/Subtraction	2.5	
Multiplication/Division	2.5	
Ratio/Proportion/Percent	1.0	

Life Skills

Participation	4.0	
Work Completion	2.0	
Behavior	3.5	
Working in Groups	2.0	

Average for Mathematics　　**2.50**

Science

Matter and Energy	2.0	
Forces of Nature	2.5	
Diversity of Life	1.5	
Human Identity	3.5	
Interdependence of Life	1.5	

Life Skills

Participation	3.0	
Work Completion	1.5	
Behavior	2.5	
Working in Groups	1.0	

Average for Science　　**2.20**

Social Studies

The Influence of Culture	3.5	
Current Events	3.0	
Personal Responsibility	4.0	
Government Representation	3.5	
Human and Civil Rights	1.5	

Figure 5: Sample Report Card (continued)

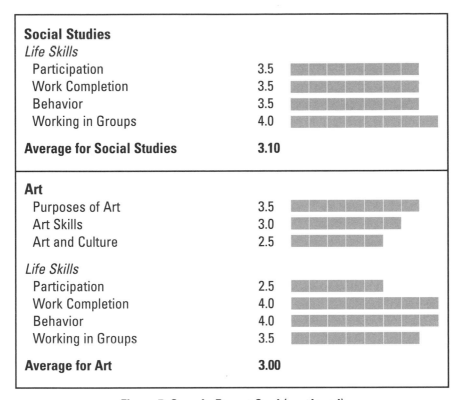

Figure 5: Sample Report Card (continued)

2006). The overall scores on the life-skills topics are computed by averaging the life-skills scores across classes.

Constructing measurement topics using the scale depicted in Figure 2, and then designing and implementing report cards, such as the one shown in Figure 5, is no small task and is not accomplished in one fell swoop. Initial steps in the design of measurement topics are best undertaken by a small group of teachers—the "vanguard group" (see Marzano, 2006)—who are willing to work through the intricacies of such a task. This is in contrast to opening up the task to all teachers whether they wish to participate or not. The complexity of the work when foisted on unwilling participants who already feel overworked can doom the project to failure. A vanguard group is also the best vehicle for experimenting with the design and scoring of formative assessments using measurement topics, the computer software necessary to keep track of formative assessments, and new practices for constructing grades based on formative assessments. Finally, it is advisable that schools and districts follow their own timelines in the design and implementation of measurement topics. School districts such as Catalina Foothills School District No. 16 in Tucson, Arizona; Township High School 211 in Palatine, Illinois; and Valparaiso Community Schools in Valparaiso, Indiana, have all approached the changes discussed in this chapter using slightly different timelines and slightly different formats.

Taking Action

This chapter has outlined five action steps—built on a foundation of four research findings—that schools and districts can take to design a comprehensive approach to formative classroom assessment. When fully implemented, the comprehensive approach described in this chapter has the potential not only of increasing the specificity and rigor of tracking and reporting student learning, but also of enhancing student learning because of the explicit feedback it provides to students and parents regarding students' areas of academic strength and growth, as well as their areas of immediate concern.

References

Bangert-Drowns, R. L., Kulik, C. C., Kulik, J. A., & Morgan, M. T. (1991). The instructional effect of feedback on test-like events. *Review of Educational Research, 61*(2), 213–238.

Bangert-Drowns, R. L., Kulik, J. A., & Kulik, C. C. (1991). Effects of classroom testing. *Journal of Educational Research, 85*(2), 89–99.

Black, P., & Wiliam, D. (1998). Assessment and classroom learning. *Assessment in Education, 5*(1), 7–75.

Consortium of National Arts Education Associations (1994). *National standards for arts education: What every young American should know and be able to do in the arts.* Reston, VA: Music Educators National Conference.

Fuchs, L. S., & Fuchs, D. (1986). Effects of systematic formative evaluation: A meta-analysis. *Exceptional Children, 53*(3), 199–208.

Hattie, J. (1984). An empirical study of various indices for determining unidimensionality. *Multivariate Behavioral Research, 19*, 49–78.

Hattie, J. (1985). Methodology review: Assessing the unidimensionality of tests and items. *Applied Psychological Measurement, 9*(2), 139–164.

Hattie, J. A. (1992). Measuring the effects of schooling. *Australian Journal of Education, 36*(1), 5–13.

Hattie, J., & Timperley, H. (2007). The power of feedback. *Review of Educational Research, 77*(1), 81–112.

Joint Committee on National Health Education Standards. (1995). *National health education standards: Achieving health literacy*. Reston, VA: Association for the Advancement of Health Education.

Kluger, A. N., & DeNisi, A. (1996). The effects of feedback interventions on performance: A historical review, a meta-analysis and a preliminary intervention theory. *Psychological Bulletin, 119*(2), 254–284.

Lord, F. M. (1959, June). Problems in mental test theory arising from errors of measurement. *Journal of the American Statistical Association, 54*(286), 472–479.

Marzano, R. J. (2002). A comparison of selected methods of scoring classroom assessments. *Applied Measurement in Education, 15*(3), 249–268.

Marzano, R. J. (2006). *Classroom assessment and grading that work*. Alexandria, VA: Association for Supervision and Curriculum Development.

Marzano, R. J., Kendall, J. S., & Gaddy, B. B. (1999). *Essential knowledge: The debate over what American students should know*. Aurora, CO: Mid-continent Regional Education Laboratory.

National Research Council. (1996). *National science education standards*. Washington, DC: National Academy Press.

Ken O'Connor

Ken O'Connor is an independent consultant on assessment, grading, and reporting. He has been a staff-development presenter and facilitator in 33 states in the U.S., eight provinces in Canada, and in seven countries outside of North America. Mr. O'Connor's 33-year teaching career included experience as a geography teacher, department head, and curriculum coordinator responsible for student assessment and evaluation. His articles have appeared in the *NASSP Bulletin, Educational Leadership,* and *Orbit.* He is the author of two books: *How to Grade Learning* (Corwin) and *A Repair Kit for Grading* (ETS Assessment Training Institute).

This chapter explores the ways in which traditional grades are counterproductive to learning. Mr. O'Connor contends that traditional grading promotes a culture of point accumulation instead of learning, encourages competition rather than collaboration, and often focuses on activities instead of results. He argues that we must adopt grading practices that are more compatible with an emphasis on learning. He presents three beliefs about grading that guide this new outlook:

- Grading is not essential for teaching and learning.

- Grading is complicated.

- Grading is subjective.

He then suggests the implementation of eight guidelines for grading to transform it to a standards-based approach, making grades compatible with the objective of learning for all. He uses real school samples to illustrate these guidelines.

Ken O'Connor can be reached at kenoc@aol.com.

Chapter 6

The Last Frontier: Tackling the Grading Dilemma

Ken O'Connor

Grading—the practice of reporting a number or letter as a summary of student performance—was virtually unknown in schools before 1850. It was only when the number of public high schools in the United States increased dramatically in the late 1800s that high-school teachers began to use percentages and other grades to rate students' accomplishments. This was the beginning of the grading system we know today. In the years that followed, schools used a variety of approaches, such as grading on the "curve" and the pass/fail system. Although different, these approaches do have something in common: They rely on a traditional approach to grading—adding up scores and then calculating a grade—which is often counterproductive to the objective of learning for all.

Grading as it has been done traditionally promotes a culture of point accumulation, not learning. It encourages competition rather than collaboration. It often focuses on activities instead of results. It makes all assessment summative (assessment *of* learning) because everything students do gets a score, and every score ends up in the grade book. In many schools, grades have achieved "cult-like status"

(Olson, 1995) where the grade is more important than whether or not students have learned anything.

Grades are not likely to disappear from schools, so it is critical that we transform our way of determining grades from the traditional culture of grading to a culture based on standards. Changing our attitudes about grades is a major undertaking, especially at the middle- and high-school levels. As DuFour, Eaker, and DuFour (2005) point out, such "significant school transformation will require more than changes in structure—the policies, programs, and procedures of a school. Substantive and lasting change will ultimately require a transformation of culture—the beliefs, assumptions, expectations, and habits that constitute the norm for the people throughout the organization" (p. 11).

We must adopt grading practices that are more compatible with an emphasis on learning. To do this, we must have a shared vision of the primary purpose of grades: to provide communication in summary format about student achievement of learning goals. This requires that grades be accurate, meaningful, consistent, and supportive of learning. Grading can be compatible with a learning-focused culture if we develop appropriate grading guidelines that become part of our regular professional practice and dialogue, and if we make those guidelines part of district and school policies and procedures.

General Beliefs About Grading

This transformation in culture requires the implementation of eight guidelines for grading. These guidelines make grades compatible with the objective of learning for all. But before I present these guidelines, it is necessary to present some beliefs about grading that underpin the guidelines.

Belief 1: Grading Is Not Essential for Teaching and Learning

Teachers do not need grades to teach well, and students can and do learn without them. What is essential to learning is that students are provided with regular and specific feedback on what they have learned well, and what problems or difficulties they are experiencing.

Belief 2: Grading Is Complicated

Teachers must acknowledge that grading is a complicated process that requires careful thought and a lot of professional dialogue and collaboration. It is not just about "crunching numbers."

Belief 3: Grading Is Subjective

Grading of student learning is inherently subjective. This is because it involves so many choices by teachers, including what is assessed, what criteria and standards it is assessed against, and the extent to which students meet the standards. Teachers must not apologize for this subjectivity, but they must also ensure that it does not translate into bias, because faulty grading damages students (and teachers). For example, a student who receives lower grades than she deserves might decide to give up on a certain subject or drop out of school, while a student who gets higher grades than he deserves might find himself in a learning situation where he cannot perform at the expected level of competence.

Eight Guidelines for Grading

The traditional approach to grading has many elements that are easily recognizable in our schools today: One grade is given for each subject at the conclusion of the grading period; the criteria for grading is often unclear; teachers use a mix of achievement, attitude, effort, and behavior to determine grades; grades record the student's average performance rather than the student's best performance; and so on. A standards-based grading system is built on eight guidelines that challenge these traditional grading approaches. Figure 1 (page 130) summarizes the eight guidelines of a traditional system versus those of a standards based system.

Traditional Grading System	Standards-Based Grading System
1. System is based on assessment methods (quizzes, tests, homework, and so on). One grade is given for each subject.	1. System is based on learning goals and performance standards. One grade is given for each learning goal.
2. Assessments are norm-referenced and based on a percentage system. Criteria are often unclear or assumed.	2. Standards are criterion-referenced and proficiency-based (using a limited number of levels to assess performance on a scale). Criteria and targets are known to all.
3. Use an uncertain mix of assessment of achievement, attitude, effort, and behavior. Use penalties and extra credit. Include group scores.	3. Measure only achievement. No penalties or bonuses are given. Includes individual evidence only.
4. Score everything—regardless of purpose.	4. Use only summative assess-ments for grading purposes.
5. Include every score, regardless of when it was collected. Assessments record the average—not the best—work.	5. Emphasize the most recent evidence of learning when grading.
6. Calculate grades using the mean.	6. Use median, mode, and professional judgment to determine grades.
7. Assessments vary in quality. Some evidence comes only from teacher recollection.	7. Use only quality assessment, and carefully record data.
8. The teacher makes decisions about grading and announces these decisions to students.	8. Discuss all aspects of grading with students.

Adapted with permission from O'Connor, K. (2002). *How to grade for learning: Linking grades to standards* (2nd ed.). Thousand Oaks, CA: Corwin Press.

Figure 1: Traditional Grading System Versus Standards-Based Grading System

Guideline 1: Base Grades on, and Provide Grades for, the Intended Learning Goals

The traditional grading system is built on assessment methods such as tests, projects, and assignments that reflect categories in the teacher's grade book. But if grades are to be meaningful, they must be built on more than these methods. Teachers should use learning goals as the basis for determining grades. Learning goals show evidence of achievement beyond a simple summary of knowledge. They provide a profile of a student's knowledge and direct evidence of his or her strengths and weaknesses. This type of assessment allows teachers to appropriately plan instruction, and allows students to focus their learning.

The difficulty in this task is determining the level of specificity at which to record and summarize data. Ideally, data should be recorded at the standard (or benchmark) level, but there are often so many standards that this is not practical. Thus, standards need to be organized into manageable groups of 7 to 15 categories. In some districts, these categories are called "power standards": the standards that matter the most. When determining these categories, districts/schools should try to include in each category standards for which the requisite knowledge, understanding, and skills are similar. Marzano (2006) calls this "covariance," which means that students would be likely to perform at a similar level on each standard included in what he calls "measurement topics" (p. 20). For example, the subject of English might have the following power standards: reading, reviewing, and responding to texts; composing in a variety of modes; controlling language; and evaluating the content, organization, and language use of texts (as shown in the example in Figure 2, page 132).

To illustrate guideline 1, Figure 2 shows a sample of a student assessment summary for Maryland's core learning goals for English (grades 1–12). Scores for each assessment are recorded by learning goal, not with a single summary score for each assessment. Tests are

CLGs	Achievement Evidence												SUMMARY
	Test 9/9	PA 9/12	PA 9/18	PA 9/23	Test 9/25	PA 9/30	Test 10/5	PA 10/8	Test 10/12	PA 10/19	PA 10/21	Exam 10/23	
Reading, Reviewing, and Responding to Texts			2		11/20 (1)		16/20 (3)			2	2	7/10 (2)	C
Composing in a Variety of Modes	19/20 (4)	4			18/20 (4)			4			2	10/10 (4)	A
Controlling Language		4		4		4				4		20/20 (4)	A
Evaluating the Content, Organization, and Language Use of Texts	13/20 (1)		1			1		1	8/15 (1)		3	6/10 (1)	D
Comments:													

Figure 2: Sample Summary of Evidence for Maryland's Core Learning Goals (CLGs) for English, Grades 1–12

scored with points, and then they are converted to levels. A score of 4 indicates excellent, 3 is proficient, 2 is approaching or partially proficient, and 1 is well below proficient. Performance assessments (PA) are scored using rubrics and recorded as level scores.

In the traditional system, we report one grade per subject. A standards-based system requires a summary symbol for each learning goal to provide a profile of each student's achievement. Note that in Figure 2, the student excels in two of the learning goals, is close to competent in a third, and is having considerable difficulty with the fourth goal. This is valuable information that cannot be gleaned from the almost meaningless single grade of B in a traditional grading system.

Standards-based report cards are the norm in the elementary grades, but they are still not used by most middle and high schools. Figure 3 (page 134) shows a high school report card that breaks down the subjects into several topic areas. Students are assessed on their proficiency in the specific subcategories of each area—not just given one grade for everything.

Guideline 2: Use Criterion-Referenced Performance Standards as Reference Points to Determine Grades

Traditionally, letter and number relationships and one- or two-word descriptors have provided the performance standards for grades: An A is 90–100% or "Excellent," a B is 80–89% or "Very Good," and so on. For there to be any real meaning to grades, and to have any possibility of consistency among teachers, the meaning of grades (whatever symbols are used) should come from clear descriptions of performance standards. The following is an example of such descriptors from the Downingtown School District in Downingtown, Pennsylvania:

> **Level 4: Advanced**—A superior, consistent performance; beyond expected achievement

Content Areas	More Than Adequate Progress	Adequate Progress	Limited Progress	No Progress	Not Applicable
Language Arts					
Reading and Literature					
Writing					
Oral Communication					
Mathematics					
Numbers and Operations					
Measurement					
Geometry and Spatial Sense					
Patterns, Functions, and Algebra					
Data Analysis, Statistics, and Probability					
Science					
The Scientific Process					
Life and Environmental Sciences					
Physical, Earth, and Space Sciences					
Social Studies					
History					
Political Science					
Cultural Anthropology					
Geography					
Economics					
Fine Arts					
Visual					
Music/Dance/Drama					

Figure 3: Sample Standards-Based Report Card

Level 3: Proficient—A solid, consistent performance; demonstrated competency of knowledge and skills

Level 2: Approaching—A partial mastery with limited to basic performance of expected achievement

Level 1: Beginning—A limited mastery of knowledge and skills; below basic expectations

Note that there are only four levels. The base is level 3—proficient. At level 4, students excel and are achieving well above proficiency. At level 2, students' achievement is partially proficient or approaching proficiency, and at level 1, their achievement is well below proficiency. These performance standards are criterion-referenced, not norm-referenced. This means that grades are determined by the actual level of achievement, not by the distribution of scores on a curve. In any one class, all students could demonstrate excellent achievement and receive As, or there may be no students excelling and achieving As.

Once the performance standards have been agreed upon, teachers must then develop and use task- or knowledge-specific rubrics that are aligned to these standards. Many examples of such rubrics can be found in Stiggins, Arter, Chappuis, and Chappuis (2004) and Arter and Chappuis (2006). Professional dialogue about the clearly described performance standards will lead to shared understanding and contribute to consistency in interpretation by teachers.

Guideline 3: Limit the Student Attributes Included in Grades to Individual Achievement

Traditionally, grades have included a variety of factors: Achievement is mixed in with effort, participation, attitude, and other behaviors. Often we do not know what a grade has actually measured. Grades should be based on achievement only, in other words, grading should be a description of students' knowledge and skills regarding the standards. Effort, participation, attitude, and other behaviors are very important, but they should be reported separately. What is needed is what I call an "expanded format" report card that provides ratings for behaviors in addition to grades for achievement.

For example, in Ontario, the provincial report cards have overall ratings for nine "learning skills" for first- to eighth-grade students (independent work, use of information, class participation, initiative, cooperation with others, problem-solving, homework completion, conflict resolution, and goal-setting to improve work) and ratings for five learning skills (works independently, teamwork, organization, work habits/homework, initiative) in each subject. (These report cards can be found at http://www.edu.gov.on.ca/eng/document/ forms/report/1998/report98.html.)

Another example of an expanded report card is shown in Figure 4. This example from Hawaii uses a set of "general learner outcomes" (GLOs), which are the broad goals of standards-based learning for students in all grade levels. Students in grades one through eight are assessed as consistently, usually, sometimes, or rarely exhibiting each GLO. This provides clear information about these behaviors separate from students' achievement of the academic learning goals in each subject.

To implement this guideline properly, nothing is permitted that distorts the grade. Teachers should not use academic penalties for behaviors such as turning work in late, nor should they provide opportunities for bonus points or extra credit unrelated to the learning goals.

It is also important to remember that there is only one student's name on the report card, so the evidence that goes into determining each student's grade must be *individual* evidence. This means that if cooperative learning is used as a teaching strategy, individual assessment must occur after group activities have been completed. It is the individual evidence that is used to determine grades.

General Learner Outcomes (GLOs)	QUARTER 1				QUARTER 2				QUARTER 3				QUARTER 4			
	Consistently	Usually	Sometimes	Rarely	Consistently	Usually	Sometimes	Rarely	Consistently	Usually	Sometimes	Rarely	Consistently	Usually	Sometimes	Rarely
GLO 1: Self-Directed Learner The ability to be responsible for one's own learning																
GLO 2: Community Contributor The understanding that it is essential for human beings to work together																
GLO 3: Complex Thinker The ability to demonstrate critical thinking and problem-solving strategies																
GLO 4: Quality Producer The ability to recognize and produce quality performance and quality products																
GLO 5: Effective Communicator The ability to communicate effectively																
GLO 6: Effective and Ethical User of Technology The ability to use a variety of technologies effectively and ethically																

Figure 4: Sample Expanded Report Card for General Learner Outcomes (GLOs)

Guideline 4: Sample Student Performance—Do Not Include All Scores in Grades

In the traditional system, almost everything students do is given a score, and every score is included in the final grade—regardless of the purpose of the activity. By doing this, we have infected our students with the "Does this count?" syndrome: Students care only about work that will affect their grade. Researchers like Black and Wiliam (1998), however, have demonstrated the value of making a clear distinction between the various purposes of assessment and their appropriate use. Learning is a process, and students (and parents) must understand—as they do in the arts and athletics—that there are different phases involved: a learning phase when students practice their knowledge, and a performance phase when students demonstrate what they know, understand, and can do. Teachers should provide feedback on formative assessments (those assessments for learning such as drafts, quizzes, and practice), but determine grades only from the evidence from varied summative assessments (assessments *of* learning). If we do this, we make grading supportive of learning.

This guideline is one of the greatest challenges to the traditional culture of schools, particularly as it relates to homework. Homework is a significant part of the grading process—especially in middle and high schools. But careful consideration needs to be given to the purpose of homework. Most homework is practice, and so any assessment of it should be considered formative, and thus has no place in grades. The only homework that should be part of the grading process is homework that requires students to extend or integrate the knowledge, understanding, and skills they have obtained in classroom learning activities—assignments or projects through which students demonstrate application and synthesis of what they have learned in class. If such assessments done outside the classroom are used to determine grades, then teachers must monitor carefully to ensure that homework represents the student's own work.

Foreign language teachers at Rutherford High School in Bay County, Florida, have been implementing this guideline since 1999. Summative assessment accounts for at least 98% of each student's grade, and they have few, if any, problems with the "Does this count?" syndrome. In fact, when students are asked about this approach, they comment that classes are less stressful because there is no grade attached to homework, and they can relax and learn. They are expected to make mistakes that help them learn, and it is obvious to students that teachers want them to learn.

Guideline 5: Keep Records That Can Be Updated Easily— "Grade in Pencil!"

As discussed in Guideline 4, in the traditional system, almost everything students do is given a score, and every score is included in grades. Guideline 5 deals with the same issue, but from the perspective of time rather than purpose. Most learning is incremental, so when we look at a student's performance on summative assessments, special emphasis must be given to more recent evidence of achievement. If a student shows today that she now knows, understands, or can do something that she did not know last week or last month, then the new evidence must replace—not just be added to— the previous evidence. This is another way we make grading supportive of learning.

This guideline means that students need to have several summative assessment opportunities to demonstrate what they know, understand, and can do in relation to each standard. This may happen as illustrated in the sample in Figure 2, but it also means that students should be given opportunities for second-chance or make-up assessments. It is of course important that students try hard and do the best they can on the first assessment; it is a waste of everyone's time for students to have a second opportunity if they have not done anything to increase their likelihood of success. Therefore, students should provide evidence of "correctives" (such as peer coaching, tutoring, and additional practice) before they are granted a second opportunity. Second opportunities do not have to be convenient for students; there might be an "opportunity cost" attached (such as having the second opportunity occur outside class time) to help students recognize that it is better to put maximum effort into the first assessment.

Laurel Floyd, a teacher a Rosenwald Middle School in Panama City, Florida, provides frequent reassessment opportunities for her sixth-grade students and always uses only their most recent scores in the determination of grades. She has found that this encourages her students to keep trying and leads to higher achievement and more positive attitudes about learning and school.

Guideline 6: "Crunch" Numbers Carefully, if at All

If a student's performance is very consistent, there is no need to number crunch. The grade he or she deserves is clear. But if a student's performance is inconsistent, the traditional method of "number crunching" does not work. Depending on the distribution of a student's scores, number crunching may not lead to the "right" grade. Traditionally grades are *calculated*: All the individual assessments are added, and the grade is the mean, or average, of all the scores. The problem with this approach is that it overemphasizes outlier scores. This works against students because outlier scores are almost always low. Grades will be more accurate if we *determine*—not just calculate—grades. Rather than averaging, teachers should consider the median (middle value) or mode (the most frequent value) as these measures of central tendency reward consistency and allow for the occasional anomalous weak performance. As educators, we must apply our professional judgment to the body of evidence each student produces, not just crunch numbers.

One very serious problem with traditional number crunching is the use of zeros (most commonly for missing or late assignments) in the calculation of grades. This is an inappropriate practice because the resulting grade is a serious misrepresentation of the student's achievement. The most common grading scale used in schools gives 60 percentage points for an F and 10 extra points for each successively higher letter grade from D up to A—an unequal scale that results in distorted grades when even one zero is included.

Instead of assigning a grade of zero, why not simply note that the evidence is missing with a blank space in the grade book? When it is time to determine a grade, decide if there is sufficient evidence to make a valid judgment. If there is sufficient evidence, determine the grade regardless of the missing evidence. (Concern about missing assignments or other evidence should be communicated prior to grading through phone calls home, email, and so on, and also on the narrative or expanded format section of the report card as suggested in Guideline 3.) If there is insufficient evidence to determine a grade, the student receives an I for "Incomplete" or "Insufficient" on his or her report card. This communicates accurately what the problem is and puts the responsibility where it should be—on the student. It gives students a second chance at success since arrangements can be made to complete the missing evidence.

Hugh O'Donnell, a retired eighth-grade social-studies teacher in Hillsboro, Oregon, included this statement in his grading policy that he shared with students and parents in the first week of the school year:

> I will not include zeros for late or missing assignments in achievement statistics, because zeros do not describe learning, and they are extreme as values. I will use the median average (or middle score) as a general indicator of achievement unless there is an unusual circumstance. In that case, I will consider the relative importance of the learning goals achieved and the recency of scores. If there is insufficient evidence of achievement, I will assign an incomplete and

expect the student to make arrangements to make up or repeat the learning experiences that were missed.

Guideline 7: Use Quality Assessments, and Properly Record Evidence of Achievement

Grading has been an "anything goes" process: Everything students do gets a score, and every score goes into the grade—regardless of the purpose of the assessment, when it occurs in the learning process, or whether it was a quality assessment. Since most teachers have unfortunately had relatively little training in assessment, classroom assessments frequently lack quality. In addition, some evidence—most notably behavioral factors such as attitude—have simply been stored in teachers' heads and retrieved when calculating grades. For grades to be accurate, assessment must meet standards of quality, and we must carefully record and maintain evidence of achievement and behaviors. The conditions necessary to ensure quality in assessment include:

- **Clear targets**—The content and performance standards must be clear, public, and identifiable by students throughout the learning process. (Guidelines 1, 2, and 3)

- **Clear purpose**—Everyone involved should understand when assessment is diagnostic, when it is formative, and when it is summative, and how the results will be used. (Guideline 4)

- **Appropriate target-method match**—To be of quality, assessments must be effective and efficient. We must attempt to ensure that any assessment is well-chosen for the learning goal(s) and the context in which it is being administered, such as the time available, number of students, and so on.

- **Appropriate sampling**—Quality assessment requires sufficient evidence to make good decisions, not too much or too little; measurement experts say that generally at least three pieces of evidence are needed, but the amount of evidence also depends on the consistency of the student's performance. Consistent performance may require less evidence, while inconsistent performance requires more evidence. (Guidelines 5 and 6)

- **Avoidance of bias and distortion**—Quality requires that everything be done to attempt to eliminate interference in the accuracy of assessment. Bias and distortion can occur if students are unwell or upset, if they lack reading skill, or if they have severe test anxiety. Sometimes there can be problems with the setting—too much noise, uncomfortable temperature, and so on—but generally these are controlled effectively. There may also be problems with the assessment itself, such as the clarity of the wording of questions or directions. Another somewhat common problem is time. If students are unable to complete an assessment in the time allotted, achievement is distorted and quality assessment has not been achieved.

Guideline 8: Discuss and Involve Students in Assessment Throughout the Teaching and Learning Process

Assessment and grading have long been shrouded in secrecy as the exclusive preserve of the teacher. Higher levels of achievement occur when students are involved in their learning (see Black and Wiliam, 1998). It is therefore important to ensure that students understand how their grades will be determined (in an age-appropriate way), and to involve them in the assessment process through record-keeping and by communicating about their achievement and progress. Teachers should provide clear explanation to young students about how their learning will be assessed and graded, and when students can read, these explanations should be in writing. Assessment and grading policies should also be shared with parents.

Following the Guidelines

Implementing these standards-based grading guidelines requires that all of the practices listed in the "traditional system" column in Figure 1 be eliminated from classrooms. If grades are to effectively serve their purpose of communicating student achievement, they must accurately depict that achievement. A standards-based approach to grading requires professional judgment, not just number crunching. Teachers must be accountable, not just accountants!

These guidelines will provide grades that are accurate, meaningful, consistent, and supportive of learning—the four conditions that must be met for effective grading. Many traditional grading practices do not meet these conditions, but they are often entrenched in our school systems—especially at the high-school level. This is particularly unfortunate because it is at this level that grades become more high-stakes as students look ahead to higher education and begin to plan their lives after high school. Thus, the need to meet the conditions for effectiveness in grading is most pressing at the high-school level. Change is always difficult, but if we recognize that how we grade makes a huge difference to students, it is obvious that we must ensure that grades are determined in ways that are logical and planned and that grades clearly communicate student achievement. "This requires nothing less than clear thinking, careful planning, excellent communication skills, and an overriding concern for the well being of students" (Guskey, 1996, p. 22).

References

Arter, J. A., & Chappuis, J. (2006). *Creating and recognizing quality rubrics.* Portland, OR: Educational Testing Service.

Black, P., & Wiliam, D. (1998). Inside the black box. *Phi Delta Kappan, 80*(2), 139–148.

DuFour, R., Eaker, R., & DuFour, R. (2005). Recurring themes of PLCs and the assumptions they challenge. In R. DuFour, R. Eaker, & R. DuFour (Eds.), *On common ground: The power of professional learning communities* (pp. 7–29). Bloomington, IN: Solution Tree (formerly National Educational Service).

Guskey, T. R. (1996). Introduction. In T. R. Guskey (Ed.), *Communicating student learning (the 1996 ASCD Yearbook,* p. 1–12*)*. Alexandria, VA: Association for Supervision and Curriculum Development.

Marzano, R. J. (2006). *Classroom assessment and grading that work.* Alexandria, VA: Association for Supervision and Curriculum Development.

O'Connor, K. (2002). *How to grade for learning: Linking grades to standards* (2nd ed.). Thousand Oaks, CA: Corwin Press.

Olson, L. (1995, June 14). Cards on the table. *Education Week, 15*(41), 23–28.

Patterson, W. (2003). Breaking out of our boxes. *Phi Delta Kappan, 84*(8), 569–574.

Stiggins, R. J., Arter, J. A., Chappuis, J., & Chappuis, S. (2004). *Classroom* assessment for *student learning: Doing it right—using it well.* Portland, OR: ETS Assessment Training Institute.

Lisa Almeida

Lisa Almeida is a senior professional development associate with The Leadership and Learning Center (formerly the Center for Performance Assessment). She was a classroom teacher, guidance teacher, and a school and district administrator in large, urban school districts. Ms. Almeida has worked with students from diverse backgrounds with differing learning needs, including English language learners, at a variety of grade levels. She continues to work with educators and students in Albuquerque Public Schools, as well as across the United States.

This chapter explores assessment practices that support English language learners (ELLs). Ms. Almeida focuses on three essential questions:

1. What do educators need to consider when preparing to meet the assessment needs of English language learners?

2. How can teachers effectively assess English language learners' learning as opposed to their ability to speak the language?

3. What are the roles of teachers and school leaders in creating and sustaining effective assessment opportunities for English language learners?

She offers practical and constructive strategies that any school can implement. She asserts that practitioners need to reflect on current English language learner assessment practices and ask if these assessments are effective measures *of* and *for* learning. She calls upon educators to replace traditional forms of assessment with more effective methods for English language learners.

For more information on Lisa Almeida and her work, contact her at lalmeida@LeadandLearn.com.

Chapter 7

The Journey Toward Effective Assessment for English Language Learners

Lisa Almeida

Many different terms have been used to identify students whose second language is English: They have been called limited English proficiency students (LEPs), English as a second language students (ESLs), and second language learners (SLLs). At present, educators refer to these students as English language learners (ELLs)—a term that more accurately reflects the process of language acquisition. Whatever the label, the number of these students in our schools has increased at exponential rates in both urban and rural districts. This dramatic demographic shift has produced many challenges for our public school system as educators struggle to meet the needs of English language learners—often without any specialized training.

In the United States, 47 million people (18% of the population) speak a language other than English at home. English language learners are the fastest growing segment of the K–12 student population (U.S. Census Bureau, 2003). One of every six children of school age is a language-minority student (National Clearinghouse for English

Language Acquisition and Language Instruction Educational Programs, 2004). Spanish speakers make up nearly 79% of English language learners; the majority of growth in this population is in the primary and intermediate grades (Kohler & Lazarín, 2007). The English language learner population is quickly becoming a majority in our communities, and therefore, in our schools. These students have a unique set of learning and assessment needs, and effective assessment practices are key to their success. Educators need reliable and valid measures to monitor their academic progress and learning.

The Expressway Versus the Toll Road

For the English language learner, our schools are often the equivalent of a "learning expressway": Students are expected to quickly get "up to speed," and they can only slow down when problems arise (such as failing grades or test scores) or when they leave the expressway (by graduating, or worse, dropping out). To successfully reach these learners, however, educators must exit the learning expressway and carefully merge onto the learning toll road. Effective assessment is a key tool in building this new road to academic success.

Envision driving on a toll road: Strategically placed stops for vehicle and personal maintenance consistently force drivers to slow down or stop. Travelers on a long journey can use these stops to check their directions, review what lies ahead, and make any necessary adjustments to get to their destinations in the most efficient way. In the same way, we can redesign our assessment practices to provide English language learners with the measured pace and continual monitoring they need to ensure they achieve at high standards.

This chapter focuses on assessing English language learners in any classroom. It will explore the elements that must be in place to effectively measure what students know and how well they know it. The chapter addresses three essential questions:

1. What do educators need to consider when preparing to meet the assessment needs of English language learners? What are the rules of the road?

2. How can teachers effectively assess English language learners' learning as opposed to their ability to speak the language? Who are the passengers on the journey?

3. What are the roles of teachers and school leaders in creating and sustaining effective assessment opportunities for English language learners? What are our responsibilities as drivers of the education process?

Rules of the Road: What Teachers Need to Know

The first rule is that there is no expressway to learning a new language. Some researchers contend that it takes 4 to 7 years for English language learners to become sufficiently fluent in their new language (Olsen, 2006). Other researchers, however, have found that with structured English-language immersion, fluency can occur much more quickly. Rather than adopting a one-size-fits-all approach with a standardized timeline, educators are well-advised to consider the linguistic, cultural, pedagogical, and cognitive needs of each individual student.

Careful determination and monitoring of students' language acquisition levels is crucial. Effective instruction and assessment for English learners requires that teachers are knowledgeable of their students' language-acquisition levels (Flynn & Hill, 2006) in both English and the students' primary language. Knowledge of students' language levels informs teachers about how students can most effectively learn content and demonstrate their understanding.

Language acquisition starts with the "beginning" or "preproduction" stage. At this stage, students have minimal comprehension skills and typically will not verbalize. The beginning level is also referred to as the "silent period." It usually lasts from 0 to 6 months after the student has started learning a new language (for students 5 years and older).

The next level is "early intermediate" or "early production," which lasts 6 months to a year. In this stage, students have partial comprehension—they can answer lower-level questions. The "intermediate" or "speech emergence" stage is next. It lasts approximately 1 to 3 years. Students at this level have good comprehension skills and respond with a phrase or short-sentence answer. These students can begin to comprehend higher-level questioning, such as why or how questions.

Within 3 to 5 years, students enter the "intermediate fluency" or "early advanced" stage. At this stage, students have above-average comprehension abilities and make few grammatical errors. These students are able to conceptually understand and effectively communicate their learning.

The final language acquisition stage is "advanced fluency," or simply "advanced," which occurs within 5 to 7 years of learning a second language. In this stage, students are able to articulate in a way similar to that of native speakers.

Knowing and understanding the characteristics of each stage of language acquisition is essential to planning effective instructional strategies and assessment formats for English language learners. Teachers must engage students at the correct level of discourse—the student's "zone of proximal development." When engaged at their current level of language ability, students can—with support from the teacher—demonstrate what they are expected to know and be able to do. When teachers are conscious of their English learners' stages of language acquisition, they can use appropriate instruction and assessment tools, which in turn support linguistic and academic achievement. For example, assessment formats for beginning students may consist of yes/no questions or one- or two-word response questions with the teacher supplying a "word bank" so students do not have to rely on their limited English vocabularies. Formats for assessing students in the early production to intermediate fluency stages might be to allow students to answer assessment questions verbally or role-play their understanding of a concept. In addition, teachers might allow students to use a translation dictionary during tests.

Knowing Our Passengers: The English Language Learners

The needs of English language learners are as diverse as the students themselves, and the challenges extend beyond language acquisition. When a student performs poorly on an assessment, is he or she struggling with language issues, cultural issues, or learning issues? Educators of English language learners face this critical question on a daily basis.

As with English-speaking students, many factors have an enormous impact on English language learners' ability to learn: which language is used (and how) in their homes and neighborhoods, their educational backgrounds, their families' socioeconomic levels, and the number of books in their homes. All of these factors contribute to the students' readiness to learn, as well as to their ability to learn in a new language.

No two English language learners have the same amount of knowledge or competency in their primary language or are in the identical stage of English-language acquisition, which adds to the challenge for educators. Some English language learners were born in the United States but reside in non-English-speaking households. Others are immigrants who have received differing amounts of formal education. Some students have been a part of the American school system for a number of years, but they may still be in the initial stages of English-language acquisition. Communication style—aside from language skills and fluency—can be a hidden issue in classroom assessment. Many cultures do not value the open style of communication that we have in our classrooms. Consequently, some

English language learners may choose to be silent or take on a passive role rather than risk making a mistake.

A small percentage of English language learners come from very primitive cultures. These students have limited social and academic experiences. They may have never been in a building with running water or used a pencil. In addition to learning *in* English while also learning the English language, they have much to learn about our educational environment; concepts such as fire drills, lunch lines, and restroom passes are all unfamiliar.

Many parents of English language learners are equally unaware of the expectations and routines of the American school system—let alone the assessment process with its battery of standardized tests. Those who have a limited education themselves often rely solely on schools to educate their children. It is not uncommon for parents to work long hours at more than one job, making participation in school functions difficult or impossible. Parents may also lack confidence in their communication skills and not feel comfortable pursuing a relationship with the school; as a result, students lose a critical support structure.

Consequently, creating inclusive, welcoming, and supportive conditions for English language learners and their families is a critical responsibility of all school staff. Parent involvement has a positive impact on all student learning, and especially on students' learning in English while they learn the English language. If students' home languages and cultures are integrated into the learning environment—in the curriculum, assessments, and school activities—parents are more likely to feel comfortable supporting their child's education by participating in school activities, such as parent-teacher conferences, English classes, the parent/teacher organization, school advisory councils, tutoring, and parent volunteer programs.

The Drivers: The Role of Teachers and School Leaders

Teachers and school leaders are in the driver's seat on the journey to effective assessment for English language learners. Educators must always be cognizant that students' conversational ability does not necessarily reflect their intellectual ability. Therefore, schools and districts need to build and implement assessment systems designed to generate summative and formative data on what English language learners know and are able to do. An effective assessment system for English language learners includes classroom measures and school-wide policies and programs.

Authentic Classroom Assessment

One crucial question looms large for classroom teachers of English language learners: How can we effectively assess English language learners' *knowledge* rather than their *fluency* in English?

Authentic or performance-based assessment instruments yield more accurate results with English language learners than traditional assessments, regardless of whether they are used to collect summative data (for a status report) or formative data (to affect learning). The results of these authentic assessments tend to be indicative of students' conceptual understanding of a concept or skill. Effective measures of English language learners' knowledge include performance assessments, cooperative learning opportunities, and the use of nonlinguistic representations (such as graphic organizers, dioramas, charts, and mental pictures), as well as teacher observations in conjunction with rubrics. Portfolios of learning are effective measures of students' oral and written language skills (Díaz-Rico & Weed, 2006).

Large-scale standardized assessments (most often used as summative measurements) tend to provide invalid data, because they rely on students' understanding of English at a certain level. More often than not, items on these assessments are selected response, extended multiple choice, and short constructed response. Without special accommodations—such as translations, a revised test format, or extra time—English language learners' knowledge and skills will not be adequately measured with these traditional assessments.

So how can we accurately assess English language learners' proficiency? Mike Schmoker (2005) makes a profound argument that "the problem is not that we do not *know* what to do—it is that we do not *do* what we know. . . . Success depends largely on *implementing what is already known* rather than on adopting new or previously unknown ways of doing things" (p. 149). We know the right thing to do. We know that authentic assessments give many students—not just English language learners—opportunities to demonstrate their conceptual understanding (or lack thereof) as active, as opposed to passive, learners (Armstrong, 1994; Coil, 2004; Darling-Hammond, 1997; Díaz-Rico & Weed, 2006; Wiggins, 2005). Students engage in higher levels of thinking when complex performances are required; therefore, they gain an innate understanding of concepts and skills rather than merely a superficial understanding. Students are expected to revise their work after obtaining specific feedback about their learning; an authentic assessment is not a one-shot approach. Authentic assessments appeal to more than the verbal/linguistic students, which instantaneously creates a successful environment for English language learners (Armstrong, 1994; Bishop 2005). Moreover, performance-based assessments are designed with the understanding that students must apply their knowledge. Therefore, the assessment is more rigorous and meaningful to students. Yet another significant advantage to using performance assessments is to provide students with opportunities to interact with one another. English language learners tend to excel in small-group settings because the environment encourages academic learning and language proficiency. In addition, the interaction helps students learn classroom routines and become active members in the culture of the classroom.

Now that we know how to assess English language learners accurately, the next step is to create and use appropriate assessment tools.

Practical Strategies for Teaching English Language Learners

Some specific strategies can help teachers in diverse schools as they plan, implement, monitor, and evaluate effective assessments for English language learners. The Center for Equity and Excellence in Education (1996) set forth two principles of effective practice for limited English proficient students. First, students should receive instruction that builds on their previous education and cognitive abilities and reflects their language proficiency levels. Second, students should be evaluated with appropriate and valid assessments that are aligned to state and local standards and take into account language acquisition stages and the cultural backgrounds of the students. When assessments are aligned to standards, teachers can more accurately infer how students are progressing towards the learning expectations.

To maximize the learning environment, and therefore, the learning opportunities for English language learners, teachers and administrators must begin by planning effective programs, lessons, and assessments that target the concepts students are required to know and the skills students must master. Planning must include specific strategies that will help teachers work with students who are learning English while also being assessed in English (Bishop, 2006).

There are critical components for preparing English language learners and teachers for success—regardless of students' stage of second-language acquisition, and regardless of the assessment format. Effective educators of English language learners do the following:

- Access and activate students' prior knowledge before administering assessments.

- Communicate with students using clear and concise language while maintaining eye contact, bearing in mind cultural differences.

- Incorporate visual aids, gestures, body movements, or pan-tomime into instruction. Nonverbal behavior can help explain or elaborate on instruction for students with limited English proficiency. However, teachers should be aware that some expressions or actions can be misunderstood by students from different cultures.

- Use shorter and simpler sentences while speaking at a slow-er speed.

- Use high-frequency vocabulary words often.

These everyday strategies can be used in all learning situations, but are especially useful when giving directions for assessments and throughout the assessment process because students who are learn-ing and being assessed in a second language need these extra lin-guistic supports.

Teachers and leaders need to continually envision and work towards creating an accountability system that is most beneficial for English language learners. Student-centered accountability is more productive than traditional accountability; it focuses on the improvement of teaching and learning instead of interpreting eval-uations and publishing reports (Reeves, 2004). What accountability system will ensure that English language learners are making progress in what they know and are able to do in critical content areas? The answer is an assessment system that includes multiple data sources for the collection of evidence of student learning.

Reeves (2004) states that "in the most successful classrooms, teachers and students understand that the purpose of assessment is the improvement of student performance. We test so that we know how to learn better and how to teach better" (p. 8). Grades, classroom performance, teacher observations and recommendations, and for-mative and summative assessment data, in addition to an array of samples of student work, are an integral part of the accountability system. Creating and sustaining a student-centered accountability system is not easy, but the effort teachers and leaders devote in this process will be rewarded with improved educational outcomes for English language learners.

Successful teachers use the following practical strategies before, during, and after assessing English language learners:

- Use more than verbal/linguistic strategies when communicating the learning objectives of the assessment with students, such as drawings, photographs, graphic organizers, and kinesthetic support.

- Ensure the assessment fits hand-to-glove with standards and curriculum and contains unbiased information.

- Provide frequent formative assessments to give students multiple opportunities to show what they know and are able to do, such as performance assessments, student-friendly rubrics, cooperative learning opportunities, nonlinguistic representations, portfolios of learning, and teacher observations.

- Provide risk-free (that is, ungraded, formative-assessment) opportunities for expression, such as interactive journals, pair-sharing, and personal timelines.

- Use assessments that generate valid data on what is truly being assessed, whether it is students' learning, English proficiency, or educational and background experiences.

- Provide timely and specific feedback to students on their assessments—not just a letter or number grade. Involve students in rubric development. English language learners will have a clearer understanding of what is expected from them, and they will feel more ownership in the process than they would after simply receiving a letter grade or using a teacher-generated rubric (Ainsworth & Christinson, 1998).

- Activate prior knowledge by using nonlinguistic representations, such as graphic organizers, physical models, or mental pictures, before asking students to complete assessments. Additionally, a K-W-L chart (what I know, what I learned, and what I want to learn) can be used. Ask students to brainstorm the "what I know" part (as a group). Then ask students to individually complete the "what I learned" portion using drawings or images.

- Provide additional time for students to complete assessments. This can be done either by allowing more time during the assessment or by creating additional time throughout the school day.

- Explain directions as many times as necessary and/or provide a translation of the test in the students' native language. It is important for teachers and students to have a strong support system for translating. Translation services and structures vary throughout schools and districts.

- If possible, include additional time in assessments to allow students to initially express their ideas in their native language and then translate their ideas into English (Tomlinson, 2001). Alternatively, allow students to dictate their answers, and if necessary, respond in their native language—especially if knowledge and skills are being assessed (as opposed to English proficiency).

- Meet with colleagues at least once a month to discuss teaching and learning strategies and results within grade levels or content areas. The data team process, a research-based five-step process, facilitates this collaboration and ensures accountability for designing the best instruction, interventions, and formative assessments for learners. This process is explained in detail in chapter 4.

- Work with students to set specific, measurable, achievable, relevant, and timely goals. Teachers and students can review and revise these goals together. This establishes a sense of urgency and maximizes progress (Echevarria & Graves, 2007). There is a strong connection between goals, motivation, and improvement for educators and students. Schmoker (1999) asserts that "good faith efforts to establish goals and then to collectively monitor and adjust actions toward them produce results" (p. 2). Working towards goals promotes logical planning and action in both teachers and students.

A Schoolwide System for Success

The challenges facing English language learners and their teachers are best met within a schoolwide support system. It is imperative that schools have a system in place to assess English language learners' educational and personal backgrounds before they start the learning journey, as well as an assessment system to continuously monitor their progress along the way. Leaders can be proactive in meeting the needs of English language learners by working with staff members to develop policies, programs, and transitional services that address many of the barriers impacting students' achievement in school. These tasks include:

- Structuring a differentiated, aligned, standards-based curriculum with regular assessment practices that allows for personalized placement and pacing depending on a student's skill and language levels, regardless of age, and where students can move into the regular curriculum when appropriate at any point in the school year

- Developing comprehensive home-language and English assessments to inform educators of students' existing knowledge and skills in both their native languages and in English

- Evaluating students' prior educational experiences

- Creating intervention services, such as intensive literacy and accelerated learning programs, for students who arrive with large gaps in their prior education

- Creating a positive and successful testing environment that allows teachers to make more accurate inferences about learning based on more student-friendly and reliable assessments

- Establishing an orientation program that includes information about the assessment structure of the school that offers easily accessible translators as well as more in-depth transitional services, such as individualized interventions and parent-education courses (a GED program and a family literacy program, for example) so parents understand the assessment process and how it impacts their child's academic progress so they can then provide support at home

- Providing health screenings with referrals to linguistically accessible and culturally appropriate services to meet the students and families' needs. Like any other students, English language learners can have health issues that are barriers to their academic performance.

- Offering counseling and support services that are linguistically accessible and culturally appropriate for students and/or families who are dealing with the challenge of assimilation into a new country, family separation, or post–traumatic stress syndrome (Olsen, 2006), all of which can have profound effects on student success as measured by formative and summative assessments

These types of programs and transitional services foster emotional security and a positive, supportive relationship with English learners and their families, who are often challenged by language, cultural, and economic barriers as they adapt to their new country and school system. Schools that build school-home connections and community partnerships can help their English language students excel in a variety of assessment scenarios.

Continuing the Journey

As we continue our educational journey toward the creation and implementation of effective measurements of English language students' learning, we must remember that most teachers in mainstream classrooms have not been prepared to teach and effectively assess English language learners. In fact, many of today's leaders have not been prepared to lead in this significant challenge. Teachers and leaders are on a steep learning curve in regards to what impacts academic success for English language learners.

Let us reflect on this popular quote: "The journey is more important than the destination." While many of the issues affecting English language learners are out of our control as educators, we do have the power to impact the quality of education for these students. Many instructional and assessment strategies and decisions—the journey—are within our control. Thus, the destination—academic achievement—is more within students' reach than we tend to recognize. What are we waiting for? I tenaciously advocate that educators act now to create and administer effective assessments for our English language learners. Guaranteeing the academic success of our country's ever-increasing population of English language learners will not only improve the lives of these students, but it will also help ensure the improved economic and social welfare of our communities.

References

Ainsworth, L., & Christinson, J. (1998). *Student generated rubrics: An assessment model to help all students succeed.* New York: Dale Seymour Publications.

Armstrong, G. (1994). *Multiple intelligences in the classroom.* Alexandria, VA: Association for Supervision and Curriculum Development.

Besser, L., Davis, D., & Peery, A. (2006). *Data teams.* Englewood, CO: The Leadership and Learning Center (formerly the Center for Performance Assessment).

Bishop, B. (2005). *Academic language acquisition for English language learners.* Englewood, CO: The Leadership and Learning Center (formerly the Center for Performance Assessment).

Bishop, B. (2006). *Academic language acquisition for English language learners.* Englewood, CO: The Leadership and Learning Center (formerly the Center for Performance Assessment).

Bravmann, S. (2004). Assessment's "fab four." *Education Week, 23*(27), 56.

Center for Equity and Excellence in Education. (1996). In the classroom: Guiding principles. Available at: www.ncela.gwu.edu (retrieved May 4, 2007).

Coil, C. (2004). *Standards-based activities and assessments for the differentiated classroom.* Marion, IL: Pieces of Learning.

Darling-Hammond, L. (1997). *The right to learn.* San Francisco: Jossey-Bass.

Díaz-Rico, L., & Weed, K. (2006). *The crosscultural, language, and academic development handbook: A complete K–12 reference guide* (3rd ed.). Boston: Pearson.

Echevarria, J., & Graves, A. (2007). *Sheltered content instruction: Teaching English language learners with diverse abilities.* Boston: Pearson.

Flynn, K., & Hill, J. (2006). *Classroom instruction that works with English language learners.* Alexandria, VA: Association for Supervision and Curriculum Development.

Gay, G. (2000). Culturally responsive teaching. Available at: www.intime.uni.edu/multiculture/curriculum/culture/Teaching.htm (retrieved May 4, 2007).

Kohler, A., & Lazarín, M. (2007). The Hispanic education in the United States. *National Council of La Raza, Statistical Brief, 8*(1), 7–8.

National Clearinghouse for English Language Acquisition and Language Instruction Educational Programs (NCELA). (2004). *ELLs and the No*

Child Left Behind Act. Available at: www.ncela.gwu.edu/about/lieps/ 5_ellnclb.html (retrieved January 28, 2007).

Olsen, L. (2006). Ensuring academic success for English learners. *University of California Linguistic Minority Research Institute Newsletter, 15*(4), 2.

Reeves, D. (2004). *Accountability for learning: How teachers and school leaders can take charge.* Alexandria, VA: Association for Supervision and Curriculum Development.

Schmoker, M. (1999). *Results: The key to continuous school improvement* (2nd ed.). Alexandria, VA: Association for Supervision and Curriculum Development.

Schmoker, M. (2005). No turning back: The ironclad case for professional learning communities. In R. DuFour, R. Eaker, & R. DuFour (Eds.), *On common ground: The power of professional learning communities.* Bloomington, IN: Solution Tree (formerly National Educational Service).

Tomlinson, C. (2001). *How to differentiate instruction in mixed-ability classrooms* (2nd ed.). Alexandria, VA: Association for Supervision and Curriculum Development.

U.S. Census Bureau. (2003). *USA quickfacts.* Available at: quickfacts.census. gov/qfd/states/00000.html (retrieved January 27, 2007).

Wiggins, G. (2005). What is understanding by design? *Understanding by design.* Available at: www.grantwiggins.org/ubd.html (retrieved May 1, 2007).

Linda A. Gregg

Dr. Linda A. Gregg is the education director for Villa Santa Maria School, a private residential treatment center in Cedar Crest, New Mexico, and an adjunct instructor at the College of Santa Fe. She has taught curriculum design courses as well as courses on educational methodology and special-education policies and procedures. She has been a regular and special-education teacher in demographically diverse schools, and worked with special-needs children and English language learners. She has served as an elementary and high-school principal and an associate superintendent of special programs. She is also a professional development associate with The Leadership and Learning Center (formerly the Center for Performance Assessment).

Dr. Gregg has won awards as an outstanding school administrator and educational leader. She has a firm commitment to lifelong learning and an unflinching belief that all children can learn.

This chapter discusses the process for effective classroom assessment from the perspective of the special-needs learner. According to the current legislation, these students are expected to take the same state tests and achieve at the same levels as their nondisabled peers, which has created considerable frustration for students, parents, and teachers. Special-needs learners often have wide gaps in their learning. Teachers can help close the gap and help students reach proficiency with specific instructional and assessment strategies. Dr. Gregg argues that effective use of assessment provides critical opportunities for teachers to enhance instruction in a timely fashion for special-needs students. She then offers practical strategies for effective assessment with special-needs students, illustrated by real-life examples.

Dr. Linda Gregg can be reached at lgregg@LeadandLearn.com.

Chapter 8

Crossing the Canyon: Helping Students With Special Needs Achieve Proficiency

Linda A. Gregg

The academic progress of special-needs students in our school systems is subject to more scrutiny now than ever before, and their teachers—both special education and general education—are feeling the pressure. The Individuals with Disabilities Education Act (IDEA) first asserted that students with disabilities must have access to the general education curriculum; No Child Left Behind (NCLB) went a step further, requiring educators to ensure that their special-needs students not only have access to the general curriculum, but also achieve *proficiency* in it. But mere exposure to the curriculum will not ensure proficiency, and it will certainly not help bridge the gap in the learning of students with special needs. These gaps occur for a variety of reasons: sensory or cognitive challenges, poor perceptual skills, and other specific physical disabilities; low school attendance or high mobility; and many others. The resulting academic gaps may appear to be as wide as the Grand Canyon. In order to cross that canyon to reach proficiency, teachers of special-needs students will need specific instructional and assessment strategies.

Both NCLB and IDEA explicitly define expectations for teachers of special-needs students. According to IDEA, special educators must develop instruction that is research-based and specifically designed to help students with disabilities access and progress towards proficiency in the general education curriculum. Individualized education programs (IEPs) require that special-needs learners participate in some form in statewide and districtwide assessments of achievement.

The expectation that students with special needs will take state tests and achieve at the same levels and in the same timeframe as their nondisabled peers has sparked controversy for school leaders—and created considerable frustration for students, parents, and teachers. Consider Julia, a seventh-grade student who performs in mathematics and reading at a third-grade level, but is still required to take the same state-mandated seventh-grade test as her nondisabled peers: How can the average teacher help Julia achieve proficiency under those circumstances?

Navigating the world of special education is much like taking a road trip for thousands of miles without a map. You may know exactly where you want to go and exactly what you want to see, but if you do not have a map to guide your journey, you cannot find landmarks that tell you how close you are to your destination. The trip will most likely take longer because you are unsure of which turns to take, or even if you are going in the right direction at all. Without appropriate planning, students with special needs may never reach their learning destination.

Effective use of assessment can create the road map for both the student and the teacher. It provides a critical opportunity to enhance instruction in a timely fashion for special-needs students. This kind of road map not only plots a course, it allows teacher and students to make adjustments when faced with various hazards or unexpected events on the road to achievement. Though teachers of special-needs students may be worried about their students passing the state assessment *of* learning, assessment *for* learning is the best, most accurate tool to plan for, stimulate, and document student success on the journey.

Assessment *for* Learning: Small Steps Count

Assessment *for* learning (Stiggins, Arter, Chappuis, & Chappuis, 2004)—formative assessment given during the learning—helps students learn more by providing crucial information about what students know and do not know while there is still time to revise the road map. Traditional forms of assessment, such as state- or district-mandated tests given at the end of the school year (summative assessment *of* learning), are not sufficient to guide instruction for students with special needs. The results of these assessments are rarely available in timely fashion or in usefully disaggregated ways that can impact day-to-day instruction. In some instances, schools have received state testing results a full year after the initial test; obviously, teachers could not use those results to help drive their instructional decisions throughout the school year. Although state and district norm- and criterion-referenced tests provide important data about student achievement, these data are usually of little assistance in determining whether school goals have been attained, evaluating the effectiveness of the curriculum and daily instruction, or ascertaining the degree and depth of student learning (Clark & Clark, 2000).

The results of assessments *for* learning are readily accessible to both the student and teacher so both can make critical decisions about the route to take toward proficiency in content, concepts, and skills. The following are typical informal classroom assessment strategies that can be used on a day-to-day basis in the classroom:

- Writing samples
- Performance assessments
- Task-specific checklists
- Work sample analyses
- Skills analyses
- Portfolios
- Computer-based presentations
- Task analyses

- Conferences and interviews
- True/false, multiple choice, short answer, fill-in-the blank, and matching exercises
- Observations
- Authentic assessments
- Checklists
- Student products
- Publisher assessments

Effective informal classroom assessments should do the following:

- Address the content, concepts, and skills required in the standard.

- Permit assessment on a periodic, ongoing basis.

- Permit tracking and monitoring of progress.

- Allow self-reflection by the student.

- Provide ample opportunities for the student to demonstrate progress.

The gaps in learning for special-needs students can be so wide that incremental improvements may be the best measure of the student's academic progress. According to McLoughlin and Lewis (2005), assessment of students with special needs must be a systematic and *ongoing* process of collecting educationally *relevant* information on student achievement and performance to help make appropriate instructional decisions. To ensure ongoing collection of relevant information, teachers can use the following five-step process for formative classroom assessment:

1. "Unwrap" or "unpack" the standard to determine the concepts, content, and skills required for instruction.

2. Determine the purpose of the assessment.

3. Select specific assessments that will provide the desired information.

4. Gather and discuss the results of the assessment with the student.

5. Use that information to make decisions about instruction.

"Unwrap" the Standard to Determine the Concepts, Content, and Skills Required for Instruction

To select an informal classroom assessment that will be beneficial, teachers must first investigate the content standards that the student must reach on his or her chronological grade level: What is the learning destination? Even though special-needs students may be performing academically on a level lower than their chronological grade level, they will still be expected to work toward proficiency at their chronological grade level.

"Unwrapping" the standard (Ainsworth & Viegut, 2006) means to systematically identify the essential content, concepts, and skills found in the standards and indicators. Unwrapping the standard helps to narrow the focus on specific content and skills within the standard and guide instruction, to target what students need to know and be able to do. Unwrapping can also help teachers decide what to assess. For example, two state standards might say:

1. Students will demonstrate the ability to summarize, paraphrase, analyze, and evaluate what they read.

2. Students will demonstrate the ability to make predictions about stories.

To unwrap these standards, identify the nouns (content or concepts) by underlining them and the verbs (skills) by circling them:

1. Demonstrate the ability to summarize, paraphrase, analyze, and evaluate what he or she reads.

2. Demonstrate the ability to make predictions about stories.

Then generate a list of the concepts and skills to be mastered from the standard. Some school districts unwrap the standards to make the information easily accessible to teachers. It is worthwhile to inquire if this information is already available at your school.

Unwrapping the standards is a valuable tool for all educators, but it is especially useful for special educators. We can choose a variety of materials and methods to teach each skill defined in the standard, but proficiency in those specific skills and abilities remains a common landmark along the road to proficiency. For example, Julia, the seventh-grade student who reads at the third-grade level, can still learn to paraphrase, analyze, evaluate, and make predictions— but she will be more successful in acquiring those skills if her teacher uses third-grade materials that she can read and comprehend. To provide the necessary content knowledge, the teacher can then present seventh-grade materials in other formats: computer programs, audio tapes, videos, or assistive technology readers. Julia would then be able to apply skills to this material that she first learned using material at her lower reading ability level. This strategy is a dynamic way to quickly help students with special needs move forward and fill in the gaps in their learning, but requires skillful assessment of the student's content knowledge, learning style, background knowledge, and skills prior to direct instruction.

Next, teachers can begin looking at which ongoing classroom assessments will provide the most valuable information to help students learn the content, concepts, and skills highlighted in the standard.

Determine the Purpose of the Assessment

When choosing assessment methods, teachers must start with the questions, "What am I trying to measure? What will be the purpose of the results I collect?" Informal classroom assessments provide instructional feedback and evaluate student needs (McLoughlin &

Lewis, 2005). They help the teacher group students for instruction, select appropriate materials, and apply focused teaching strategies. Students with special needs frequently exhibit gaps in their learning or splintered educational skills. Fortunately, effective assessments can provide objective, tangible data with which to make appropriate instructional decisions. Consider the purpose of the assessment before choosing the method. There are many reasons for selecting a particular assessment tool: to determine if a student is entitled or eligible for specific programs, for preassessment (to collect baseline data), for accountability, or to measure students' learning towards a learning goal or standard, to name a few. For example, Roger is a new student in Ms. Cartwright's classroom. She determines a need to preassess Roger's abilities in reading. She chooses to first do an informal classroom observation. This informal observation will help lead her to the next assessment step and gather additional assessment information about Roger. She may decide to conduct a formal error-analysis assessment to help determine the extent of Roger's reading issues. The results of the error analysis can help her focus on the specific skills Roger lacks to help him move forward successfully in reading.

Select Specific Assessments That Will Provide the Desired Information

There are so many informal classroom assessments to choose from—how will a teacher of students with special needs know which instrument will yield the most appropriate information about student learning? Remember, informal classroom assessments take place during learning—not after. Therefore, the assessment should allow the student and teacher to see immediate or incremental progress towards proficiency of the standard being measured. It should yield information that will provide immediate feedback to the student and ultimately help the teacher select appropriate instructional strategies that will help the student reach the learning target. Using a variety of assessment opportunities, teaching appropriate test-taking skills, teaching new skills at current ability levels, and involving students in the creation of the assessments will produce the best results for students with special needs.

Because students with special needs often do not generalize information well, it is important to provide clear examples and ample opportunities for them to interact with the information in a variety of assessment formats. Identify each format (multiple choice, extended response, and true/false, to name a few) for students as you instruct them in how to respond. Provide students with a graphic organizer, if necessary, to help them manage the information. Provide samples, and help or ask students to design a nonlinguistic representation that is meaningful to them. Provide plenty of practice and constant immediate specific feedback.

As students advance in the concepts and skills for a standard, the teacher should investigate the format and manner in which the student will ultimately be assessed on state and district tests and align some classroom assessments to that format. For example, if the state or district format is multiple choice, it will be necessary to specifically teach students test-taking strategies to respond appropriately using this format. For students with special needs, low test scores can be a reflection of a change in test format. To return to our sample standard for seventh grade—"Students can demonstrate the ability to summarize, paraphrase, analyze, and evaluate what they read"—even though Julia demonstrated proficiency in her ability to summarize a story, she might receive a low score when the same standard is presented on a state test as a multiple-choice question.

When introducing a new concept such as rubrics or scoring guides to students, teachers should base instruction on samples and materials at the student's ability level, just as in the previous step, Julia learned to summarize using third-grade reading material. Students should not struggle to comprehend content when they are trying to develop new skills. In creating an effective rubric, for example, students should be able to focus on the task of designing or following the rubric without struggling to read the content.

The teacher should actively involve students in the process of using assessments to improve their own learning. A well-constructed scoring guide for a rubric can be used for day-to-day assessment throughout instruction to help monitor and guide student progress towards the specific skills of the content standard. Students can help create the guide; whenever possible, use the students' own words on the rubric by asking them to describe their understanding of what is expected and how they can achieve success. Teachers should also give students a sample of excellent work to illustrate what is expected of them.

Another helpful self-assessment strategy for students with special needs is a personal strategy log. This is a small booklet with a list of key strategies taught by the teacher throughout the week. The student should be given time in class to write in the log, which might include the strategy, a nonlinguistic representation or graphic organizer, a drawn or written model, and step-by-step ideas. Students can maintain this log from elementary through secondary school for each subject and use these logs on a daily basis to reference models, problem-solve, edit, share in small groups, or engage in deliberate conversation with peers. Students must begin to see them as personal tools to help them advance more independently in their studies. The teacher should provide multiple opportunities for students to actively use their strategy logs throughout the day.

Gather and Discuss the Results of the Assessment

Feedback is an important aspect of assessment, and it plays a critical role in the teaching and learning process (Konold, 2004). After selecting and administering the appropriate assessments, the next step is to share the results with students. Feedback should include positive comments indicating what the student is doing well, with specific information about what the student should continue doing. At this point, the teacher considers his or her next steps, such as direct instruction, reteaching, additional exemplars, conferences with the student, more practice, change in technique, or electronic tutorials. Allow opportunities for students to self-assess and reflect on their work. Another option is peer review, where a student works with a peer in the class to check the rubric and discuss strategies for improvement.

As mentioned earlier, actively involving the special-needs student in his or her progress is critical. Students need to see where they are on the road to proficiency. While it is true that many students with special needs will require accommodations and may take longer to reach proficiency, the goal is still to provide them with the same opportunities as general education students to work towards the general education curriculum.

Remember, at this point in the learning process, we are not assigning final grades. Instead, we are identifying proficiency benchmarks to help students navigate their own learning of content, concepts, and skills. Gather the assessment results, and discuss with students their progress. They should receive immediate feedback with opportunities to make corrections, especially since generalization is often an issue for students with learning disabilities. Additional opportunities for interaction with the content, concepts, and skills will prove invaluable.

Use Assessment Information to Make Decisions About Instruction

According to Reeves (2004), a fundamental truth in effective teaching is that assessment strategies, both formal and informal, must do more than assess student progress: They must help the teacher determine the most appropriate instruction. This issue is especially critical for teachers of students with special needs. Focused daily, weekly, and monthly classroom formative assessment and constant monitoring of the student's skills will provide the immediate information needed to appropriately drive instruction so that special-needs students can succeed on state tests along with their nondisabled peers. Effective use of assessment information improves teacher as well as student learning.

An effective way to use assessment data to enhance teacher learning is through structured weekly or bimonthly data team meetings. The Leadership and Learning Center (formerly the Center for Performance Assessment) has described collaborative, structured, scheduled meetings that focus on the effectiveness of teaching and learning. Both general and special-education teachers attend these meetings. Typically, elementary school teams meet at grade level, and secondary schools by subject area. Teachers of self-contained special-education classes should definitely be encouraged to attend data team meetings. The special-education teacher can select an area of greatest concern such as mathematics, science, or reading, and join the team. Special educators provide invaluable information to the team regarding differentiation of instruction, modifications, and strategies specific to students with academic challenges. Additionally, everyone on the team can share strategies for concepts and content.

Another strategy for using assessment information to enhance instruction is with an academic review team (ART). An ART is made up of at least one general and one special educator who meet on a weekly basis for approximately 20 minutes to share assessment data with one another. The ART then suggests interventions and shares them with the students, parents, and administrators. Students should become active participants in this process as well. The purpose of the ART is to provide clear benchmarks and interventions on a weekly basis, rather than waiting until the annual Individual Education Program (IEP) team meeting. The ART process provides active, ongoing weekly information to help the teacher.

Assessment Mapping

Another strategy for using assessment information to enhance instruction for special-needs students is assessment mapping. An assessment map identifies assessment practices and documents the key information gained from each item or practice. The map provides an overview of the student's strengths, weaknesses, and proficiencies, which can then be used to plan and alter instruction as needed at the start of instruction and during the learning process. Mapping starts with a review of the previous assessment information found in the student's files, then moves on to an observation and interview with the student. It continues with assessment of the student's work and performance during the learning process. All of this information comes together to create a map that the student and teacher can use to help guide the student's learning journey. Let us use the example of Dwayne to illustrate the mapping process.

Dwayne Smith is a ninth-grade student. He strongly dislikes school, but attends every day. He primarily enjoys social interaction. His reading comprehension is 3.0, his vocabulary score is 3.5, and his math is at a 3.4 level. Dwayne's teacher, Ms. Williams, observed him, conducted an initial interview, and obtained the following information: He enjoys music, art, sports, and board games. His passion is computer games, and he has excellent keyboarding, gross, and fine motor skills. Dwayne is popular at school. However, he has expressed embarrassment about the need to attend special-education classes. He loves action and science fiction movies. His iPod is packed with an eclectic range of music. He is a multimodality learner who appears to learn best with auditory, visual, kinesthetic, and tactile strategies. According to his school records, Dwayne was identified in the third grade as a student with specific learning disabilities in math calculations and reading (decoding and comprehension). His goal is to become a computer game designer. His parents are supportive and indicate that he uses his computer at home several hours a day.

Ms. Williams used the assessment mapping process to document the information gleaned from the interview and the documentation in Dwayne's file, and then she mapped a plan with Dwayne to help him on his academic journey. Figure 1 (page 178) shows Dwayne's assessment map. Teachers should make every attempt to gather the baseline data shown in Figure 1 as early in the school year as possible.

After completing the map, Ms. Williams is able to discuss the information with Dwayne and develop a strategic map or plan of action. First, she will use the strengths described in the map to obtain curriculum materials that will match his learning style preference. Next, she will employ skills in the effective teaching strategies to help Dwayne maximize his skills in the classroom.

Dwayne can first learn specific skills, such as how to retell information and how to predict and analyze information, on his ability level of 3.5. Dwayne can then access the learning in a variety of methods at his chronological grade level. For example, based on the information obtained from the assessment map, Ms. Williams may decide to provide Dwayne with a book for a reading assignment in audio format. He might be asked to use graphic organizers to chart information found in a video of the social studies content. Dwayne can create a PowerPoint® of the learning with pictures and captions. Dwayne and Ms. Williams can create a scoring guide or rubric to make sure that he addresses the state standards and benchmarks for his grade level.

Although Dwayne has a specific learning disability, the same assessment map process can be used for students with low cognitive abilities as well. The key is to gather as much early assessment data as possible as shown in the assessment map (Figure 1). Create a clear list of the content, concepts, and skills required from the state standards. Armed with this information, teachers can create a road map to guide instruction and make appropriate professional decisions for each student. It is important to involve the student in the process so

| Student: | _Dwayne Smith_ | | Grade: | _9_ |
| Teacher: | _Ms. Williams_ | | | |

Date	Assessment Strategy	Key Information
9/1	Document present levels of academic performance (see current IEP).	_Dwayne's KeyMath assessment is at 3.4 grade level. He struggles with application of computation. His Woodcock reading score is 3.0 for comprehension. His vocabulary score is 3.5._
9/1	Documented accommodations (see IEP)	_Read instructions to the student, provide frequent breaks, test in small group, and provide a quiet environment._
9/5	Review previous assessment information in cumulative records, IEP form, health card, and attendance record.	_He missed one day of school last year, is in excellent health, and has good vision and hearing._
9/8	Interview and/or observe student to learn academic preferences, hobbies, and leisure activities.	_He prefers art, music, and physical education classes. He enjoys sports, movies, and computer games._
9/13	Interview previous teacher (if possible) and parents to learn student's strengths and challenges and successful experiences.	_His strengths include computer skills and tactile hands-on activities. He exhibits challenges in reading and math calculations._
9/15	Assess multiple intelligence area(s).	_He has strong art, music, spatial, and interpersonal skills._

Figure 1: Sample Assessment Map for Special-Needs Students

Date	Assessment Strategy	Key Information
9/15	Assess the most effective instructional strategies in core content areas (math, language arts, science, and social studies).	• *Tape recorder for note-taking* • *Reviewing notes with a classmate* • *Developing nonlinguistic representations for math lessons* • *Using a personal math journal* • *Participating in collaborative activities*
9/20	Observe and document learning style preferences.	*He enjoys small-group activities and station work (learning centers). He prefers interactive computer learning programs.*
On-going	Document classroom assessments *for* learning.	*Dwayne struggles with multiple choice and true/false tests. He has not developed a strategy for approaching these types of tests. His preferred method is student- or teacher-developed rubrics.*
On-going	Assess modality preference in language arts.	*His dominant modalities in language arts appear to be auditory, visual, and tactile.*
On-going	Assess modality preference in mathematics.	*His primary modalities in mathematics are visual, kinesthetic, and tactile.*
10/1	Determine best assistive technologies.	*Use WYNN Reader, Cardex Reader, tape recorder/CD player, video and audio content area tape on grade level. Use word prediction and dictation software. Practice activities with calculator as well as pencil and paper.*

Figure 1: Sample Assessment Map for Special-Needs Students (continued)

he or she can clearly understand why assessments are given and how the information gathered will help the student succeed.

Reading the Road Map

Assessment does not interrupt the normal flow of classroom instruction. Effective assessments should be included seamlessly in the daily instruction and everyday activities in the classroom: Assessment is *part of* instruction. Assessment results can be used immediately to make appropriate instructional decisions, including adjusting assignments, selecting materials, and modifying the instructional focus as needed, targeting specific content areas, and helping to bridge the gap and providing a clear path and successful journey towards the goal of academic proficiency.

The student with special needs has a long and sometimes bumpy road to travel, with learning gaps that at times appear to be as wide as canyons. But this road can be navigated safely with ongoing assessments *for* learning. Appropriate application of the information obtained from informal classroom assessment is the key to helping the special-needs learner reach the learning destination. There are so many assessment considerations for students with special needs that one might easily become detoured on the road to academic achievement. It is much easier to first look at the big picture and then take one step at a time.

References

Ainsworth, L., & Viegut, D. (2006). *Common formative assessments: How to connect standards-based instruction and assessment.* Thousand Oaks, CA: Corwin Press.

Bloom, B. S. (1984). *Taxonomy of educational objectives: The classification of educational goals: Handbook 1, cognitive domain.* New York: Longman.

Clark, D. C., & Clark, S. N. (March/April 2000). Appropriate assessment strategies for young adolescents in the era of standards-based reform. *The Clearing House, 73*(4), 201–204.

Hoy, C., & Gregg, N. (1994). *Assessment: The special educator's role*. Pacific Grove, CA: Brooks/Cole Publishing.

Konold, K. E. (July/August 2004). Using teacher feedback to enhance student learning. *Teaching Exceptional Children, 36*(6), 64–69.

Marzano, R. J., & Kendal, J. S. (2007). *The new taxonomy of educational objectives* (2nd ed.). Thousand Oaks, CA: Corwin Press.

McLouglin, J. A., & Lewis, R. B. (2005). *Assessing students with special needs* (6th ed.). Upper Saddle River, NJ: Prentice Hall.

Oosterhof, A. (2003). *Developing and using classroom assessment* (3rd ed.). Upper Saddle River, NJ: Prentice Hall.

Reeves, D. B. (2004) *Accountability for learning: How teachers and school leaders can take charge*. Alexandria, VA: Association for Supervision and Curriculum Development.

Stiggins, R. J., Arter, J. A., Chappuis, J., & Chappuis, S. (2004). *Classroom assessment for student learning: Doing it right—using it well* (3rd ed.). Portland, OR: ETS Assessment Training Institute.

Salvia, J., Ysseldyke, J., & Bolt, S. (2007). *Assessment in special and inclusive education* (10th ed.). Boston: Houghton Mifflin.

U. S. Department of Education. (2001). *The No Child Left Behind Act of 2001*. Washington, DC: Author. Available at: http://www.ed.gov/policy/elsec/leg/esea02/index.html

U. S. Department of Education. (2004). *The Individuals with Disabilities Education Act (IDEA)*. Washington, DC: Author. Available at: http://idea.ed.gov/download/statute.html

Dylan Wiliam

Dr. Dylan Wiliam is deputy director of the Institute of Education, University of London. He has been a teacher at both private and public urban schools in London. Dr. Wiliam developed innovative assessment schemes in mathematics before taking over leadership of the mathematics teacher education program at King's College, University of London. He has served as the dean of the school of education and assistant principal of the college. He also served as senior research director in the research and development division of the Educational Testing Service in Princeton, New Jersey. His recent work has focused on supporting teachers to make greater use of assessment to support learning (sometimes called formative assessment). He is the coauthor, with Paul Black, of a major review of the research evidence on formative assessment, published in 1998, and has subsequently worked with many groups of teachers in both the United Kingdom and the United States on developing formative assessment practices.

In this chapter, Dr. Wiliam contends that if we are serious about improving student achievement, we must focus on changing those things that teachers do that are the most critical: the minute-to-minute and day-by-day use of assessment to adjust instruction. This deep change requires a different form of teacher professional development: building-based teacher learning communities. The author gives five key strategies for effective formative assessment and illustrates these strategies with specific techniques:

- Clarifying learning intentions and sharing criteria for success
- Engineering effective classroom discussions, questions, and learning tasks that elicit evidence of learning
- Providing feedback that moves learners forward
- Activating students as the owners of their own learning
- Activating students as instructional resources for one another

For more information about Dr. Dylan Wiliam and details about how to contact him, visit dylanwiliam.com.

Chapter 9

Content *Then* Process: Teacher Learning Communities in the Service of Formative Assessment

Dylan Wiliam

Raising student achievement is important, but not for the reasons many educators think. Forget No Child Left Behind and adequate yearly progress. Forget district and state reports that rank schools by proportion of proficient students. Raising achievement is important because it matters for individuals and society. If you achieve at a higher level, you live longer, are healthier, and earn more money. For those with only a high school diploma, the standard of living in the United States is lower today than it was in 1975; for those with degrees, it is 25 to 50% higher.

In addition, people who earn more money pay more taxes, are less likely to depend on Medicaid or welfare, and are less likely to be in prison. It has been calculated that if a student who drops out of high school would stay to graduate, the benefit to society would be $209,000 (Levin, Belfield, Muennig, & Rouse, 2007). This sum is made up of $139,000 in extra tax revenue, $40,500 savings in public health costs, $26,600 savings in law-enforcement and prison costs, and $3,000 in welfare savings. Eric Hanushek (2004), a leading economist of education in the United States, has calculated that if we could raise each student's achievement by one standard deviation (equivalent to raising a student from the 50th to the 84th percentile), over 30 years, the economy would grow by an additional 10%, and just the *additional* taxes being paid by everyone would more than pay for the whole of K–12 education.

For these reasons, it is clear that we need to raise student achievement in our schools, but how do we do this? We too often rely on quick fixes, which rarely produce success. To successfully raise student achievement, we must improve the quality of the teachers working in our schools—specifically, we must work to improve the teachers we already have. We must look carefully at both the costs and the benefits of possible reforms. An analysis of the research reveals that helping teachers develop minute-by-minute and day-by-day formative assessment practices is more cost-effective than any other strategy. However, changing what teachers do, day in and day out, cannot be done effectively through traditional methods, such as the summer workshop. This chapter argues that to raise student achievement, educators must form building-based learning communities in which teachers use a format of five strategies for formative assessment, hold each other accountable, and provide support for one another.

The Search for Solutions

Given the gravity of the benefits of increased student achievement, both for individuals and society, it is not surprising that we have been looking for solutions to improve the effectiveness of our schools. The problem is that we have been looking in the wrong places. The first generation of school effectiveness research just looked at outputs: Some schools achieved good results, and others achieved less good results. The rather simplistic conclusion drawn from this was that schools made a difference, so the search commenced for features of effective schools (see, for example, Chubb & Moe, 1990). However, a second generation of school effectiveness research showed that demographic factors accounted for most of the differences between schools. Most of the schools getting good results were in affluent areas, and most of the schools with low student achievement were in areas of poverty. The conclusion based on this research was that maybe schools did not make so much of a difference, and the reasons for low student achievement were demographic (see, for example, Thrupp, 1999).

More recently, a third generation of school effectiveness research has looked not only at the outputs of schools, but at the difference in what students knew when they started at the school compared to when they left—the so-called value added. What this research shows is that it does not matter very much which school students attend. What matters very much is which classrooms they are in in that school. If a student is in one of the most effective classrooms, he or she will learn in 6 months what those in an average classroom will take a year to learn. And if a student is in one of the least effective classrooms in that school, the same amount of learning will take 2 years. Students in the most effective classrooms learn at four times the speed of those in the least effective classrooms (Hanushek, 2004).

What accounts for these very different rates of learning? One obvious factor is class size, but it turns out that the effects of class-size reduction programs on student achievement are quite small, and such programs are very expensive (Hattie, 2005). Jepsen and Rivkin (2002) found that, for example, teaching 120 third-grade students in classes of 20 rather than 30 would result in just five additional students passing a standardized test, at a cost of around $120,000. In general, class-size reduction programs are most effective for younger students (kindergarten, first, and possibly second grade), and then only if class size is reduced to 13 to 15 students (Mosteller, 1995). For most students, the effect of class-size reduction is small.

Other reform efforts have centered on the structures of our schools, such as size or different governance and funding models. Much time, effort, and money has been invested in the creation of smaller schools, and while in some cases, improvements in student engagement and attitudes have been found, there appears to be little or no impact on student achievement (Gewertz, 2006a; 2006b). The charter school movement has claimed some successes, but once the demographic factors are taken into account, the impact on student achievement seems to be small, if not negligible (Carnoy, Jacobsen, Mishel, & Rothstein, 2005; Lubienski & Lubienski, 2006).

What about teacher subject knowledge? In a study of almost 3,000 students in 115 classrooms, Hill, Rowan, and Ball (2005) found that higher levels of what they called "mathematical knowledge for teaching" *were* associated with increased student progress, but the effects were, again, small. Over a year, the students taught by the most knowledgeable teachers (in other words, the top 5%) learned about 25% faster than the students taught by the least knowledgeable teachers (those in the bottom 5%). This difference was statistically significant, and bigger than the impact of socioeconomic factors, but nowhere near the 400% speed-of-learning differential between students in the most and least effective classrooms.

It appears that the most important difference between the most and the least effective classrooms is the teacher, but the most important variable appears to be what they *do*, rather than what they *know* (Monk, 1994). If we want better teachers, we can achieve this in a number of ways: If we do it gradually, by increasing the thresholds at which teachers enter the profession, it takes many years to have any effect (Hanushek, 2004). If we try to do it quickly, for example by allowing people to teach even though they have not completed a teacher-preparation program, then these teachers turn out to be no better than those trained in traditional ways (Darling-Hammond, Holtzman, Gatlin, & Vasquez Heilig, 2005).

To sum up the argument so far: We need to raise student achievement, because it matters for individuals and for society. To raise student achievement, we need to improve teacher quality, and the only way to do this, at least in the short to medium term, is to invest in the teachers we have already—what my colleague Marnie Thompson calls the "love the one you're with" strategy. In other words, if we are serious about improving student achievement, we have to invest in the right professional development for teachers.

This is an important point, because too often, professional development is presented as a fringe benefit—part of a compensation package to make teachers feel better about their jobs. This certainly seems to be the way teacher professional development is viewed by many outside the world of education, and also, sometimes, by policymakers.

The question is this: Can we do it? Can we improve teacher quality through professional development? Asked 20 or even 10 years ago, the answer would probably have been, "No." While investment in teacher professional development has been a feature of the educational landscape for many years, there was depressingly little evidence that it made any difference to student achievement: "Nothing has promised so much and has been so frustratingly wasteful as the thousands of workshops and conferences that led to no significant change in practice when teachers returned to their classrooms" (Fullan, 1991, p. 315). However, in recent years, it has become clear that the main reason teacher professional development has largely failed to impact student achievement is because we have not been doing what the research shows makes a difference to student learning. So now the question is this: What do we need to be doing to improve teacher quality and thus improve student achievement, and how do we go about doing it?

In recent years, there has been a growing acceptance that to be successful, teacher professional development needs to concentrate on both content *and* process (Reeves, McCall, & MacGilchrist, 2001; Wilson & Berne, 1999). In other words, we need to focus on *what* we want teachers to change, or change about what they do, and we have to understand *how* to support teachers in making these changes. However, in practice, this often gets implemented through unfocused models. Teacher coaching is one example. This strategy can be used to change things about the way teachers teach that do affect student learning, but it can also be used to change things that do not make any difference to student learning. For instance, a teacher might want to learn how to implement "jigsaw" groups, despite the absence of evidence that this is likely to make a difference to student achievement (indeed, according to Slavin, Hurley, & Chamberlain, 2003, not only is there an absence of evidence of an effect; there is, in fact, evidence of the absence of an effect). Similarly, there has been marked interest among educators in such strategies as "brain-based education" or learning styles despite the absence of evidence that these models make a difference to student achievement (see, respectively, Bruer, 1999; Adey, Fairbrother, & Wiliam, 1999).

If we are serious about improving student achievement, we have to focus relentlessly on changing those things that teachers do that are the most important to change: those things that, when we focus on them, and change them, improve student learning.

The remainder of this chapter shows that, measured in terms of impact on student achievement, the single most important thing to change in teachers' practice is the minute-to-minute and day-by-day use of assessment to adjust instruction. Because this involves sustained change in deeply ingrained practices and habits, this will necessitate a different type of teacher professional development: building-based teacher learning communities. But note that the teacher learning communities are a means to an end, not an end in themselves: content, *then* process.

Formative Assessment: The Evidence

The term "formative assessment" has been with us for 40 years (see Wiliam, 2007, for an extended account of the origins of the term), but the underlying idea—that we should use evidence of learning to adjust instruction—has been around for thousands of years. Reviews of research in this area by Natriello (1987) and Crooks (1988) were updated by Black and Wiliam (1998), who concluded that regular use of classroom formative assessment would raise student achievement by 0.4 to 0.7 standard deviations— enough to raise the United States into the top five countries in the international rankings for math achievement, for example. Subsequent longer-term implementation studies (those at least 1 year in duration), with tests that are less sensitive to instruction than those typically used in research studies, have found smaller effect sizes— typically around 0.3 standard deviations (Wiliam, Lee, Harrison, & Black, 2004)—but even these are large effects. To see how large, it is useful to compare the effects of teachers' use of formative assessment with other kinds of educational interventions.

Table 1 (page 190) shows the effect, in the number of additional months progress per year, of three different educational interventions, and the cost per classroom per year. The estimate of the effects of class size is based on the data generated by Jepsen and Rivkin (2002), and the estimate for teacher content knowledge is derived from Hill, Rowan, and Ball (2005). (The cost of increasing teacher content knowledge is unknown. We know it increases student achievement, but we do not know how to raise teachers' pedagogical content knowledge by this much.) The estimate for formative assessment is derived from Wiliam, Harrison, & Black (2004), and other small-scale studies. The data in Table 1 suggest that investing in teacher professional development is 20 to 30 times more cost-effective than class-size reduction, at least beyond the second grade.

Intervention	Extra Months of Learning Gained per Year	Classroom Cost per Year
Class-size reduction by 30% (for example, from 30 to 20 students)	3	$30,000
Increase teacher content knowledge from weak to strong (2 standard deviations)	1.5	Unknown
Formative assessment	6 to 9	$3,000

Table 1: Cost-Effect Comparisons for Three Educational Interventions

The substantial cost-effectiveness of formative assessment as a lever for school improvement has, of course, attracted considerable attention, and a number of test publishers have produced what they call "formative assessment systems." Typically, these systems provide for assessment of student progress at regular intervals (generally every 4 to 9 weeks) and provide reports that identify students or particular aspects of the curriculum that require special attention.

These systems *are* formative, in the sense that they provide evidence about student achievement that can be used to adapt instruction to better meet student learning needs. However, they are very different from the research reviewed by Natriello (1987), Crooks (1988), and Black and Wiliam (1998), which found that regular use of classroom assessment increases student achievement. Such formative assessment systems have a role to play in the effective monitoring of student progress. Indeed, I would argue that some means of tracking student progress over the medium term and taking action to address any problems identified are essential components of any comprehensive assessment system. But it is disingenuous at least, and possibly mendacious, to claim that the research literature provides evidence of the effectiveness of such systems. Quite simply, it does not (Popham, 2006; Shepard, 2007). That is not to say that such evidence will not be forthcoming in the future—it may well be—but no such evidence has been assembled to date. So if we are serious about a relentless focus on the things that we know will work to raise student achievement, these formative assessment systems have only a marginal role to play. They will not by themselves result in substantial increases in student achievement, nor are they even necessary. Such systems have a role in supporting good management and supervision, but in terms of improving—as opposed to monitoring—student learning, they are almost irrelevant.

What is needed, rather, is a focus on what actually goes on inside the classroom (Black & Wiliam, 1998). The kinds of formative assessment practices that profoundly impact student achievement cannot wait until the end of a marking period, or even to the end of an instructional unit. If students have left the classroom before teachers have made adjustments to their teaching on the basis of what they have learned about the students' achievement, then they are already playing catch-up. If teachers do not make adjustments before students come back the next day, it is probably too late. This is why the most important formative assessments are those that occur minute-by-minute and day-by-day (Leahy, Lyon, Thompson, & Wiliam, 2005).

So the big idea of formative assessment is that evidence about student learning is used to adjust instruction to better meet student needs; in other words, teaching is *adaptive* to the student's learning needs, and assessment is done in real time. More explicitly (Thompson & Wiliam, 2007, p. 6), formative assessment is:

Students and teachers
Using evidence of learning
To adapt teaching and learning
To meet immediate learning needs
Minute to minute and day by day

An important feature of this definition is that it shares the responsibility for formative assessment between teachers and students. While this definition succeeds in explaining what effective formative assessment is not, it provides few clues about how effective assessment should be done. A careful analysis of the theoretical and empirical work in this area (Wiliam & Leahy, 2007; Wiliam & Thompson, 2007) suggests that effective formative assessment consists of five key strategies:

1. Clarifying learning intentions and sharing criteria for success

2. Engineering effective classroom discussions, questions, and learning tasks that elicit evidence of learning

3. Providing feedback that moves learners forward

4. Activating students as the owners of their own learning

5. Activating students as instructional resources for one another

(A comprehensive review of the research underlying this analysis can be found in Wiliam, 2007.)

These strategies clarify what effective assessment is, but they still provide relatively little guidance for the teacher about how to apply these strategies in the classroom. For that reason, I draw a careful distinction between *strategies* and *techniques*. These five strategies are "no-brainers"—they are always smart things to do in the classroom; however, the techniques used to implement these strategies require careful thought by the teacher. What might work for one class in one context might not be appropriate for another class—regardless of how similar they appear to be. Through work with teachers and researchers in dozens of schools, my colleagues and I have developed a list of more than 100 of these techniques across the five strategies. Five of these techniques follow, one for each of the five strategies.

Strategy 1:   Clarifying Learning Intentions and Sharing Criteria for Success

Technique: Sharing Exemplars

Before asking students to write a new kind of assignment such as a lab report, the teacher gives each student four sample lab reports that represent varying degrees of quality. These samples can be student work from earlier years—with the names removed, of course—or teacher-produced samples. Students are asked to place the pieces in order of quality and identify what is good about the good ones and what is missing or weak about those that are not as good.

Strategy 2:   Engineering Effective Classroom Discussions, Questions, and Learning Tasks That Elicit Evidence of Learning

Technique: Dry-Erase Boards

During a lesson on equivalent fractions, the teacher asks the class a question such as, "Write down a fraction between ⅙ and ½," and asks all students to hold up their responses on the count of three. Using this kind of "all-student response system" helps the teacher to quickly get a sense of what students know or understand while requiring all students in the class to engage in the task. If all the answers are correct, the teacher moves on. If none of the answers are correct, the teacher may choose to reteach the concept in a different way. If there are a variety of answers, the teacher can then use the information gleaned from student responses to direct the subsequent discussion.

Strategy 3:   Providing Feedback That Moves Learners Forward

Technique: Find It and Fix It

Rather than checking all correct answers in an exercise and putting a check mark next to those that are incorrect, the teacher directs the student to identify them him- or herself: "Five of these are incorrect; find them and fix them." This kind of feedback requires the student to engage cognitively in responding to the feedback, rather that just reacting emotionally to his or her score or grade.

Strategy 4:   Activating Students as the Owners of Their Own Learning
Technique: Traffic Lighting

After they complete a piece of work, students go back to the learning intention or success criteria provided at the beginning of the lesson and indicate their level of understanding with a colored circle: Green means "I understand," yellow means "I'm not sure," and red means "I do not understand." Younger students can use emoticons such as ☺, ☺, and ☹. At regular intervals, the teacher provides time in class for students to move their learning forward by turning their reds to yellow and their yellows to green.

Strategy 5:   Activating Students as Instructional Resources for One Another
Technique: Pre-Flight Checklist

Before students can turn in an assignment, they must trade papers with a peer. Each student then completes a "pre-flight checklist" by comparing the peer's document against a list of required elements. For example, the pre-flight checklist for a lab report might require, among other things, a title, a date, diagrams drawn in pencil and labeled, and results that are clearly separated from conclusions. Only when the peer has signed off on the checklist can the work be turned in to the teacher. (Note that the peer is not involved in grading the work; only in providing feedback for improvement.)

By using these specific techniques for formative assessment (among others), teachers can begin to integrate the five strategies into their classroom practice. But this is only the beginning of the process. Through reflection, teachers begin to develop a new conceptualization of their practice. In some ways, this teacher professional development process echoes the remarks of Millard Fuller, the founder of Habitat for Humanity, who said, "It's easier to act your way into a new way of thinking than to think your way into a new way of acting." The traditional, workshop-based approach to professional development has two drawbacks. First, it does nothing to involve teachers in the process and tailor their work to their own students in their own schools and classrooms. Second, as any quarterback can attest, knowing what you want to do, and actually being able to do it, are two very different things.

In this new model, teachers start with the practical components, such as the five sample techniques mentioned previously. As they adopt and integrate these techniques and others into their own practice, they find a new synergy and see their own practice in new ways, which in turn leads to new thinking. In other words, rather than trying to transfer a researcher's thinking straight to the teacher, this new approach to formative assessment emphasizes content, *then* process.

Embedding Formative Assessment With Learning Communities

If the use of minute-to-minute and day-by-day formative assessment brings such benefits, and what needs to be done is so clear, why is it not common practice in every American classroom? There are two main reasons: The first is that many of the practices identified in the research as necessary to effective implementation have to go up against long-established traditions. For example, the tradition of grading student work with letter grades is so ingrained in schools that many teachers cannot envision doing business any other way. However, there are ways of assessing that provide useful information to the teacher and can still be used to assign grades at the end of a marking period (see Clymer & Wiliam, 2006/2007). Too often, the prevailing attitude is that one should not countenance change because things are bad enough as they are, and effective leadership is very difficult to deliver when superintendents hold their position on average for less than 2½ years (Snider, 2006). The second reason is that the changes are hard to implement. These are not superficial changes like learning to teach new units or adopting different lesson structures. The adoption of minute-to-minute and day-by-day formative assessment requires deep changes in the way that teachers teach, and this is much harder than it appears.

For example, a teacher with 20 years of experience will have asked approximately half a million questions in her career. When one has done something a certain way half a million times, doing it another way is very difficult. But there is a deeper reason why change is difficult, even for inexperienced teachers: Teachers learn most of what they know about teaching before they are 18 years old. In the same way that most of us learn what we know about parenting through being parented, teachers have internalized the "scripts" of school from when they themselves were students. Even the best 4-year teacher-education programs will find it hard to overcome the models of practice their future teachers learned in the 13 or 14 years they spent in school as students.

If we are to have any chance of really changing teacher practice, we have to take seriously that implementing minute-to-minute and day-by-day formative assessment is not primarily a matter of providing teachers with new knowledge, although some knowledge will be important. The crucial thing is to change habits, and traditional teaching structures do not change habits. The adoption of coaching in many districts is an example of this, but as noted previously, you can coach teachers to change aspects of practice that have little impact on student achievement. After many false starts and blind alleys, I have become convinced that the best way to support teachers in adopting minute-to-minute and day-by-day formative assessment is through building-based teacher learning communities. This is not because of an ideological commitment to the benefits of teachers talking to each other, but because of the nature of the changes we are seeking to produce. If we were trying to increase teacher subject knowledge, then teacher learning communities would not be a very sensible approach—it would be far better to arrange for high-quality direct instruction. But when we are trying to change deeply ingrained, routinized practices, then it seems that teacher learning communities offer the best hope.

Over the last 3 years, my colleagues and I have explored a number of different approaches to establishing and sustaining teacher learning communities, and as a result of this experimentation, it appears that five principles are particularly important: gradualism, flexibility, choice, accountability, and support (Wiliam, 2006).

Gradualism

Asking teachers to change what they do is rather like asking a golfer to change his swing in the middle of a tournament. Teachers who try to add more than two or three techniques to their teaching at the same time almost invariably find that their teaching routines fall apart, and they go back to doing what they know how to do. In the long-term, they achieve less change than teachers who take smaller steps.

Flexibility

Techniques that work in one context may not work, or may not be appropriate, in others. Only the teacher is able to judge this, so he or she must be able to make adjustments to the techniques. Sticking within the framework of the five strategies reduces the chance that a teacher's modifications weaken the power of the technique. For example, one teacher used colored disks—green on one side and red on the other—to encourage students to do "real-time" traffic lighting. At the start of the lesson, all disks are green side up, but if a student wants to ask a question, he or she must turn the disk over to show red. Another teacher tried this, but found it hard to see the disks from the front of the classroom, so she purchased sets of red, yellow, and green cups (enough for each student to get one of each). At the beginning of the lesson, the yellow and red cups are nested inside the green cup. If a student thinks the teacher is going too fast, he or she shows the yellow cup, and if the student wants to ask the teacher a question, he or she shows the red cup. This teacher then introduced a new variation: As soon as one student shows a red cup, the teacher chooses at random from the students showing yellow and green, and the selected student has to answer the question posed by the student with the red cup. This modification by the teacher not only made the "traffic lights" more visible, but it also increased students' accountability for their learning.

Choice

The initial reaction of most teachers to being asked to adopt minute-to-minute and day-by-day formative assessment techniques is that it is scary. Putting teachers in control of choosing which techniques they will try appears to make this challenge a little less daunting, and it also allows teachers to emphasize the techniques that best suit their teaching style. For example, my colleagues and I (Black, Harrison, Lee, Marshall, & Wiliam, 2003) describe two middle-school science teachers in the same school with very different styles. Derek is a charismatic teacher with a substantial classroom presence—a "larger-than-life character," so to speak. He chose to focus on student questioning as his priority for personal development. He is now an extraordinarily skilled leader of classroom discussions—one of the best I have ever seen—but he is very firmly in the middle of everything, much like the conductor of an orchestra. Another teacher, Philip, has a very different classroom style. When you walk into his classroom, he is often hard to spot, since he is usually in the midst of a discussion with a small group of students, while the others in the classroom work purposefully at their allotted tasks. Philip chose to focus on activating students as owners of their own learning, and as instructional resources for one another, and now creates a highly effective learning environment for his students. The important point here is that Derek would be far less successful if he were forced to emphasize peer- and self-assessment, and Philip would be far less successful if he were forced to prioritize questioning. Teaching is a highly personal activity, and choice in implementing formative assessment is essential if teachers are to integrate it into their practice.

Accountability

Although in this process teachers are free to choose how to change or adapt their techniques, they remain accountable to the teacher learning community for the changes they have made. In other words, although they are free to choose what to change, they are accountable to the teacher learning community for the change, and, just as importantly, they have to be able to justify that what they change is likely to improve student learning by being clearly related to at least one of the five key strategies. Teachers have repeatedly told us that the fact that they had promised to their colleagues to try something out is what made them prioritize this over all the other things they had to do.

Support

The flip side of accountability is support. In fact, in our work with teachers, we have used the term "supportive accountability" to indicate the learning community's effectiveness. The learning community offers both support and accountability, but with two conditions: First, the teacher learning community builds trust among its members so that members can move beyond "polite serial turn-taking" and begin genuinely to engage in each other's professional development (Grossman, Wineburg, & Woolworth, 2000). Second, the teacher learning community is genuinely a meeting of equals, at least in terms of power. In our experience, when one member of the community sets him- or herself up as the formative assessment "expert," the learning of the other members is compromised. While there is a valuable role for those who are not currently teaching—supporting the group, running interference, providing advocacy, and so forth— they can never be full participants in such a community.

Content *Then* Process

In this chapter, I have argued that increasing student achievement must be a priority, both for our students individually and for society as a whole. In the past, policymakers have focused on quick-fix solutions, such as curriculum reform, textbook replacement, changes in governance, altering school structures and timetables, and investing large amounts of money in information technology. Even when implemented properly (as few are), these kinds of initiatives have little impact on student achievement. They encourage us to come to the plate because the team is losing to try to hit a home run. But we end up striking out instead. What the research shows us is that the only answer is continuous small improvements—"small ball," if you like. We need to worry about getting to first base before we can make it home. We need to do this not because the solution is elegant or attractive, but because there is nothing else that we currently know of that works anything near as well.

The research shows that it is what teachers do in the classroom that really matters—not having teachers meet in workshops to talk about how to assess student work or what students' scores on tests mean for the curriculum. If the research on professional development over the last 20 years has shown us anything, it is that we can change teacher thinking without changing teacher practice, and the only thing that impacts student achievement is teacher practice. So if we are serious about raising student achievement, we must focus on helping teachers change what they do in the classroom.

Moreover, we must also be careful to focus on the things that make a difference. Teacher change for the sake of change is inadequate. The research summarized in this chapter shows that changing teachers' minute-to-minute and day-by-day formative assessment practices is the most powerful way to increase student achievement, and it is 20 to 30 times more cost effective than, for example, class-size reduction programs.

However, being clear about what needs to be done is only the first step, although it has to be the first step: content, *then* process. Once we are clear about what needs to be done, we must figure out ways to do it, and this is where the research on teacher expertise is so important. The necessary changes are *not* changes in teacher knowledge—teachers know much of what they need to know already. The changes we need are changes in the habits and rituals of teachers' practice that have been ingrained over many years. This requires different pedagogical models. Specifically, it requires building-based teacher learning communities. If we can concentrate on doing what is right, rather than what is expedient or easy, unprecedented increases in student achievement and teacher satisfaction are within our grasp. The question is whether we have the courage to reach.

References

Adey, P. S., Fairbrother, R. W., & Wiliam, D. (1999). *A review of research related to learning styles and strategies.* London: King's College London Centre for the Advancement of Thinking.

Black, P., Harrison, C., Lee, C., Marshall, B., & Wiliam, D. (2003). *Assessment for learning: Putting it into practice.* Buckingham, UK: Open University Press.

Black, P., Harrison, C., Lee, C., Marshall, B., & Wiliam, D. (2004). Working inside the black box: Assessment for learning in the classroom. *Phi Delta Kappan, 86*(1), 8–21.

Black, P. J., & Wiliam, D. (1998). Inside the black box: Raising standards through classroom assessment. *Phi Delta Kappan, 80*(2), 139–148.

Bruer, J. T. (1999). In search of … brain-based education. *Phi Delta Kappan, 80*(9), 648–657.

Carnoy, M., Jacobsen, R., Mishel, L., & Rothstein, R. (2005). *The charter school dust-up: Examining the evidence on enrollment and achievement.* Washington, DC: Economic Policy Institute.

Crooks, T. J. (1988). The impact of classroom evaluation practices on students. *Review of Educational Research, 58*(4), 438–481.

Chubb, J. E., & Moe, T. M. (1990). *Politics, markets and America's schools.* Washington, DC: The Brookings Institution.

Clymer, J. B., & Wiliam, D. (2006/2007). Improving the way we grade science. *Educational Leadership, 64*(4), 36–42.

Darling-Hammond, L., Holtzman, D. J., Gatlin, S. J., & Vasquez Heilig, J. (2005). Does teacher preparation matter? Evidence about teacher certification, Teach for America, and teacher effectiveness. *Education Policy Analysis Archives, 13*(42).

Fullan, M. (1991). The new meaning of educational change. London: Cassell.

Gewertz, C. (2006a, March 8). Failed breakup in Denver offering lessons. *Education Week, 25*(27), pp. 1, 18.

Gewertz, C. (2006b, August 9). Chicago's small schools see gains, but not on tests. *Education Week, 25*(44), pp. 5, 18.

Grossman, P., Wineburg, S., & Woolworth, S. (2000). *What makes teacher communities different from a gathering of teachers?* Seattle: University of Washington Center for the Study of Teaching and Policy.

Hanushek, E. A. (2004). *Some simple analytics of school quality* (Vol. W10229). Washington, DC: National Bureau of Economic Research.

Hattie, J. (2005). The paradox of reducing class size and improving learning outcomes. *International Journal of Educational Research, 43*(6), 387–425.

Jepsen, C., & Rivkin, S. G. (2002). *What is the tradeoff between smaller classes and teacher quality?* (NBER Working Paper #9205). Cambridge, MA: National Bureau of Economic Research.

Hill, H. C., Rowan, B., & Ball, D. L. (2005). Effects of teachers' mathematical knowledge for teaching on student achievement. *American Educational Research Journal, 42*(2), 371–406.

Leahy, S., Lyon, C., Thompson, M., & Wiliam, D. (2005). Classroom assessment: Minute by minute, day by day. *Educational Leadership, 63*(3), 18–24.

Levin, H. M., Belfield, C., Muennig, P., & Rouse, C. (2007). *The costs and benefits of an excellent education for all of America's children.* New York: Teachers College Press.

Lubienski, C., & Lubienski, S. T. (2006). *Charter, private, public schools and academic achievement: New evidence from NAEP mathematics data 2006.* New York: National Center for the Study of Privatization in Education.

Monk, D. H. (1994). Subject area preparation of secondary mathematics and science teachers and student achievement. *Economics of Education Review, 13*(2), 125–145.

Mosteller, F. W. (1995). The Tennessee study of class size in the early school grades. *The Future of Children (Special issue: Critical issues for children and youths), 5*(2), 113–127.

Natriello, G. (1987). The impact of evaluation processes on students. *Educational Psychologist, 22*(2), 155–175.

Popham, W. J. (2006). Phony formative assessments: Buyer beware! *Educational Leadership, 64*(3), 86–87.

Reeves, J., McCall, J., & MacGilchrist, B. (2001). Change leadership: Planning, conceptualization and perception. In J. MacBeath & P. Mortimore (Eds.), *Improving school effectiveness* (pp. 122–137). Buckingham, UK: Open University Press.

Shepard, L. A. (2007). Will commercialism enable or destroy formative assessment? In C. A. Dwyer (Ed.), *The future of assessment: Shaping teaching and learning.* Mahwah, NJ: Lawrence Erlbaum Associates.

Slavin, R. E., Hurley, E. A., & Chamberlain, A. M. (2003). Cooperative learning and achievement. In W. M. Reynolds & G. J. Miller (Eds.), *Handbook of psychology, volume 7: Educational psychology* (pp. 177–198). Hoboken, NJ: Wiley.

Snider, J. II. (2006, January 11). The superintendent as scapegoat. *Education Week, 25*(18), 40, 31.

Thompson, M., & Wiliam, D. (2007). *Tight but loose: A conceptual framework for scaling up school reforms.* Paper presented at a Symposium entitled "Tight but loose: Scaling up teacher professional development in diverse contexts" at the annual conference of the American Educational Research Association, Chicago, IL.

Thrupp, M. (1999). *Schools making a difference: Let's be realistic!* Buckingham, UK: Open University Press.

Wiliam, D. (2006). Assessment: Learning communities can use it to engineer a bridge connecting teaching and learning. *Journal of Staff Development, 27*(1), 16–20.

Wiliam, D. (2007). Keeping learning on track: Formative assessment and the regulation of learning. In F. K. Lester, Jr. (Ed.), *Second handbook of mathematics teaching and learning* (pp. 1053–1098). Greenwich, CT: Information Age Publishing.

Wiliam, D., & Leahy, S. (2007). A theoretical foundation for formative assessment. In J. H. McMillan (Ed.), *Formative classroom assessment: Research, theory and practice.* New York: Teachers College Press.

Wiliam, D., Lee, C., Harrison, C., & Black, P. J. (2004). Teachers developing assessment *for* learning: Impact on student achievement. *Assessment in Education: Principles, Policy, and Practice, 11*(1), 49–65.

Wiliam, D., & Thompson, M. (2007). Integrating assessment with instruction: What will it take to make it work? In C. A. Dwyer (Ed.), *The future of assessment: Shaping teaching and learning.* Mahwah, NJ: Lawrence Erlbaum Associates.

Wilson, S. M., & Berne, J. (1999). Teacher learning and the acquisition of professional knowledge: An examination of research on contemporary professional development. In A. Iran-Nejad & P. D. Pearson (Eds.), *Review of research in education* (Vol. 24, pp. 173–209). Washington, DC: American Educational Research Association.

Stephen White

Dr. Stephen White is a nationally known educational consultant whose expertise in data analysis, systems, leadership assessment, and school improvement is helping to change the way educators view themselves and manage data in an era of high-stakes accountability and testing.

He is the author of two award-winning books, numerous articles, and is a contributor to leading publications. As a former superintendent and high school principal, Dr. White brings more than 35 years of experience at all levels. He is the primary author of the PIM™ school improvement framework, the Leadership Map, and has reviewed over 1,400 school improvement plans since 2005.

In this chapter, Dr. White describes a purposeful, collaborative approach to data collection and analysis. This *data on purpose* leads not only to direct changes in classroom practice and individual student achievement, but also to system-level changes in school culture that will benefit all students. He contends that powerful assessments are more than just isolated attempts to measure progress toward a goal—rather, they must be embedded in the practices used throughout the learning process.

This chapter defines and examines four types of data—learning, teaching, leadership, and persuasive data. Dr. White then describes how to use triangulation to extract meaning from the raw data—to find the critical information, see the big picture, and identify key interactions between variables. He uses real examples to illustrate this process for data collection and analysis.

For more information about Dr. Stephen White, visit www.Leadand Learn.com or contact him at swhite@LeadandLearn.com.

Chapter 10

Data on Purpose: Due Diligence to Increase Student Achievement

Stephen White

"Get the habits of analysis—analysis will in time enable synthesis to become your habit of mind."

Frank Lloyd Wright (1867–1959)

Powerful assessment is more than an isolated attempt to measure progress toward a goal; it is embedded in the practices used throughout the learning process. As the contributors to this book have shown, effective assessment practices can inform instruction, provide guidance about quality and format to students, and create a synergistic relationship between assessment, curriculum, standards, and instruction. A purposeful, collaborative approach to data collection and analysis is a key piece of a holistic approach to teaching and learning. *Data on purpose* leads not only to first-order, direct changes in classroom practice and individual student achievement, but also to second-order, system-level changes in school culture that ultimately benefit all students.

The notion of second-order change is most closely associated with development and application of key leadership attributes that help leaders realize and sustain change at higher levels (Fullan, Hill, & Crévola, 2006; Marzano, Waters, & McNulty, 2005; Reeves, 2006). The same phenomenon is found when data teams operate effectively in schools.

Data teams use the results from common formative assessments to create a framework for making instructional decisions at the classroom level, a first-order change (Besser et al., 2006). When the work of these data teams produces a collective sense of efficacy, and collaboration becomes part of a school's culture, however, second-order change occurs (DuFour, Eaker, & DuFour, 2005; Hoy, Tarter, & Hoy, 2006; Murphy & Lick, 2004).

This chapter describes how a purposeful, precise approach to selecting, analyzing, and understanding data can augment a comprehensive assessment framework and produce this second-order change. Data on purpose ensures that key attributes of learning and implementation are applied at all levels to inform learning, teaching, and leading. It goes beyond first-order analysis of achievement patterns for curriculum alignment and creates second-order understanding and application of *antecedents*—adult actions that consistently lead to improved achievement (Reeves, 2006; White, 2005.)

Selecting the Right Data

If we know the antecedents—the best strategies, the best working environments, and the best ways to allocate resources—and focus our efforts to achieve them, we are much more likely to influence results positively. Antecedents can be identified and implemented through the analysis of the appropriate data. Data are more relevant for answering some inquiry questions than others. For example, not all data will help a team identify teaching antecedents such as promoting writing across the curriculum, using high-yield instructional strategies, and implementing classroom walk-through observations; to succeed, the team will need to examine data relevant to their purpose. Data can be generally classified, according to its relevance, as *learning* data, *teaching* data, *leadership* data, or *persuasive* data.

Learning Data

Every time students complete an assessment, learning data are generated. The results of formative, summative, traditional, and high-quality embedded assessments of students are all learning data, including results from commercially developed assessments, teacher-generated formative assessments, short-cycle assessments, and performance assessments. We are most familiar with and most focused on this type of data; learning data serve as our barometer of effectiveness. For many, this is the only kind of data that informs instructional decisions.

The purpose of analyzing learning data is to acquire meaningful information about students, curriculum, alignment, sequencing, and by inference, about instruction and motivation. The ability to disaggregate results by subgroup, content standard, and subscale over time provides rich insights into both learning and teaching. The most effective student learning assessments are designed to provide evidence of the following:

- Thinking
- Knowledge of essential questions
- Understanding of big ideas
- Progress towards a standard

Learning data are most useful in determining how students respond to the curriculum, its pace, and its major areas of focus. They are less precise in identifying what instructional strategies are most effective simply because the assessments that produce these data do not monitor teaching. Learning data are by definition data collected "after the fact," and changes we implement as a result of analyzing learning data are responsive rather than proactive. Formative, short-cycle assessments are designed specifically for the purpose of early, responsive adjustments to instruction, but to be proactive requires data about teaching and about learning.

Teaching Data

Data on teaching encompass the range of teacher actions and practices, from daily routines to high-yield instructional strategies. Schools across the country are beginning in earnest to supplement their assessment battery with routine measures of teaching. Such data answer the questions:

- What practices are working well to improve student achievement?

- To what degree are they working well?

- What practices are not working as well as anticipated and need to be discarded or modified?

- How can I augment my current teaching practices to be more effective?

Teaching data allow us to supplement learning data and make informed decisions about changes in practice that lead, in turn, to second-order change. Research has established which instructional strategies have high yields in student achievement, and it is critical that teachers are equipped to target these strategies to student needs in the context of the local school. The purpose of teaching data is to improve understanding and implementation of those practices. The most useful data on teaching measure:

- Quality of delivery (what percentage of the strategy's components were delivered)

- Frequency of delivery (number of times the strategies were implemented as planned)

- Consistency of delivery (percentage of teachers participating in the strategies)

- Quality of corrective feedback (how often given, after how much lag time, and whether it identified strengths or areas for growth)

Teaching data help educators make informed inferences as to why there is variability across content standards and among student subgroups, but conclusions and decisions will be based on effects, not causes. Whereas learning data clearly identify differences in performance, teaching data explain these differences with greater clarity in terms of teachers' actions and choices.

Leadership Data

Data on leadership are the least prevalent today, but the most needed. Research clearly indicates the impact of leadership on student achievement (Boyatzis & McKee, 2005; Marzano, Waters, & McNulty, 2005; Quinn, 2004; Reeves, 2006). The purpose of leadership data is to help determine the quality and consistency of leadership practices. These data add insight into which leadership practices are most effective in building capacity, creating culture, and sustaining student achievement. As fundamental as learning data are, and as useful as teaching data can be to our understanding, leadership data add a level of precision to the analysis that cannot be achieved without them. Figure 1 (page 212) shows 10 powerful acts of leadership that lend themselves to relatively easy and embedded data gathering and analysis.

To the degree an administrator self-monitors or surveys staff and students on a regular basis about the degree to which these leadership actions occur, they can provide a valuable source of data and discipline for second-order change.

For example, Cherie O'Day, principal of Bridgeport Elementary in the Metropolitan School District of Wayne Township, Indianapolis, instituted a 3-week instruction, 1-week remediation/enrichment schedule across core content areas schoolwide. This ensured that the entire faculty was providing midcourse corrections to struggling students at least every 3 weeks. This was an act of leadership. Others monitored the quality and quantity of feedback as well as shifts in resources, time, and training to add meaning to any extrapolation of antecedent data from student achievement results.

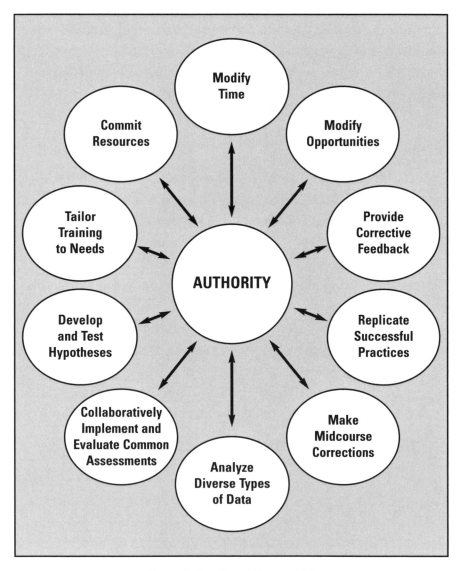

Figure 1: Ten Acts of Leadership

Each of these 10 acts of leadership lends itself to data collection by school leaders. At Bridgeport, the 3 week instruction/1-week remediation/enrichment structure allows the school to monitor the number of midcourse corrections at least monthly by grade level or by classroom. They could also use a protocol for professional development that allows them to monitor the degree to which professional development is differentiated based on faculty needs (tailored training). Those that assess their own actions are much better equipped to determine what is working to improve student achievement than those who fail to monitor their own acts of leadership.

Persuasive Data

The purpose of these data is to build support for necessary changes in professional practice with evidence that will satisfy the skeptics. This requires at a minimum pre- and post-test frameworks, and preferably experimental and control-group evidence as well. When schools or districts are reluctant to embrace a novel but powerful initiative, data collected both from classrooms that are implementing the initiative and from status-quo classrooms can be very useful in at least starting a conversation, or directing attention to appropriate action research protocols. When choosing data for the purpose of persuading, one can select key indicators from each type of data—learning, teaching, or leadership—as needed to validate emerging practices.

All four types of data are available at any time. When we strategically select data from the universe of possibilities to inform our decisions at a level that allows us to make and sustain improvements at a higher, second-order level, we are using data on purpose. By first identifying the purpose of the data to be gathered and analyzed, practitioners will be able to leverage assessments to make extraordinary improvements and implement second-order changes in their practice. The tool to unlock those improvements is triangulation.

Triangulation

Triangulation is used by a variety of specialists, from engineers to navigators, to extrapolate from known data points to make reliable conclusions about other points that cannot be known directly. For example, a sailor can establish his or her location by taking bearings on two geographical features or two stars. Triangulation is a means of determining precise targets with limited information—a way to gain meaning from raw data, find critical information, see the big picture, and identify key interactions among variables.

Teachers frequently triangulate student achievement data when they compare district criterion-referenced tests or end-of-course assessments with grades or short-cycle formative assessments. Do grades actually align with the standards? To what degree does the district test align with the state standards? Are there gaps in the curriculum or problems with its pacing? Triangulating different forms of student achievement data generally results in better alignment, sequencing, and content-area focus. It has many benefits, including early recognition of content subscale learning gaps in individual children.

The next step is to triangulate these student achievement results with data about teaching practices. Only then can we determine whether teachers are using power standards or developing lessons from "unwrapped" standards. (For a detailed discussion of unwrapping and power standards, see Larry Ainsworth's chapter 4.) Table 1 illustrates how a grade-level team could analyze learning data (in this case, from an assessment using extending response to measure student proficiency in number sense) and teaching data (in this case, on the frequency of reciprocal teaching during this unit) to determine the impact of an instructional strategy.

Classroom	Pretest Results	Number of Days Reciprocal Teaching Was Used (As Observed in 15 Days)	Posttest Results
A	43% proficient or above	3	55% proficient or above
B	17% proficient or above	13	50% proficient or above
C	65% proficient or above	12	90% proficient or above

**Table 1: Triangulation of Short-Cycle Assessment
With Reciprocal Teaching, Grade 4**

Classrooms B and C showed much greater gains than classroom A. Was the use of reciprocal teaching the only antecedent that influenced this improvement? Obviously not. The data, however, indicate that the consistent implementation of reciprocal teaching is strongly correlated with improved achievement on this common formative assessment. The limited data are illustrative of all data analysis in three ways:

1. Examination of data in isolation of its context can lead to erroneous conclusions.

2. Educators must interpret the data available to them.

3. If we adhere to data-driven decision-making, we will make decisions based on the best data available at the time.

Collaborative scoring of student work requires some degree of calibration among teachers to ensure interrater reliability. Despite its potential for variation, collaborative scoring not only creates more precise analysis of writing, but also informs instruction and shares data among collaborative teaching teams. All data are limited and incomplete, and perfection is not an option (Reeves, 2006). To ignore the findings in Table 1 and dismiss the influence of reciprocal teaching would mean to defer to a "factless" approach to teaching and learning. Effective assessments such as those described throughout this book require that decisions be made on the basis of available data and evidence.

Because teaching and learning are so complex, it is important to remember that educational cause-and-effect relationships are not laws of physics, and correlation is not causality. We do not know which other high-yield strategies might produce a similar result, but we do know that reciprocal teaching correlated highly with improved achievement at this grade level and for this standard. Selection of teaching practices to monitor and triangulate with learning data requires professional judgment. The following are some important points to keep in mind:

- Which high-yield instructional strategy has been supported by professional development at your school?

- Do all participants have a common understanding of its implementation protocol and terminology?

- Which strategy has been supported and reinforced by modeling, coaching, mentoring, or peer observation?

- Which strategy lends itself to routine and reliable data collection?

- Is the strategy an appropriate fit for the academic content standard being pursued?

Teaching data can be used to analyze more than the effects of formal teaching strategies. The way teachers begin lessons, transition between activities, and manage classrooms may also be antecedents or predictors of excellence. Because the single most powerful influence on student achievement is the teacher (Wenglinsky, 2002), every teacher interaction with students and with other teachers qualifies as potential data on teaching. The purpose of teaching data is to ascertain the degree to which some teaching practices work and others do not.

To determine with confidence the relative impact of specific teaching strategies, we need to add data about leading. Table 2 presents data about learning, teaching, and leading to triangulate a more complete picture of what is happening at the school and answer questions about where to commit resources and how to sustain current improvement efforts. Grade 4 represents the composite of classrooms A–C from Table 1.

Class	Strategy	Pretest Percentage Proficient or Above	Posttest Percentage Proficient or Above	Number of Days Strategy Was Used (As Self-Reported During 45 Days)	Number of Classroom Walk-Throughs With Same-Day Feedback (Out of 15)
Grade 4	Reciprocal Teaching	42%	65%	28	15
Grade 5	Cooperative Learning	36%	45%	30	8
Grade 6	Graphic Organizers	58%	60%	26	10

Table 2: Triangulation of Short-Cycle Assessments With High-Yield Instructional Strategies and Daily Disciplines of Leadership

What meaningful insights can be gleaned from the new data? Counting acts of leadership like classroom walk-throughs (CWTs) with same-day feedback reveals the lack of consistency between grades. Note the gains made when consistency of feedback, implementation of high-yield strategies, and frequency of implementation are combined. These additional data suggest that classroom walk-throughs may have had as much impact on scores as any of the high-yield strategies: Grade 4 received the most feedback from CWTs and showed the greatest gains in achievement, even though Grade 5 implemented its strategy more often. Reciprocal teaching gains may have been even greater with more consistent implementation and feedback from the principal. By triangulating results in learning with leadership data and teaching data, we can better understand those factors that influence student achievement and adjust our practices for improvement. This triangulation has the following implications:

- The combination of reciprocal teaching and same-day feedback contributes to improved achievement in math (for the standard on number sense).

- More consistent same-day feedback would likely lead to gains in student achievement.

- More consistent implementation of high-yield strategies would likely lead to gains in student achievement.

By monitoring a limited number of teaching and leading activities, much greater confidence and precision can be achieved for each short-cycle assessment, with more refined guidance for learning, teaching, and leading. The level of sophistication is only limited by the quality of data gathered, disaggregated, and analyzed.

A final scenario demonstrates how easily teachers and principals can triangulate data for specific purposes.

AYP Township was concerned about the effectiveness of its writing program. The township had made a 3-year investment in the instructional strategy known as 6+1 Trait Writing, added full-time literacy coaches at each elementary school, and provided for extensive professional development and coaching. Before the new program started, AYP students scored 58% proficient or above on the state writing assessment, and the latest results from after the program had been underway for 3 years indicated only 67.33% of students scored at proficient or advanced levels. The school board, superintendent, and assistant superintendent for teaching and learning were very disappointed with the results of their investment.

An inquiry was begun to determine what was working and what was not, and to provide a rationale for keeping, modifying, or discarding the program. Discussions on alternative programs had already begun, but the assistant superintendent believed strongly in the current program. She needed data to help persuade her boss and the school board—and to restore her own confidence in the model. She hoped the data analysis would provide some evidence of success and was pleased that a number of measures of learning, teaching, and leading were in place. The most recent results of those measures are delineated in Table 3 (page 220).

The assistant superintendent was relieved at the depth of implementation at School C. She was surprised at the wide variation among schools, and puzzled because all three K–6 principals worked so closely together—or so she thought. She was particularly surprised to find such differences in numbers of grade-level teams and disappointed to see such a lackluster attention to student conferences. The results were clear: Collaborative practices and public display of data correlated closely with improved student achievement. She was able to convince the superintendent to advocate for the literacy coaching positions to continue, with the understanding that collaborative practices and public display were no longer optional and would be central to the leadership evaluation process.

Due Diligence in Data Analysis

Given the dozens of sources, how does one select the most meaningful and informative learning data? We face the same challenge when selecting data on teaching practices that range from greeting students at the door to grading to a wide range of high-yield instructional strategies. Leadership practices are equally ubiquitous and varied. A common process for data selection and analysis

Measure	School A	School B	School C
Percentage of classrooms displaying student work by trait weekly	19	51	100
Number of grade-level teams rotating student scoring by trait four times a year	2	7	7
Percentage of student-led conferences explaining 6 traits of writing	14	73	25
Percentage of special subject teachers (art, music, and so on) using traits at least weekly (self-reported)	60	75	40
Percentage of teachers posting rubrics on traits each month	43	60	90
Percentage of teachers using collaborative scoring each month	75	94	88
Percentage of students showing writing gains in monthly writing prompts	53	80	90
Percentage of students scoring at least at the proficient level in state assessment	58	65	79

Table 3: AYP Township 6+1 Trait Writing Program—Three-Year Results

is recommended here that every teacher, teacher team, and administrator can logically apply to the growing range of available data.

In the business world, "due diligence" is the process of scrutinizing important information (financial data, market data, and so on) before making key decisions of long-term consequence. Due diligence makes an assumption that data are critical evidence and interprets data in the context of known measures of success. In education, the research showing the effectiveness of high-yield instructional strategies, collaboration, and accountability provides that context. This ensures that the analysis is guided by both research and the best practices of a standards-based framework. There may be other pertinent factors, but analysis should begin with a due diligence examination of the learning, teaching, and leadership data on these three issues.

High-Yield Instructional Strategies

The first step in the educational due diligence process is to determine the relationship of instructional strategies to student achievement. Instructional strategies should always engage students in thinking. Examples include use of provocative writing prompts, cogent use of metaphors and similes, problem-solving multistep problems with the scientific method, and mathematical analysis of relationships in time and space. Instructional strategies have established protocols for delivering instruction. They require professional development to acquire competence, and practice to achieve mastery. Many powerful programs are sound in their pedagogy, but efforts to replicate them are often ineffective because they are not implemented as designed, monitored as created, or followed with fidelity over time (Elmore, 2004; Sparks, 2004; Steiner, 2000).

Instructional strategies are measured by learning and teaching data. Important aspects to measure include type of strategy employed, degree to which protocols are implemented, and evidence of success in student work.

Collaboration

Peter Senge (2000) suggested that team thinking was as essential to the success of schools as it was to any other organization in business, government, or health care. The most powerful collaborative structures elicit team thinking and candor, ensure transparent meeting processes, and designate distinct times for reflection and analysis (Lencioni, 2002; White, 2005). Collaborative peer observations promote improved teaching practice (Buchanan & Khamis, 1999), and sustained longitudinal gains in achievement occur when collaborative structures are present and encouraged (Kannapel, Clements, Taylor, & Hibpschman, 2005; Langer, Colton, & Goff, 2003).

Examining data on collaboration is the second step in the due diligence of understanding student achievement antecedents. Collaboration is measured by either the teaching or leading data. Important aspects of collaboration to measure include the frequency of collaboration, time devoted to examining student work, degree to which teams develop and refine assessments, and adherence to norms regarding candor and team thinking.

Accountability

Tables 1–3 illustrate how valuable it can be to triangulate data about high-yield strategies and collaboration. Yet sometimes an excellent strategy with collective backing can still yield lackluster results; in such cases the problem may be lack of accountability. Accountability is the sum of follow-through, feedback, rewards, transparency, and even sanctions.

Accountability is measured by leadership data. Important aspects of accountability to measure include the proportion of schools and classrooms that display data through data walls, how frequently action steps or implementation protocols are monitored, and how consistently professional development is linked to supervision.

Due diligence requires examining all three areas: high-yield instructional strategies, collaboration, and accountability. The analysis portrayed in Table 3 addressed two of the three essential categories: collaboration (grade-level teaming and collaborative scoring) and accountability (display of student work and display of writing data), but failed to examine a high-yield instructional strategy (for example, reciprocal teaching). As a result, although that study yielded some valuable information, it failed to achieve true due diligence.

Analysis as Discovery

The evidence discussed in this chapter is all generated internally—within schools, grade levels, and departments. Our work will be most successful when we base it on evidence from our experience rather than on another's research or reference. Meaningful data on learning, teaching, and leadership are waiting to be captured and analyzed in every district, school, and classroom—by those who approach data with a sense of purpose. We need only add our professional judgment and collective wisdom to bring forth the insights on best practices that our students need to achieve at high levels. Using data on purpose brings us closer to developing a standard for due diligence in education, a standard by which we will seek out the most relevant data and analyze them in the context of proven best practice before discarding effective approaches or adopting ineffective ones.

By pursuing data on purpose, educators can turn data analysis into a process of discovery—a treasure hunt for insight. When we combine our talents and energies at this higher, second-order level, we can achieve a breakthrough not only in our thinking, but also in our ability to meet the needs of all students.

References

Besser, L., Anderson-Davis, D., Peery, A., Almeida, L., Flach, T., Nielson, K., Trujillo, J., & Woodson, N. (2006). *Data teams seminar.* Englewood, CO: Advanced Learning Press.

Boyatzis, R., & McKee, A. (2005). *Resonant leadership: Renewing yourself and connecting with others through mindfulness, hope, and compassion.* Boston: Harvard Business School.

Buchanan, J., & Khamis, M. (1999). Teacher renewal, peer observations and the pursuit of best practice. *Issues in Educational Research, 9*(1), 1–14.

DuFour, R., Eaker, R., & DuFour, R. (Eds.). (2005). *On common ground: The power of professional learning communities.* Bloomington, IN: Solution Tree (formerly National Educational Service).

Elmore, R. (2004). The right thing to do: School improvement and performance-based accountability. Harvard Graduate School of Education and Consortium for Policy Research in Education (CPRE). Washington, DC: National Governors' Association Center for Best Practices.

Fullan, M., Hill, P., & Crévola, C. (2006). *Breakthrough.* Thousand Oaks, CA: Corwin Press.

Hoy, W. K., Tarter, C. J., & Hoy, A. W. (2006). Academic optimism of schools: A force for student achievement. *American Educational Research Journal, 43*(3), pp. 425–446.

Kannapel, P. J., Clements, S. K., Taylor, D., & Hibpschman, T. (2005). *Inside the black box of high-performing high-poverty schools.* Lexington, Kentucky: A report from the Prichard Committee for Academic Excellence.

Langer, G. M., Colton, A. B., & Goff, L. S. (2003). *Collaborative analysis of student work: Improving teaching and learning.* Alexandria, VA: Association for Supervision and Curriculum Development.

Lencioni, P. (2002). *The five dysfunctions of a team: A leadership fable.* San Francisco: Jossey-Bass.

Marzano, R. J., Waters, T., & McNulty, B. A. (2005). *School leadership that works: From research to results.* Alexandria, VA: Association for Supervision and Curriculum Development.

Murphy, C. U., & Lick, D. W. (2004). *Whole-faculty study groups: Creating professional learning communities that target student learning* (3rd ed.). Thousand Oaks, CA: Corwin Press.

Reeves, D. B. (2006). *The learning leader: How to focus school improvement for better results.* Alexandria, VA: Association for Supervision and Curriculum Development.

Schmoker, M. (2006). *Results now: How we can achieve unprecedented improvements in teaching and learning.* Alexandria, VA: Association for Supervision and Curriculum Development.

Senge, P. (2000). *Schools that learn: A fifth discipline fieldbook for educators, parents, and everyone who cares about education.* New York: Doubleday.

Sparks, D. (2004, March). Closing the knowing-doing gap requires acting on what we already know. *Results.* Oxford, OH: National Staff Development Council.

Steiner, L. (2000). *A review of the research literature on scaling up in education: The problem of scaling up in education.* Chicago: North Central Regional Educational Laboratory.

Quinn, R. E. (2004). *Building the bridge as you walk on it: A guide for leading change.* San Francisco: Jossey-Bass.

Wenglinsky, H. (2002, February 13). How schools matter: The link between teacher classroom practices and student academic performance. *Education Policy Analysis Archives, 10*(12). Available at http://epaa.asu.edu/epaa/v10n12/.

White, S. H. (2005). *Beyond the numbers: Making data work for teachers and school leaders.* Englewood, CO: Advanced Learning Press.

Douglas Reeves

Dr. Douglas Reeves is founder of The Leadership and Learning Center (formerly the Center for Performance Assessment). Dr. Reeves is also a frequent keynote speaker in the United States and abroad for education, government, and business organizations. Beyond his work in large-scale assessment and research, Dr. Reeves has devoted many years to classroom teaching with students of all ages. He is the author of many articles and more than 20 books.

Dr. Reeves was twice selected for the Harvard Distinguished Authors Series. He won the Parent's Choice Award for his writing for children and parents and was named the 2006 Brock International Laureate. His work appears in numerous national journals, magazines, and newspapers.

In this chapter, Dr. Reeves tackles the question, "How do we implement and sustain practices and policies that support improved student achievement?" The research is clear: We know what to do to improve student achievement. But the question of how leaders can facilitate this change is not always as clear. This chapter addresses the essential issue of implementation of effective practice and the role that leaders play in defining, supporting, and instituting effective practice.

Dr. Reeves begins by discussing the use of assessment and feedback, and then he describes five choices leaders make that affect the quality of assessment *for* learning within their schools:

- Power standards or frantic coverage?
- Practical utility or psychometric perfection?
- The primacy of literacy or the pursuit of popularity?
- Collaboration or "the blob"?
- Evidence or tradition?

To learn more about Dr. Douglas Reeves, visit www.LeadAndLearn.com.

Chapter 11

Challenges and Choices: The Role of Educational Leaders in Effective Assessment

Douglas Reeves

While many areas of educational practice and leadership are subject to debate, speculation, and uncertainty, there are at least a few areas in which the preponderance of the research evidence, the weight of opinion, and common sense all converge to support a particular conclusion. The role of assessment in education is one such area. Three conclusions based on the evidence have emerged: Feedback must be accurate and timely; inaccurate feedback is counterproductive; and current practices are, to put it charitably, inconsistent. Equipped with these evidence-based conclusions, the question we must address as educational leaders is not, "What shall we do to improve student achievement?" This is already clear. Rather, we must focus on the remaining question: "How do we implement and sustain practices and policies that support improved student achievement?" This chapter addresses the essential issue of implementation of effective practice and the role that leaders play in defining, supporting, and instituting effective practice.

What We Know About Assessment and Feedback

"It's still a mystery. We just don't know what to do," an eminent professor lamented in a meeting I attended. I was thunderstruck. Had he not been in a library in the past decade or two? While there are raging controversies in many areas of education, I doubt many readers of this book could object to the following widely supported conclusions:

1. Feedback is most useful to students when it is accurate, timely, and specific.

2. Feedback that is inaccurate and untimely is counterproductive.

3. Feedback practices are inconsistent within and among schools.

First, consider the positive role of feedback in improving student achievement. While Marzano (2006) and Marzano, Pickering, and Pollock (2001) noted the primacy of feedback as an influence on improved student achievement, one hardly needs academic research to support this conclusion. Watch any child play an electronic game, where the supply of accurate, timely, and specific feedback seems endless: He sits, transfixed and immobile, for hours at a time as the steady stream of feedback lures him, in the parlance of the gamer, to "get to the next level." This same student is inattentive and disengaged in class.

No student would remain so engaged if feedback were inaccurate or differed based on whether the student is male, female, rich, or poor. No student would be so engaged and devoted to an electronic game if the manufacturer sent the scores by mail to the student days or weeks after the student played the game. No student would stare at a game for hours if, after each defeat, the feedback was only "you lost the game," rather than the rich array of feedback on time, available resources, alien attackers, and strategy that games routinely provide. Effective feedback not only tells students how they performed, but how to improve the next time they engage the task. Effective feedback is provided in such a timely manner that the next opportunity to perform the task is measured in seconds, not weeks or months.

Before dismissing the electronic game example as unworthy of schools or impossible in practical application, consider other examples of effective feedback that occur in schools every day. Watch, for example, the outstanding music teacher at work. Within seconds, the out-of-tune cello or the slightly flat tenor can be stopped and corrected. At first, the feedback might be provided individually, then in a small group (just the cellos or the tenors), and then in a large group (the entire orchestra or chorus). Each student leaves the rehearsal knowing that his or her individual and group performance has improved. It is quite unlikely that, at any time during the rehearsal, the teacher retrieved a grade book and recorded data to be transmitted to students weeks later.

Athletic coaches, theatrical directors, chess club advisors, and many other exemplars of effective feedback are all around our schools, if only we would take time to notice and replicate their strategies. Students remain engaged in basketball in an environment where the standards are clear and consistent, the feedback is instantaneous, and every missed shot is followed by the opportunity to literally and figuratively rebound. That the same students fail English and algebra is not due to a cognitive deficit (consider the complexity of offensive and defensive maneuvers in contemporary basketball), but to a lack of accurate, timely, and specific feedback.

Second, consider the role of feedback when used incorrectly. It is worse than a waste of the teacher's time and energy: Ineffective feedback is inversely related to student achievement. Guskey (2000, 2002), Guskey and Bailey (2001), Marzano (2006), and I (2004a, 2006a) have addressed feedback practices that are not only ineffective but counterproductive. As with effective feedback strategies, however, one hardly needs the imprimatur of research to establish the obvious. People know that dogs, horses, guinea pigs, and toddlers respond to encouragement and incentives better than to punishment, yet some people remain indifferent to nearly a century of evidence that establishes that grading as punishment does not work.

Most fifth-grade students learn the difference between mean, median, and mode, and thus gain the insight that the arithmetic mean, or average, may not be the best representation of a set of data. Yet the teachers of those students can remain stubbornly allegiant to the average. While we know that immediate feedback is essential for improvement, schools continue to maintain the practice of "final" exams, with the implicit message that feedback from the teacher in this context is irrelevant and futile.

Third, feedback practices are inconsistent within and among schools. Grading practices remain, in most schools, the exclusive province of the classroom teacher, with grading policies varying wildly from classroom to classroom and school to school. Sometimes, this creativity is used to provide superior feedback and improve achievement. Other times, however, this creativity is the academic equivalent of the football coach creatively changing the dimensions of the field or the height of the goal posts.

In the latter case, no thoughtful person would defend the creative prerogatives of the coach; students, parents, and colleagues would denounce such manipulations as unfair. "Kids won't play the game," they would protest, "if the coach changes the rules and conditions. The players will just become discouraged and give up. Besides, the kids will never get better if the coach doesn't provide a clear framework and consistent guidance." Indeed, the certainty of these protests ensures that every football field in the nation remains uniform, while those domains about which feelings are less intense—the classrooms—remain a sea of ambiguity and inconsistency.

There are two reasons educational leaders fail to emphasize consistency in the classroom as much as they do on the athletic field: They have the wrong criteria for decision-making, and they have the wrong information on which to make critical decisions. Guskey and Bailey (2001) concluded that the problems of inconsistency are compounded by a range of potential biases, from culture to gender to handwriting to the sequence in which a piece of student work is evaluated. These inconsistencies and their consequences have persisted for a century, these researchers demonstrate, because the decision-making processes are stubbornly indifferent to evidence.

The reasons for this indifference are not malice, but rather result from misplaced priorities. The most common reason I hear that schools have not changed toxic and counterproductive grading policies is a lack of "buy-in," a reference that most frequently applies to classroom teachers and activist parents whose children have been well-served by the current assessment and grading regime. When the standard by which decisions are made is not the evidence of impact on student achievement, but instead the perception of popularity or discontent among adults, then leadership priorities are wrong. Leaders who follow the lure of popularity will achieve no more than a Pyrrhic victory, gaining short-term affirmation from adults at the expense of long-term losses in equity and educational achievement. None of the compelling evidence and arguments in this volume will have a scintilla of impact if the essential question leaders ask is, "Do I have buy-in from all the adults?" rather than, "Is it the right decision for students?"

The second reason that leaders make inappropriate decisions about assessment is that they have the wrong information. As Popham (2006a, 2006b) suggests, leaders and teachers misuse the term "assessment" and many related concepts such as "validity." Thus it is not surprising that even well-intentioned efforts to improve feedback systems for student achievement are easily derailed.

Each of these elements—decision-making criteria and accurate information about assessments—are necessary but insufficient elements for effective leadership. A well-intentioned change in decision-making frameworks without an improvement in assessment literacy will yield only frustration, with bad decisions made with great sincerity. Similarly, all the training seminars in the world about assessment literacy without a corresponding change in decision criteria will yield only hypocrisy, with bad decisions made with sighs of reluctance and resignation, while leaders once again confirm the hypothesis that evidence is merely a tiny gnat on the back of the elephant resistant to change.

Choices and Tradeoffs for Leaders

We know that feedback, when provided in an accurate and timely manner, is related to improved student achievement. We further know that inaccurate and ineffective feedback is counterproductive. Finally, the educational landscape is littered with a broad range of inconsistent and contradictory feedback systems, including idiosyncratic grading and assessment practices and policies. What can school leaders do about it? The rest of this chapter focuses not on easy solutions, but on choices and tradeoffs that leaders must make.

Perfection is not an option, and leaders who delay the pursuit of progress as they pursue perfection in assessment policies will doom themselves and their school to what Tom Peters and Robert Waterman (1982) decried as analysis paralysis. Change is delayed as perfection remains the enemy of progress, while toxic and ineffective practices remain entrenched. There is a better way, and this section describes five choices leaders can make to improve the quality of assessment *for* learning within their schools.

Choice 1: Power Standards or Frantic Coverage?

The primary obstacle to successful assessment is the sheer quantity of academic standards educators must address. Since Marzano and Kendall (1998) first addressed the mismatch between the time available in schools and the time required by prevailing standards, the trend among state departments of education has been, perversely, to increase the quantity and specificity of standards, guaranteeing haste and superficiality rather than focus and depth.

Because the establishment of standards is inherently a political process, representing the accumulation of ideas from a variety of different stakeholders, it is unlikely that standards will be winnowed. Social studies standards, in particular, reflect the need of political authorities to create the illusion that they represent a growing number of viewpoints, events, historical figures, and contemporary ideas in school curricula.

To test whether the standards-time mismatch affects the assessment agenda in your school, simply ask a group of teachers to fill in the blank in the following sentence: "We would like to do a better job on assessment and feedback, but we just don't have the _____." It is unlikely that they will suggest "intellect" or "ability" or "desire"—or even "money." By far the most common reason classroom teachers do not have more frequent and effective assessments is that they lack the time to cover the curriculum, develop assessments that match the curriculum, and provide feedback that is detailed and specific.

While a growing number of leaders are creatively using time previously allocated to meetings and administrative matters to give teachers greater opportunities to improve assessment, this strategy is only a part of the solution. School leaders who wish to create time for classroom teachers must clearly and deliberately "pull the weeds before they plant the flowers." Specifically, they must guide the faculty through a process that identifies which academic standards meet the criteria for "power standards" (Ainsworth, 2003; Reeves, 2004b). Only when the faculty has identified those standards that are most essential will they be able to make the decision, with leadership endorsement and support, that it is more important and effective to assess a few standards well and frequently than to assess all standards in a manner that is, inevitably, superficial and late.

To identify power standards, the faculty must address three questions: First, which standards have endurance? That is, which standards appear to be of lasting value from one grade level to the next? Reading comprehension is obviously included in this criteria, while just about anything involving plastic volcanoes is not. Second, which standards provide leverage? That is, which standards have applicability in multiple disciplines? Nonfiction writing and the ability to create and draw inferences from graphs and charts clearly have multidisciplinary leverage, while the ability to distinguish the trapezoid from the rhombus is of more limited utility.

Third, which standards are most essential for the next level of instruction? The answer to this question is tricky, because if I ask a group of fourth-grade teachers, "What are you willing to give up?" the typical response is, "Nothing. Everything we do is important, and besides, the kids need it for next year." But when I walk down the hall and ask a group of fifth-grade teachers what I would need to do as a fourth-grade teacher so that my students could enter fifth grade with confidence and success, the answer is almost always a very brief set of requirements. Never, in the course of posing this question hundreds of times, has the fifth-grade faculty told me that I would need to cover every sentence of the fourth-grade standards. There is, in other words, an intuitive understanding of the need for power standards, but human nature reliably tells us that it is easier to give advice than to take it. As a former math teacher, I hold the rhombus, trapezoid, and parallelogram dear to my heart. Nevertheless, were I advising a fellow middle-school math teacher on the subject of power standards, I would suggest that mastery of triangles and rectangles—the building blocks of every polygon—is a more productive use of time than memorizing the qualities of my favorite trapezoid. In other words, we must be able to distinguish what teachers love from what students need.

Choice 2: Practical Utility or Psychometric Perfection?

Even after the scope of the curriculum has been narrowed through the use of power standards, time remains an unbearable burden when it comes to creating classroom assessments. Indeed, I have seen some classroom assessments that were designed to provide timely and effective feedback for students and teachers, but because the assessments required 2 hours to administer and a week to evaluate, they became a waste of time.

Why were the assessments so long? Certainly there was no malicious intent to waste teachers' and students' time. Rather, the teachers and administrators constructing the assessments recalled their college assessment classes in which they were admonished to construct tests with adequate domain sampling (Crocker & Algina, 1986) and a sufficient number of items so as to achieve a high degree of reliability.

The problem is that these standards for test construction apply to high-stakes norm-referenced tests designed to carefully separate the performance of one student from another. If our purpose is the selection of students for a limited number of places in next fall's Yale Law School class, then a focus on extensive domain sampling and high reliability would be appropriate. But when our purpose is a quick determination of the extent to which students understand skills and concepts, and the equally important purpose of adjusting teaching strategies to help students who have not yet mastered those skills and concepts, then practical utility takes precedence over psychometric perfection.

Skeptics will no doubt argue that if we do not pursue statistical reliability in classroom assessments, then all of the teaching adjustments will be a waste of time. After all, if the test fails to yield accurate results, and the instructional interventions are applied to the wrong students or in the wrong domains of learning, then what good are they? This is a fair challenge, and the answer is not that a 10-item test designed by teachers, with results returned in hours rather than weeks, is superior to a 100-item test designed by professional test writers. The answer, rather, is that school leaders must choose which error has the least risk for their students.

Of course, there is a risk in losing psychometric perfection. By supplanting elegance with practicality, educational leaders may make the mistake of giving some students extra help in an area in which the students really did not need it. Suppose the assessment insufficiently samples the domain of "reading comprehension" and the results suggest, incorrectly, that a student needs to do extra work in this domain. Consider what the risk really is. If the teacher makes such an error, the very worst that will happen is that students will receive extra instruction in reading comprehension—hardly the worst error teachers and leaders can make. Moreover, because assessments are frequent, the error will be quickly caught and corrected. If, by contrast, leaders make the mistake of failing to notice a student needs help when, in fact, the student desperately needs help, then the consequences are far more serious. This typically happens because leaders want psychometric perfection, and they make the error of supplanting practical, if imperfect information, with the mythical ideal of the perfect test. In such circumstances, leaders can be almost certain that students will never receive meaningful feedback because 1) the assessments may not be administered in the first place; 2) teachers will be intellectually and emotionally detached from the assessments and will telegraph those feelings to students; 3) the feedback will be inscrutable for both teachers and students; and 4) the feedback, even if provided in a clear manner, will be late and voluminous.

Leaders who choose practical utility will help teachers and students learn that "Doug needs to work on the properties of the right triangle." Those who pursue psychometric perfection will receive a ream of paper from the assessment office or a series of endless tables and graphs attached to emails. Said one principal faced with such a pile of shrink-wrapped paper: "My faculty just isn't ready for this." Thus ended the usefulness of a huge investment of time and resources by that school system. In contrast, some schools in Broad Award-winning Norfolk (Virginia) Public Schools use 10-item biweekly assessments to provide same-day feedback to students and teachers. While critics might denigrate those assessments as failing to pass muster with educational measurement experts, the record speaks for itself. Norfolk's use of brief and frequent assessments has been directly linked to a stunning and sustained improvement in achievement and equity (Reeves, 2004a).

Choice 3: The Primacy of Literacy or the Pursuit of Popularity?

When asked to share the secrets of high-performing schools, I am always taken aback. There are no secrets, no proprietary models, no mystical wisdom that can only be acquired with deep insight and deeper pockets. Indeed, research accumulated on thousands of students in high-performing schools is freely available on the Internet from a wide variety of sources and political perspectives. (This research information can be found at the noncommercial sites www.allthingsassessment.info and www.allthingsplc.info.) The challenge is not a lack of knowledge; the challenge is implementation.

One thing that high-performing schools uniformly do is establish literacy as their primary pursuit (Reeves, 2004a, 2004b). These schools rightly believe that literacy is as important as the safety and health of their students. Because they know that the health and safety risks of students who drop out of school are markedly higher than the risks of students who succeed in school, these educators and leaders know that the analogy between literacy and health is a sound one.

Consider the evidence on the relationship between time and student literacy. In what some readers may regard as a "blinding flash of the obvious," we have observed that elementary schools that devote more time to literacy experience higher levels of student achievement. Specifically, in one school system we studied, we found that in schools that devoted an average of 90 minutes per day to literacy instruction, 55% of the students scored at the proficient level or higher on state tests of reading comprehension in schools averaging 120 minutes of daily instruction, and 72% of the students scored at the proficient level or higher; in schools averaging 180 minutes per day of instruction, more than 80% of the students scored at the proficient level or higher.

Of particular interest is the fact that the last group of schools began the year with the lowest performing students. The teachers and leaders knew that to catch up, they would have to make dramatic changes in their schedule. We have found the same phenomenon in secondary schools. When reviewing the failure rate for 9th- and 10th-grade English classes, we compared two groups of students. Both groups had the same curriculum, textbooks, teachers, and final exam. The only difference was that one group had double periods while the other group had the traditional one-period-per-day schedule.

The results were stunning. In composition, 37% of the students in the one-period class failed, while 18% of the students in the two-period class failed. In literature, 36% of students failed the one-period class, while 18% failed the two-period class (Reeves, 2004a). We found similar results in mathematics. When students had the opportunity to spend more time on math, their failure rate was substantially lower.

While it is easy to offer the rejoinder that time alone is not enough, and how one uses time is important, such a discussion is beside the point if we do not first give teachers the time that they need to help students catch up to where they need to be and also receive grade-level instruction.

If these findings are so obvious, why do schools so rarely give priority to literacy? Why is the prevailing model in school schedules the presumption that all subjects are of equal value and thus deserve equal time? I have interviewed many high school science and social studies teachers. In response to the question, "What is the most important thing we can do in elementary and middle school to help students be successful in your class?" the nearly unanimous response has been, "Please send me students who can read my textbook— then I can help them understand the content."

Particularly compelling is the evidence that eighth-grade students who are not reading on grade level have an 85% probability of remaining below grade level in reading throughout high school (Capella & Weinstein, 2001). Thus one would think that middle-school leaders would err on the side of caution, routinely providing additional literacy instruction for their students—perhaps twice to three times as much time for literacy as for other subjects. Of course, such a schedule is exceptional, and when it does occur, it is typically provided only on a remedial basis.

Frequently school leaders ask, "Why is it that students appear to be making progress in literacy in elementary school and then decline in middle school?" A quick examination of most school schedules reveals that middle-school students receive from one-third to one-half the time each day devoted to literacy as their elementary-school counterparts. The explanation for the decline in literacy during the middle-school years is plainly leadership decision-making, not adolescent hormones.

To find more time for literacy, leaders must give up their tenuous grip on the popular illusion that every subject is of equal value. Some schools alternate science and social studies, music, and art, thereby giving all students instruction in these important areas while maintaining an extra portion of instruction in reading and writing. It is important to note that the mantra of "reading across the curriculum" is not a sufficient replacement for direct instruction in reading and writing. I challenge you to look at a dozen randomly selected samples of student writing at any grade level in your system, and then make the claim that students will be harmed by additional explicit instruction in reading and writing.

Rather than embrace the evidence that supports the primacy of literacy, some state legislatures have bowed to political pressure from subject-matter interest groups, requiring schools to provide minimum numbers of hours of instruction in a wide variety of subjects. Such a fragmentation of the curriculum guarantees that students who need extra literacy intervention will be required to receive it after school or in summer school, the two venues least likely to be used by the most needy students, who may have childcare responsibilities after school and during the summer, or whose parents may not be able to help them take advantage of those interventions.

Perhaps the least effective argument by the advocates of other subjects is that an excessive emphasis on literacy will hurt elective subjects. While no doubt well-intentioned, these advocates appear to forget that most elective courses are offered in 11th and 12th grade, and thus the first step to providing more elective opportunities in school is to ensure that we have more 11th- and 12th-grade students. The only way to achieve that objective is to reduce failures in middle school and the first 2 years of high school. A step on the path to reducing failures is acknowledging the primacy of literacy.

Choice 4: Collaboration or the Blob?

Waters and Marzano (2007) suggest that leadership can be either part of the solution or what they call "the blob"—a disparaging reference to the "bloated educational bureaucracy" made in the 1980s by then Secretary of Education William J. Bennett. The characterization hit a raw nerve, particularly among hardworking and sincere school leaders. Nevertheless, the amount of time wasted in administrative meetings is staggering, particularly considering how much of it is devoted to the delivery of information that would be more efficiently and accurately delivered in print.

If we expect a culture of collaboration to develop in schools—and collaboration is at the very heart of professional learning communities that are committed to fair and consistent assessments—then leaders must reallocate time from the least productive parts of administrative meetings to collaboration.

Leaders have an enormous discretion to waste time or use it wisely. I asked one Virginia school leader how she had found the time to examine student work, create common assessments, and review data, all within a school day, a schedule, and a teacher contract that led her counterparts to regard such activities as impossible. The principal shot me a piercing glance and said firmly, "Well, perhaps it's because I haven't made an administrative announcement in a faculty meeting for about 3 years." It is only a matter of tradition that meetings are reserved for announcements. Leaders in collaborative cultures dispense with the formalities and invest time in genuine collaboration.

How much time does effective collaboration take? First, we must be absolutely clear about what "collaboration" means in the context of creating and implementing effective assessments. At the very least, teachers must create common assessments (Ainsworth & Viegut, 2006; Reeves, 2002); examine the results of those assessments to improve teaching practices (White, 2005a, 2005b); and examine student work (Reeves, 2004a).

Roland Barth, founder of the Harvard Principals' Center, famously distinguished between congeniality and collegiality as characteristics of effective collaboration (1990). Barth, a true scholar and a "gentle man," knows well the value of congeniality. But he also knows the value of engagement, contention, and genuine collegiality. While I prefer congenial company as much as the next person, the heart of effective collaboration is the difficult and challenging work of resolving disagreements. Consider the evidence on how 50 educators examined anonymous samples of student work and, using the same scoring rubric, came to strikingly different conclusions. In the course of six 4-hour meetings—a total of 24 hours—the same group's level of agreement rose from 19% to 92% (Reeves, 2006b). While it is easy to say that collaboration is essential for fair assessment, and that effective collaboration requires time and practice, consider how the last 24 hours of faculty meeting time were spent in your school.

Collaboration time is required not only for achieving assessment excellence, but also for closing the equity gap. There is a stunning difference between schools that were successful in closing the achievement gap and those that were not (Oberman & Symonds, 2005). While all claimed to engage in reviews of student data and all had engaged in the required workshops and consumed copious amounts of coffee and bagels, only those schools where administrators provided extensive time for collaboration were able to apply that professional development in a way that led to closing the achievement gap.

The evidence indicates that it was not a difference of teacher training or desire—it was a difference of leadership decision-making in providing time for meaningful collaboration. Specifically, about 35% of gap-closing schools examined student data "a few times a week," while fewer than 5% of non-gap-closing schools monitored achievement and equity data with that degree of frequency. By contrast, almost 50% of the non gap closing schools admitted to examining data only "a few times a year," while a little more than 20% of the gap-closing schools were in that category.

When considering why so many school reform ideas fail, the typical cheap shot is to blame a resistant culture, unchanging veteran teachers, and intractable habits. But before casting any further blame, school leaders must look in the mirror and ask whether they have provided the time not only for professional development, but for implementation of professional ideas, concepts, and skills every single week of the year. In his influential leadership book *Good to Great*, Jim Collins (2001) emphasizes the need to move organizations from mere compliance with regulatory requirements to a set of norms that are so ingrained that they are simply "the way we do business around here."

When The Broad Education Foundation was considering selections for their annual award for the best urban school system in the nation, their panel of judges visited Norfolk Public Schools. Over the course of several years, Norfolk had created and implemented an accountability system that used data in a remarkably constructive and effective way, with clear links to improved student achievement (Reeves, 2004a). While visiting a school, one of the Broad judges asked a teacher, "When the leadership of the school district changes, will you stop doing all of this analysis of data and student work?" The teacher replied, "We don't do it because the central office is telling us to. We do it because it's how we know what to teach and how to teach it."

I have observed that particular school from 1998 to the present, and it is fair to say that enthusiasm for data analysis and teacher collaboration was not something that came naturally. But when you watch a video of authentic teacher collaboration in action today at Ocean View Elementary School in Norfolk, Virginia (Reeves, 2006a), you witness a group that laughs, applauds, encourages, and confronts, all in a compact period of 30 minutes. It is, as a result of long-term persistent efforts by principal Lauren Campsen and the entire faculty, just the way that they do business.

Choice 5: Evidence or Tradition?

Stanford professors Jeffrey Pfeffer and Robert I. Sutton (2006) ask how we might respond if a hospital administrator announced, with breathless enthusiasm, that after much consideration, the hospital intended to embark on a new course of action. Specifically, the hospital had decided to start using evidence to do less of what killed patients and more of what improved the health of patients. Your reaction, like mine, might be one of incredulity. "Aren't they doing that now?" we would wonder. If that is our reaction, the researchers respond, then we do not know very much about how medicine is practiced. With a shocking litany of examples from medical care, business, professional practices and yes, education, Pfeffer and Sutton demonstrate how even well-educated professionals are seduced by what they term "dangerous half-truths and total nonsense."

Creating an evidence-based culture is difficult, because schools are frequently accustomed to equating creativity and freedom—including the freedom to make fact-free decisions—with professional respect. If, for example, we challenge a teaching practice or grading system, it is not merely a discussion of alternative points of view and a comparison of the evidence supporting each point of view, but rather a potential affront to the professionalism and respect of the individual engaging in the practice under consideration.

Just as in some cultures the word of the patriarch, clergy, or monarch stands as sufficient justification for action, the prerogative to choose lectures over interactivity, zeroes over appropriate consequences for failed work, or summative over formative assessment is a potentially destructive choice too often left to the authority of the individual teacher. Challenges to that traditional prerogative are not seen as questions about teaching and assessment strategies, but rather as strikes at the heart of nearly sacred beliefs. The evidence on the matter cannot be heard over shouts alleging micromanagement and disrespect.

Fortunately, schools that are committed to assessment excellence bring to conversations about teaching, leadership, and student achievement not only their ingrained belief systems, but also abundant evidence on student achievement. When both the creation of assessments and the evaluation of student work are the result of collaborative processes, teachers and school leaders can quickly evaluate the effectiveness of strategies, make mid-course corrections, express some new hypotheses about what actions they might take to improve student learning, and, within days or weeks, have additional evidence with which the new hypotheses can be tested. Their model of teaching professionalism is neither submission to administrative dictates nor blind adherence to the holy writ of tradition and personal preference, but rather a commitment to a continuous cycle of "try it, test it, improve it."

The commitment to evidence is more than the elevation of rationality over superstition. Indeed, even superstition can be supported by observation and apparent evidence. Many stories, from Greek mythology to Rudyard Kipling's "Just So" stories, associate natural phenomena with imaginative causes. The enduring nature of these associations is best evidenced by names of constellations that remain in use to this day, though Kipling's explanation of "How the Camel Got His Hump" was less enduring.

What about the mythology of the classroom? Just as Pfeffer and Sutton (2006) found physicians who applied their observations from a medical residency 3 decades old as if they represented the most contemporary research, so also there are teachers and school leaders whose own experiences as students and whose formative teaching experiences continue to dictate their professional decision-making, even as the conditions of school have changed remarkably. Consider the profound changes in society between 1987 and 2007 in technology, global politics, biomedical research, and almost every other area of life—changes to which curriculum, assessment, and instruction have remained stunningly indifferent.

This indifference to evidence carries with it an enormous cost. When teachers and school leaders believe that the primary causes of student achievement are factors outside of their control, it becomes a self-fulfilling prophecy. In a study involving more than 300 schools and more than 300,000 students (Reeves, 2006b), we asked the simple question, "What are the causes of student achievement?" When teachers and leaders attributed the causes to factors beyond their control, their students lived down to those expectations. When considering the percentage of students scoring at the proficient or higher level on 25 separate measurements of student achievement, the students in schools where the causes of achievement were attributed to student factors averaged 43.6%, while the students in schools where the causes of achievement were attributed to teaching and leadership averaged 64.8%.

Recently, my colleagues and I revisited the data and examined the gain scores from 2005 to 2006. In schools where teachers examined the evidence of the impact of teaching effectiveness on student achievement and regarded their professional practices as the primary causes of student achievement, the gains in student achievement were three times higher than in those schools where the faculty and leaders attributed the causes to factors beyond their control.

Using a completely separate methodology, Marzano, Waters, and McNulty (2005) conducted a meta-analysis of 21 separate leadership practices associated with improved student achievement. Only three of those factors were associated with both first-order change— relatively quick and easy reforms—and second-order changes that produced lasting systemic improvements. Those three were belief systems about the efficacy of leaders and teachers, research-based practices, and monitoring and evaluation.

In sum, the commitment to evidence over tradition is not merely an homage to rationalism and enlightenment. It is an essential foundation for any school committed to improving student achievement.

Speaking With Actions

Since the days of the Lyceum of Socrates, discussions of school reform have been dominated by two themes: First is the function of schools themselves, as institutions that not only shape young minds but also contribute to society as a whole. Though contemporary debates fail to match the eloquence of the ancients, the subjects are strikingly similar. The second theme of school reform is one of universal complaint. That schools are inadequate to their task is the complaint of generations of school critics, starting with those who served hemlock to the teacher who corrupted the youth of the day with challenging ideas. Complaints also come in the form of the lamentation of generations of exasperated teachers that youth is wasted on the young.

Somewhere between the extremes of complaints and debate, far from the free-fire zones of rhetorical combat unburdened by evidence, lies the opportunity for genuine progress. Schmoker (2006) noted that the confluence of research, technology, and dissemination about professional practices gives us the historic opportunity to realize the promise of education. In this chapter, we have considered only a few pebbles on the mountain of evidence that demonstrates that teaching and leadership not only improve assessment practice, but shape in profound ways educational excellence and equity for generations to come.

Only a few decades ago, the world of education faced a different change, one brought about by a young girl named Linda Brown who, in my hometown of Topeka, Kansas, was required to walk past a school designated for white students to attend the school to which she had been assigned. Thanks to her courageous father, Oliver Brown, and a young attorney named Thurgood Marshall, her name was forever associated with the landmark case of *Brown v. Board of Education of Topeka.* Less well-known than the case name is the argument that preceded the decision. On a cold December day in 1952, one of the nation's preeminent attorneys and a former candidate for vice president of the United States, Charles Davis, argued that Linda Brown's case was a futile attempt to change 300 years of attitudes that were, in the view of Mr. Davis, so culturally ingrained as to be unchangeable. But Davis's peroration was interrupted by Justice Felix Frankfurter, who said from the bench of the Supreme Court words that should resonate in every school today:

> Attitudes in this world are not changed abstractly, as it were, by reading something. . . . Attitudes are partly the result of working, attitudes are partly the result of action. . . . You do not fold your hands and wait for attitude to change by itself. (Friedman, 1969, pp. 412–413)

As this book goes to press, the United States Supreme Court has ruled that policies in place in thousands of schools achieving desegregation are invalid (Greenhouse, 2007). Therefore the words of Justice Frankfurter are particularly relevant more than 55 years after they were spoken. Educators and school leaders can depend upon neither public policy nor court decisions nor prevailing attitudes to create the reality of equity and excellence in education. Similarly, neither my words nor those of the most persuasive and powerful school leaders will change every mind, nor will they unite every faculty, nor should we entertain fantasies of universal agreement or acceptance of challenging reforms in schools. Rather, we must be emboldened by Frankfurter's words, Marshall's arguments, and the courage of the Brown family, and let our actions speak.

References

Ainsworth, L. (2003). *Power standards: Identifying the standards that matter the most.* Englewood, CO: Advanced Learning Press.

Ainsworth, L., & Viegut, D. (2006). *Common formative assessments: How to connect standards-based instruction and assessment.* Thousand Oaks, CA: Corwin Press.

Barth, R. S. (1990). *Improving schools from within: Teachers, parents, and principals can make the difference.* San Francisco: Jossey-Bass.

Capella, E., & Weinstein, R. S. (2001, December). Turning around reading achievement: Predictors of high school students' academic resilience. *Journal of Educational Psychology, 93*(4), 758–771.

Collins, J. (2001). *Good to great: Why some companies make the leap . . . and others don't.* New York: HarperCollins.

Crocker, L., & Algina, J. (1986). *Introduction to classical and modern test theory.* New York: Holt, Rinehart and Winston.

Friedman, L. (1969). *Argument: The complete oral argument before the supreme court in Brown v. Board of Education of Topeka, 1952–55.* New York: Chelsea House.

Greenhouse, L. (2007, July 1). In steps big and small, Supreme Court moved right. *The New York Times,* p. A1.

Guskey, T. R. (2000, December). Grading policies that work against standards . . . and how to fix them. *NASSP Bulletin, 84*(620), 20–29.

Guskey, T. R. (2002). *How's my kid doing? A parents' guide to grades, marks, and report cards.* San Francisco: Jossey-Bass.

Guskey, T. R., & Bailey, J. M. (2001). *Developing grading and reporting systems for student learning.* Thousand Oaks, CA: Corwin Press.

Marzano, R. J. (2006). *Classroom assessment and grading that work.* Alexandria, VA: Association for Supervision and Curriculum Development.

Marzano, R. J., & Kendall, J. S. (1998). *Implementing standards-based education*. Student Assessment Series. Washington, DC: National Education Association.

Marzano, R. J., Pickering, D., & Pollock, J. E. (2001). *Classroom instruction that works: Research-based strategies for increasing student achievement*. Alexandria, VA: Association for Supervision and Curriculum Development.

Marzano, R. J., Waters, T., & McNulty, B. A. (2005). *School leadership that works: From research to results*. Alexandria, VA: Association for Supervision and Curriculum Development.

Oberman, I., & Symonds, K.W. (2005, January–February). What matters most in closing the gaps. *Leadership*, 8–11.

Peters, T. J., & Waterman, Jr., R. H. (1982). *In search of excellence: Lessons from America's best-run companies*. New York: Warner Books.

Pfeffer, J., & Sutton, R. I. (2006). *Hard facts, dangerous half-truths, and total nonsense: Profiting from evidence-based management*. Boston: Harvard Business School Publishing.

Popham, W. J. (2006a, February). *Assessment for learning: An endangered species? Educational Leadership, 63*(5), 82–83.

Popham, W. J. (2006b, March). Needed: A dose of assessment literacy. *Educational Leadership, 63*(6), 84–85.

Reeves, D. B. (2002). *Making standards work: How to implement standards-based assessments in the classroom, school, and district* (3rd ed.). Denver, CO: Advanced Learning Press.

Reeves, D. B. (2004a). *Accountability for learning: How teachers and school leaders can take charge*. Alexandria, VA: Association for Supervision and Curriculum Development.

Reeves, D. B. (2004b). *Accountability in action: A blueprint for learning organizations* (2nd ed.). Englewood, CO: Advanced Learning Press.

Reeves, D. B. (2004c). The case against zero. *Phi Delta Kappan, 86*(4), 324–325.

Reeves, D. B. (2006a). *Data for learning: A blueprint for improving student achievement using data teams* [DVD]. Englewood, CO: Advanced Learning Press.

Reeves, D. B. (2006b). *The learning leader: How to focus school improvement for better results.* Alexandria, VA: Association for Supervision and Curriculum Development.

Schmoker, M. (2006). *Results now: How we can achieve unprecedented improvements in teaching and learning.* Alexandria, VA: Association for Supervision and Curriculum Development.

Waters, T., & Marzano, R. J. (2007, March 19). *From part of the "blob" to part of the solution: Balanced leadership, the district office, and student achievement.* Paper presented at the Association for Supervision and Curriculum Development Annual Conference, Anaheim, CA.

White, S. (2005a). *Beyond the numbers: Making data work for teachers and school leaders.* Englewood, CO: Advanced Learning Press.

White, S. (2005b). *Show me the proof! Tools and strategies to make data work for you.* Englewood, CO: Advanced Learning Press.

Richard DuFour

Dr. Richard DuFour is one of the nation's foremost authorities on applying the principles of professional learning communities in the real world of schools. He draws upon 34 years of experience as a public school educator—as a teacher, principal, and superintendent—and his two decades as a leader of one of the most recognized and celebrated schools in America, Adlai E. Stevenson High School District 125 in Lincolnshire, Illinois.

Dr. DuFour is the author of eight books, numerous videos, and more than tinguished educational service and scholarship, including the National Staff Development Council's Distinguished Service Award. He consults with school districts, state departments of education, and professional organizations throughout North America on strategies for improving schools.

In this chapter, Dr. DuFour paints a picture of the power of effective assessment practices in a real school setting. He conveys not only the "how" of effective assessment, but also the "why." In this chapter, a veteran teacher has the opportunity to reexamine not only his practices, but also some of his fundamental assumptions about assessment. He learns that assessment does not require a multitude of new resources, but rather something even more rare—the willingness to change the fundamental assumptions and practices that have characterized public education for decades. When done well, he discovers, assessment can help build a collaborative culture, monitor the learning of each student on a timely basis, provide information essential to an effective system of academic intervention, inform the practice of individual teachers and teams, provide feedback to students on their progress in meeting standards, motivate students by demonstrating next steps in their learning, fuel continuous improvement processes—and serve as the driving engine for transforming a school.

Dr. Rick DuFour can be reached at rdufour@district125.k12.il.us.

Epilogue

Once Upon a Time: A Tale of Excellence in Assessment

Richard DuFour

The distinguished authors contributing to this book offer extraordinary insight and expertise in the exploration of what represents "excellence in assessment." My contribution is not designed to examine the technical aspects of assessment, but rather to illustrate the potential power of effective assessment practices through the oldest teaching vehicle known to man—a story. Richard Axelrod once wrote: "Universities come to know about things through studies, organizations come to know about things through reports, and people come to know about things through stories" (p. 112). Good stories teach us. They convey not only how something should be done, but more importantly, why it should be done. They communicate priorities and clarify what is significant, valued, and appreciated.

The following story offers a model of what I consider to be excellence in assessment in a school setting. The protagonist of the story is a high-school teacher, but the message applies equally and with little revision to middle and elementary schools as well.

After 10 years as a high-school social studies teacher, Peter Miller was convinced that kids were kids and schools were schools. So when his wife suggested they move across the country to be closer to her family, he willingly agreed. He applied at several schools and was offered an interview at Russell Burnette High School.

The interview process at Burnette intrigued Peter. At every stage of the process, the selection committee stressed that the school had created a collaborative culture in which teachers worked together to help all students learn. Teacher teams had created a "guaranteed and viable curriculum" that specified the knowledge, skills, and dispositions all students were to acquire in each course. Peter was asked to review the "Essential Learnings" established by the U.S. history team and was struck by the fact that the curriculum stressed only 10 key concepts each semester, rather than the long list of discrete facts he had been expected to teach at his former school.

The selection committee also gave Peter copies of the curriculum pacing guide, the common assessment calendar, examples of preassessments for several units, examples of common assessments, and the rubrics for evaluating student essays and term papers—all of which had been created by the U.S. history team. The committee asked Peter to critique each document and to express his concerns as well as suggestions for improvement. Peter was impressed by the active role the other history teachers played in the interview process, and equally impressed that he had been required to spend a day at the school teaching prior to being offered the job. He gladly accepted the offer to join the staff at Burnette and looked forward to establishing himself in his new school. He had none of the trepidation and self-doubt that had characterized his first year as a teacher. He was a veteran who knew how schools worked.

The school year at Burnette began with 3 full days for teachers to work prior to students arriving on campus. Peter was delighted; he would have plenty of time to get his room ready and to prepare his first unit. His enthusiasm diminished when he learned that mornings were reserved for teachers to meet in their collaborative teams. Peter had had little use for the faculty and department meetings in his previous school, and he quietly resented that team meetings at Burnette would intrude upon his personal time at such a busy point in the school year.

The first U.S. history team meeting, however, was nothing like the meetings at Peter's old school. Each member of the team studied the school's results from both the state assessment and the national ACT exam in social studies. The team also reviewed an analysis of the very strong correlation between results on their common assessments with the results of the high-stakes state and national exams.

"We know we are on the right track," Ambrose, the team leader, observed. "If we can help every student be successful on our ongoing common assessments, we can be very confident they will be successful on state and national assessments as well. We can continue to assess students in other concepts we deem important, but we have an obligation to help our students be successful on the high-stakes tests they must take." The team devoted the remainder of the morning meeting to identifying the areas where students had experienced difficulty on the two external exams and brainstorming instructional, curricular, and assessment strategies to address those areas.

The second U.S. history team meeting was devoted to reviewing the results of the common assessment students had taken at the end of the first unit in the previous school year. The team had analyzed the results at the end of that unit, and now they reviewed their findings and their ideas for addressing the concepts and skills where students had performed least well. Peter was puzzled. The results looked quite good to him.

"I think you should congratulate yourselves," Peter told his teammates. "Why are you taking time to review this exam? I don't see any evidence here of serious problems in student learning."

"It's just what we do here," his teammate Miriam explained. "We are always looking to get better, and even on a test where students did well, there's always a concept or a few items where they do least well. If our team can identify effective strategies for addressing those areas, we can become even more effective and help more students achieve at higher levels every year."

It was evident that the team did not merely consider student performance on the overall test. Members had identified the specific skills and concepts students were to learn and had established the score a student must obtain on each to be deemed proficient. This shift of emphasis from general performance to skill-by-skill analysis helped Peter to see that on one area of the test, many students failed to demonstrate proficiency. The team spent the rest of the meeting reviewing each component of the test and offering ideas for teaching and assessing the concepts and skills of the unit. Ambrose asked Peter to develop test items for the unit and to present them to the team for possible inclusion in the common assessment.

The third team meeting was devoted to a discussion of the prerequisite knowledge students would need to be successful in the first unit and how the team would determine which students lacked that knowledge. The team had reviewed key terms and concepts recommended by the National Center for History in the Schools and the National Council of Social Studies Teachers, had selected the terms they felt were most essential to their curriculum, and then had assigned the terms to different units of instruction. The key vocabulary terms for the first unit included:

assimilation	expansionism	neutrality
autonomy	federal	protective tariff
cartography	imperialism	republicanism
colonization	inalienable	salutary neglect
constitutionalism	mercantilism	sovereign
culture	monarchy	sphere of influence
dissent	nationalism	

Miriam explained to Peter that at the start of every unit, teachers administered a brief preassessment of those terms to their students. Because there were at least two sections of history taught each hour, and because the history classrooms were next to one another, teachers were able to divide students into two different groups based on their proficiency with the vocabulary.

"So in my case, students who lacked the prerequisite vocabulary went with Frank," Miriam explained. "He introduced key terms with brief explanations, then asked students to define the term in their own words in the section of their history notebook devoted to terms and concepts. He helped them create graphic organizers and put them into pairs to review the terms."

"Meanwhile," Frank said, "students who were already proficient went with Miriam. She presented them with a high-interest article on the major themes of the unit and then led a discussion of the article."

The team then reviewed examples of some of the graphic organizers students had used in the past and discussed different strategies for presenting key vocabulary in terms students could understand. They also discussed questions they could use to stimulate discussion of the article to be presented to the second group of students.

By the end of this third day of preparation, Peter was growing uneasy. He had always enjoyed virtually unfettered autonomy in his teaching. He had been free to teach what he wanted, when he wanted, how he wanted, and to assess students in whatever manner he saw fit. Now he was part of a team that made those decisions collectively. Peter was not convinced that all this teaming and collective decision-making was in the best interests of teachers or students. On the eve of his first day of classes, he was less confident of his ability to fit in at his new school, and he questioned whether he had made the right choice in accepting the position there.

Once the students arrived, however, Peter felt far more comfortable. He discovered that he still enjoyed great autonomy in how he conducted his classroom and how he taught his content on a day-to-day basis. His concern that his instruction and daily pacing would be prescribed proved to be unfounded. His team had helped clarify what students were to learn in the unit, and he knew that each U.S. history teacher would present, review, and discuss those same essential learnings with students in the first few days of class. He also knew that all U.S. history students would take the team's common assessment on the same day at the end of the third week of class. In the meantime, however, Peter was free to make decisions each day regarding how to teach and how to check for student understanding.

Peter's team continued to meet for 1 hour each week. On Monday mornings, teachers reported to work 15 minutes earlier than usual, and the start of classes was delayed 30 minutes in order to create this collaborative time. Teachers were then allowed to leave 15 minutes earlier than usual on Mondays, so they were not required to work longer hours or to sacrifice personal time in order to collaborate with their colleagues.

The first few minutes of each meeting were spent debriefing members of the team on how they felt the unit was going. Members were encouraged to express any concerns. The team then turned its attention to the five-point rubric that had been created to score student responses to essay questions. Members reviewed the criteria they had established for assessing the quality of student essays and then examined different anchor essays that reflected each score. At subsequent meetings, they individually scored the same student essay and then shared their conclusions.

"We're willing to accept a difference of one point on the five-point scale," Ambrose explained, "but if two members present scores with a variance of more than one point, we'll discuss the variance, review our rubric and the anchor essays, and then determine an appropriate score." Peter was somewhat chagrined when he was the only team member whose score deviated from the rest of the team the first two times they practiced applying the rubric. His colleagues, however, were very supportive. They explained the thought process they used in scoring the sample and encouraged him to articulate his reasoning. The dialogue was helpful, and on the third attempt to review a sample essay, his score was consistent with his colleagues.

The ability to write a well-reasoned, persuasive essay that incorporated historical evidence was one of the essential outcomes all history students were expected to achieve. So Peter followed the lead of his teammates and taught his students the rubric to ensure they understood the criteria they should use in judging the quality of their own work. He devoted class time to reviewing the rubric with his students, providing them with sample essays from the past, and leading the class in scoring essays of different quality.

Peter had already discovered the importance of checking for student understanding on an ongoing basis. He felt he was proficient in using classroom questions and dialogues for that purpose. He directed questions to students randomly, rather than relying primarily upon volunteers. He extended wait time whenever students struggled and refused to let any student simply declare he or she did not know the answer. He would prod, rephrase, ask them to explain their thought process, and insist they clarify exactly what they did understand and exactly where they were confused. Students soon learned that a simple shrug would not suffice for Mr. Miller. They also learned that he rarely affirmed or corrected an answer immediately. Instead, he would provide more wait time and then direct a student's response to several other students for analysis and comment. He encouraged debate and insisted that students explain their thought process.

Peter did not limit his strategies for checking student understanding to questioning during class. He would typically begin each class by directing students to write in their notes, "At the end of today's class, I will be able to . . . " and asking them to explain how that day's lesson was linked to the essential learnings of the course. At the conclusion of the class he would pose a question, ask students to write a response in their notes, and quickly check each student's response to see if there was confusion. He frequently called upon students to identify similarities and differences between historical events and eras or to develop analogies between historical situations and contemporary events. He often presented a statement, challenged students to explain whether or not they agreed, and then used disagreements or confusion as an opportunity to clarify. He did not believe in giving homework every day, but when he did assign homework, he made a point of providing specific feedback to students. In short, Peter was confident his students were well-prepared when they took the team's first common assessment.

The assessment was in two parts. The first section included multiple choice and matching items, while the second presented an essay question. Peter presented the results from the first part of the assessment to his department chairman and received two printouts the next day. The first showed how his students had performed on each skill and concept the team had assessed, compared to the performance of all the students who completed the assessment. The second printout presented an item analysis that compared the results of his students to all students on each item on the assessment.

The night before the next team meeting, Peter's wife asked how his classes were going. "Well, I'm generally pleased," Peter told her, "but on our common assessment, my students struggled with one concept—distinguishing between different forms of government. Their scores prevented our team from achieving its target for that concept." He grimaced. "I'm not looking forward to admitting that tomorrow." Privately, he hoped he would be able to avoid saying anything.

The next team meeting was a revelation to Peter. Although each teacher had received only the analysis for his or her own students compared to the total group, teachers were extremely open with their results. "My students obviously didn't get the concept of republicanism," Miriam said. "How did the rest of you teach that?" Various team members shared their strategies, then brought up the weak spots in their own students' performance.

Encouraged by their openness, Peter shared his concerns about his students' understanding of different forms of government. The team's response could not have been more positive. Frank and Miriam suggested instructional strategies. Ambrose offered a graphic organizer he had developed that had helped students use comparison and contrast to understand the concept. Skill by skill, concept by concept, the team reviewed student performance, identified whose students had excelled and whose students had struggled, and engaged in lively dialogue about strategies for teaching concepts more effectively.

The team then turned its attention to the item analysis and identified three items on the 30-item test that warranted review. The team quickly discovered that all three items assessed the same skill and that one of the items had been poorly written. They also discovered that the skill had been the last one taught in the unit. The team decided to rewrite the poorly written item and to change the pacing of the unit so members could devote more time to the skill prior to giving the next assessment.

Following the meeting, Peter asked Miriam, "What happens if we use all these strategies and as result, student performance on that skill reaches proficiency?'"

"Why, we'll celebrate our success, of course," she said. "And then we'll look for the next items where students did less well. There will always be 'the lowest 10 percent' of items on any assessment we give. We attack those items, implement improvement strategies, celebrate our success, and then look for the next items. That is the beauty of continuous improvement. You never really arrive, but there is always a lot to celebrate."

Peter was perplexed by the team's policy regarding the essay portion of the assessment. Teachers were expected to provide specific feedback to each student regarding how he or she could improve the essay according to the team rubric, but they did not assign a specific grade to the essay. Students were then required to prepare a second draft of the essay that incorporated the recommendations before they would receive a grade.

"I don't understand the rationale behind this process," Peter said. "Why not grade the first essay and average the scores?"

"Well," Frank said, "we just don't think it's reasonable to assign a grade to skills students are attempting to use for the first time. We want our kids to have the benefit of specific feedback before we grade their efforts."

"We think giving feedback tells students that we expect them to achieve a standard," Miriam chimed in, "and that we'll ask them to refine and improve their work until they reach it. Later in the year, they won't have this chance, but for now, early in the learning process, we feel it's imperative that students benefit from practice and specific feedback before we assign grades to their work."

This feedback was part of a systematic structure to ensure learning. Shortly after the team administered the common assessment, teachers were required to complete progress reports sent to counselors, advisors, and parents. Students in danger of failing were required to report to the tutoring center, where they devoted extra time to their studies and received small-group and individualized tutoring—during the school day. Burnette High had created a schedule that ensured each student had one period available each day to receive this additional time and support for learning. Upperclassmen who did not require this intervention were given the privilege of unstructured time, while freshmen and sophomores were assigned to study halls.

Two weeks later, the students who had completed this first intervention were given another opportunity to demonstrate they had learned the key concepts of the previous unit by taking another form of the assessment. If they performed well, their failing grade was dropped and replaced with the higher grade for students. Miriam explained, "We say we want them all to learn; we don't say that we want them all to learn *fast* or the *first time*. If some students have to work harder and take longer before they demonstrate proficiency, so be it. In the final analysis, if they demonstrate proficiency, we give them a grade that reflects that."

Peter was still a little skeptical. He thought that an opportunity to take a second assessment would cause students to "blow off" the first test. Afterwards, however, he had to admit that he was wrong. His juniors truly valued their unstructured time. They knew that poor performance on the first assessment would mean not only the loss of that privilege, but also an extra commitment of time and effort to learning what they should have learned in the first place. Peter could see no evidence that students were indifferent to the results of their first test. In fact, there was a palpable sense of academic press—a clear expectation that students must demonstrate they had actually acquired the essential knowledge and skills of the unit—that he had never experienced before.

By the end of his first month at Burnette, Peter had come to the realization that he was not in Kansas anymore—this school was very different from those in which he had worked in the past. He had never experienced practices like working in teams, developing common assessments, aligning those assessments with state and national tests, using the results from previous assessments to guide instruction, identifying prerequisite knowledge for success in the unit, regrouping and sharing students, providing students with specific feedback rather than grades, providing systematic interventions when students were unsuccessful, and allowing students additional opportunities to demonstrate proficiency.

The difference in the use of assessments was one of the most striking contrasts between Peter's past practice and his new school environment. In his former school, individual teachers had either developed their own assessments or simply used the assessments provided in the textbook and teacher's manual. There, administering a test signaled the end of a unit, and the purpose of the test was to assign grades. Students who did not do well were exhorted to do better and try harder, but they rarely received specific feedback on how to improve—and almost never were given a second chance to demonstrate their learning. Students and teachers alike understood that taking a test meant the unit was over, and the class would move forward.

At Burnette, however, assessments were used to determine if students needed assistance in acquiring prerequisite skills prior to teaching each unit, to inform individual teachers of the strengths and weaknesses in their instruction, to help teams identify areas of concern in the curriculum, to identify students who needed additional time and support for learning, and to give students additional opportunities to demonstrate that they had learned. Assessment seemed to represent the most critical component of the collaborative culture that characterized the school, and the way teachers used assessments sent students a clear message that they were required, rather than invited, to learn.

By the end of his first semester, Peter considered Burnette's practices so powerful and practical that he questioned why he and his colleagues had not implemented them in his former schools. If certain background knowledge was an essential prerequisite for success in a unit, it just made sense to identify students who did not have that knowledge and to intervene on their behalf at the outset of the unit. If all the teachers of a course were expected to teach the same concept, it was certainly more efficient to work collaboratively in planning the unit, gathering materials, and developing assessments than to work in isolation and duplicate each other's efforts.

"In my old school," Peter told the U.S. history team one day, "what students learned, the rigor of their assessments, and the criteria used to judge the quality of their work depended on who their teacher was. We each worked in isolation. Here, however, our approach is so much more equitable. Students have access to the same curriculum and assessments of equal rigor, and we judge their work according to the same standard. At Burnette, I know all students are receiving the best education possible, in every classroom."

Peter had come to recognize the power of assessments in the service of learning—for students and teachers alike. The common assessments provided him with timely feedback on the success of his students in meeting an agreed-upon standard, on a valid assessment, in comparison to other similar students attempting to achieve the same standard. For the first time in his career, he was able to identify areas of strengths and weaknesses in his teaching and to use that insight in his dialogue with teammates to improve his instruction. Assessments had become a powerful tool in informing his practice.

More importantly, however, Peter had discovered the potential of assessments to enhance the learning of his students. By administering common assessments at the end of each unit, the members of his team were able to identify students who needed additional time and support for learning. Burnette's systematic intervention process required those students to continue to work on acquiring the essential skills in the tutoring center. Tutors then used the assessments to identify the specific skills and concepts a student had been unable to master and to provide precise instruction and feedback in a small group setting to assist the student. It certainly made sense to Peter to use assessments not only to point out that a student had not learned, but also to provide the student with the specific feedback and information to improve upon the learning. Because assessments in his former school had been regarded as the conclusion of a unit rather than a critical element in the learning process, poor performance on an assessment sometimes had a devastating effect on a student's motivation. A series of bad test scores early in the semester could doom a student to a failing grade. Burnette's practice of allowing additional opportunities to demonstrate learning never deprived students of hope.

It had been a semester of growth for Peter. He had reexamined not only his practices, but also some of his fundamental assumptions. Not all schools were alike. Some school cultures and structures are far more effective in helping students learn. Even a veteran teacher like himself could learn to approach his profession from a new perspective. He had made the right choice in coming to Burnette, because this school had taken the assertion, "All Kids Can Learn," and added an even bolder proposition: School can be a place where even the adults could learn.

Burnette High School's assessment story is not a utopian ideal. It takes place in real schools with real teachers and real students. It does not require a windfall of new resources. It does, however, require something even more rare—the willingness to change the fundamental assumptions and practices that have characterized public education for decades.

Attention to this vital area must be a cornerstone of any school improvement effort. Schools simply cannot meet the challenges they face unless educators unleash the potential of effective assessment. To limit the use of this powerful instrument to ranking, sorting, and selecting students is analogous to using a computer as paperweight. When done well, however, assessment can help build a collaborative culture, monitor the learning of each student on a timely basis, provide information essential to an effective system of academic intervention, inform the practice of individual teachers and teams, provide feedback to students on their progress in meeting standards, motivate students by demonstrating next steps in their learning, fuel continuous improvement processes—and serve as the driving engine for transforming a school.

Reference

Axelrod, R. (2002). *Terms of engagement: Changing the way we change organizations.* San Francisco: Berrett-Koehler.

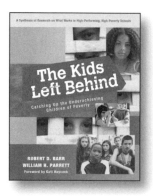